Kenneth Frampton was born in 1930 and trained as an architect at
the Architectural Association School of Architecture, London. He
has worked as an architect and as an architectural historian and critic,
and is now Ware Professor at the Graduate School of Architecture
and Planning, Columbia University, New York. He has taught at a number
of leading institutions in the field, including the Royal College of Art
in London, the ETH in Zurich, the Berlage Institute in Amsterdam,
EPFL in Lausanne and, most recently, the Accademia di Architettura in
Mendrisio, Switzerland. He has also served on many international juries
for architectural awards and building commissions. His writings include
the bestselling *Modern Architecture: A Critical History* in the World of Art
series, and *Studies in Tectonic Culture* (1995).

Thames & Hudson world of art

This famous series provides the widest available range
of illustrated books on art in all its aspects. If you would like
to receive a complete list of titles in print please write to:

THAMES & HUDSON
181A High Holborn
London WC1V 7QX

In the United States please write to:

THAMES & HUDSON INC.
500 Fifth Avenue
New York, New York 10110

Printed in Singapore

I. Le Corbusier and Pierre Jeanneret with a model of the Palace of the Soviets, 1931.

Kenneth Frampton

Le Corbusier

with 191 illustrations

Thames & Hudson world of art

For my son Maxim

First published in the United Kingdom in 2001 by
Thames & Hudson Ltd, 181A High Holborn, London WC1V 7QX

www.thamesandhudson.com

British Library Cataloguing-in-Publication Data
A catalogue record for this book is available from the British Library

ISBN 0-500-20341-5

Designed by Derek Birdsall
Typeset by Omnific

Printed and bound in Singapore by C. S. Graphics

Contents

Introduction *6*

1   The Formative Years 1887–1916   *8*

2   Towards a New Architecture 1917–1927   *20*

3   The City of Tomorrow 1910–1933   *46*

4   Decorative Art Today 1925–1937   *58*

5   A House, A Palace 1923–1929   *70*

6   World Architect: Czechoslovakia, Russia, Brazil,
     North Africa, North America, France and Switzerland
     1928–1936   *88*

7   The Politics of the Unpolitical: Le Corbusier and
     Saint-Simonian Technocracy 1923–1947   *116*

8   From Intermediate Technology to Regional Urbanization
     1929–1946   *130*

9   Towards a New Habitat 1922–1960   *150*

10   The Sacred and the Profane:
     Le Corbusier and Spiritual Form 1948–1965   *167*

11   Passage to India 1950–1965   *184*

12   *Le Poème de l'Angle Droit*   *200*

13   Fin d'un Monde: The Last Works 1939–1965   *214*

Notes   *230*
Bibliography   *234*
Acknowledgments   *235*
Index   *236*

Introduction

To publish another book on Le Corbusier after so much has been written by himself and by others is to run the risk of redundancy; yet it will be a long time before we shall free ourselves from the fertility of his vision and the range of his influence. In fact, as the new century unfolds and as our knowledge of his overall achievement continues to grow, by virtue of ever more meticulous scholarship, we have all the more reason to feel that we will never quite finish with the labyrinthine scope of his production. Architect, urbanist, painter, graphic designer and writer, polemicist and mystic, Le Corbusier was a figure of many guises, to such a degree that it is hard to know where one role ends and the other begins. At the same time, we are aware that a reconciliation of opposites was an irreducible aspect of his method.

This synoptic account of Le Corbusier's overall production is part thematic, part chronological, in an attempt to trace the evolution of his architectural thought at different scales and in different modes of acting and reacting. It has been written for the informed general reader and also for graduate students in architecture and art who have need of a primer in order to pursue studies in depth focused on a particular aspect of his career. Thus emphasis has been placed as much upon the interplay between ideological influences and conceptual intentions as upon the realization of actual buildings. This brings one to acknowledge a quality that is all but unique to Le Corbusier – namely that he is an architect whose projects are so rigorously developed as prototypes as to exercise an influence that is more than equal to that of his built work. This character bestows a lasting didactic value on the eight volumes of his *Oeuvre complète*, which are still extensively sought by tyro architects throughout the world. Perhaps only K. F. Schinkel's *Sammlung Architektonischer Entwürfe* of 1840 has enjoyed a comparable pedagogical status. What Le Corbusier often failed to realize through force of circumstances came to be accorded viability in typological terms. This canonical dimension partly accounts for the number of line drawings included in this study; indeed, one has to admit that in his case the essential concept, even when realized, is often more economically and comprehensively conveyed through orthogonal projection than through a photograph.

In my account, after an initial chapter treating with Le Corbusier's origins, the next four chapters refer to the titles and themes of his polemical texts of the 1920s, culminating in the traditional reciprocity that he saw as obtaining between the monumentality of the *palace* and the convenience of the *house* and his demonstration through his invention of the *free plan* of the way in which the deportment of the one and the comfort of the other could be combined.

Le Corbusier's dialogical habit of mind took a totally different turn around 1930 when he began to think of revitalizing vernacular culture through its subtle integration with modern technology. Shortly after the Crash of 1929 he began to lose his faith in the manifest destiny of the machine age, and it is just this doubt that came to be played out in his return to primitive constructional methods in the mid-1930s. His faith in what he then characterized as the 'spirit of solidarity', while neither populist nor Marxist, grew out of a conviction that some form of hybrid technique combined with the welfare state of the Popular Front could bring about a new, less unrealistically utopian state of harmony. In this regard one of the most intriguing things about Le Corbusier's reformulation of the new was the way in which he constantly strove to come to terms with the ever escalating reality of modernization, acknowledging, by the mid-1930s, that the bounded domain of the traditional city was a lost cause and going on to posit, as a more viable paradigm, a regional urban fabric comprised of linear industrial settlements running between the nodes of pre-existing towns, leaving the interstitial countryside unencumbered.

After the Second World War Le Corbusier became increasingly involved with the idea of 'intermediate technology', capable of reconciling the split between modernization and local building culture wherever this could be found, be it in Latin America, India, or his beloved Mediterranean. In the last twenty years of his life this caused him to embrace a pantheistic spirituality seemingly capable of overcoming the confrontation between traditional cultural form and the relentless onslaught of ever more volatile technology. It is this perhaps that accounts for the tragic cast lying just beneath the plastic lyricism of his later work. As he put it below his fictitious coat of arms, comprising a sword, a cloud and a star, *la vie est sans pitié* - 'life is without pity'.

KF
New York, Winter 2000

7

Chapter 1 　The Formative Years 1887–1916

It is hard to imagine a more provincial setting than the horological town of La Chaux-de-Fonds, with its population of 27,500, locked away in the Swiss Jura, at the end of the last century. This was where Charles Édouard Jeanneret-Gris (he would assume the pseudonym 'Le Corbusier' in 1920) was born in 1887 to a bourgeois-artisan family, comprising his meticulous father, Georges Édouard Jeanneret-Gris, who was a watch-enameller by trade, and his equally strong-willed mother, Marie-Charlotte-Amélie Perret, who supplemented the family income by teaching piano. Édouard, as he was familiarly known in his youth, was the second son in more ways than one, his brother Albert being greatly favoured by the parents for his evident musical gifts. At the same time, Édouard was the more complex and quixotic personality. He was at once affable and introspective, convivial and solitary, socially inept and yet blessed with a boisterous sense of humour. He was fiercely loyal in friendship and yet, at times, blatantly opportunistic. He oscillated throughout his teens and early twenties between flaunting his artistic ability and suffering bouts of extreme insecurity. At the same time, he was extremely idealistic and burdened throughout his life with a romantic disposition that was exacerbated in early manhood by the assumptions of a Nietzschean self-image. In this respect, he was not beyond distorting the truth as far as his early formation was concerned (in *Vers une architecture* of 1923, for instance, he claimed to have met the great Lyons urbanist Tony Garnier in 1907, whereas we now know the meeting did not take place until 1919[1]).

While he was always close to his family, he was at the same time rather independent, and although passionately attached to La Chaux-de-Fonds he continually escaped its provincialism by travelling throughout Europe for months at a time. All in all, he possessed a markedly dichotomous character that found expression in his later professional career in a particular way. Of all the leading architects of the twentieth century, he was the only one to maintain a double métier throughout his life, dividing his daily routine between painting and architecture. In his maturity, that is from 1924 to 1952, he was in the habit of devoting the mornings to painting and writing and the afternoons to architecture, while from 1953 until

2. Engraved watch case, 1903.

his death in 1965 the sequence was reversed. This alternating regimen contributed in the long run not only to his capacity as an architect but more directly to his stature as a 20th-century painter of consequence, particularly for the works of his Purist period. The same schismatic nature found expression in his youthful years in many different ways, most dramatically perhaps in the engraved watch-case that he made as a school exercise in 1903, in which an Art Nouveau Lalique-like bee is depicted emerging from the abstract Hoffmannesque scales that enclose the rest of the case.[2] There is no more curious example of his dialogical disposition than his professional calling card of 1913, where he advertised his services as both an interior decorator and a specialist in reinforced concrete construction.

28, 32

2

3

One cannot emphasize too strongly the seminal role played in Jeanneret's early life by his teacher in the art school in La Chaux-de-Fonds, the artistic polymath Charles L'Éplattenier. The latter had studied fine and applied art first in Budapest and then more systematically in Paris at the École des Arts Décoratifs and the École des Beaux Arts, before returning to La Chaux-de-Fonds in 1898 to become a leading member of the faculty in the school of art. Jeanneret first came under his influence in 1902 when, at the age of fifteen, he registered for a four-year course in watch engraving, then being taught by L'Éplattenier. As things turned out, it was also L'Éplattenier who later persuaded him to turn his artistic talents towards the field of architecture. That career shift took place in 1905, the year in which L'Éplattenier established his élite *Cours supérieur* (advanced course) under the auspices of the school. The initiative confirmed him as a man of vision who, in the Jugendstil

3. The future Le Corbusier's visiting card, 1913, displaying at a professional level his early predilection for dialogical oppositions.

9

manner of the epoch, was determined to create a new Jura culture largely based on the flora and fauna of the region. To this end he exposed his students to the emerging Anglo-French Arts and Crafts ideology of the epoch, to the writings of the theorists John Ruskin, Owen Jones, Eugène Grasset, and above all Charles Blanc, author of the 1867 *Grammaire des arts du dessin*.

Dedicating himself almost overnight to the practice of architecture, in 1906 the nineteen-year-old Jeanneret designed his first house, the Villa Fallet in La Chaux-de-Fonds, with the help of a local architect named René Chapallaz. The general configuration of the building, the furnishing, and above all the decoration and the sgraffitto relief on its gable front were all from Jeanneret's hand. Following the inductive decorative method set forth in Owen Jones's *The Grammar of Ornament* of 1856, the young Jeanneret covered the gable in a conventionalized pattern derived from the local flora – specifically from the structure, fruit and foliage of the pine tree. As a result of this successful collaboration a partnership was established between Chapallaz and Jeanneret in order to facilitate the detailing and supervision of the next two villas to come from the young architect's hand. These houses, the Villas Stotzer and Jacquemet, erected close to the Villa Fallet for relatives of the Fallet family, were designed in 1908 while Jeanneret was staying in Vienna. All three of these chalet-style villas, along with the Arts and Crafts house that Chapallaz designed for L'Éplattenier in 1904, were intended to display the domestic ethos of a new Jura culture.

Around 1909, much to L'Éplattenier's chagrin, Jeanneret began to distance himself from this regional endeavour, in part because of what he had seen in Italy in 1907, during a tour he made with his sculptor friend Léon Perrin, and in part because of a period that he spent in Paris working in the atelier of Auguste and Gustave Perret, between midsummer 1908 and November 1909. Both of these experiences brought him into contact with the classical tradition, particularly the trip to Italy, where he visited Siena, Ravenna, Padua,

4. Three houses realized in La Chaux-de-Fonds, Switzerland: Villa Fallet, 1906; Villa Stotzer, 1908; and Villa Jacquemet, 1908.

Verona and Florence, although we now know that he initially found the Renaissance to be somewhat antithetical to his Gothic predisposition. Aside from introducing him to French classicism, his apprenticeship with Perret Frères encouraged his latent technocratic bent, above all by exposing him to their experimental work in the development of reinforced concrete construction, Perret Frères being closely associated at the time with the pioneer reinforced concrete contractor François Hennebique. Cutting across these influences was Jeanneret's earlier visit to the Charterhouse of Ema in Tuscany in 1907, an experience that afforded him a generic societal model that would greatly influence the rest of his career. He wrote in retrospect of Ema that there 'I encountered an authentic and overwhelming human aspiration, silence and solitude but also daily contact with men and yet at the same time opening out towards the ineffable.'[3]

Between the Italian journey and his Parisian apprenticeship Jeanneret visited Vienna where, to L'Éplattenier's disappointment, he turned down an opportunity to work with the Wagnerschule master Josef Hoffmann. Notwithstanding the musical culture of the city which he greatly appreciated, he found the decorative Jugendstil climate quite stifling, and after a stay of some weeks he left for Paris. There, a frustrating, inexplicably dilatory search for employment, during which he casually contacted Eugène Grasset, ended when he found part-time work in the office of Auguste Perret, which left him free to pursue his own research in the libraries and museums of the city in the afternoons. On Perret's advice he also studied mathematics and engineering, although not until the last months of his stay in Paris when he was systematically tutored in these subjects by an engineer named Pagès.[4]

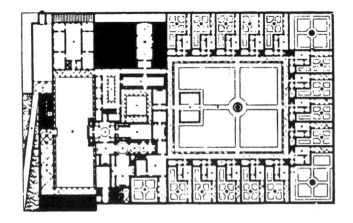

5. The Charterhouse of Ema, near Florence, Italy, 14th century: plan, showing the typical Carthusian monks' cells, each assuming an L-shaped plan formation around a reciprocally L-shaped garden court.

In December 1909 he returned briefly to La Chaux-de-Fonds to present his proposal for the Ateliers d'Art Réunis, which was yet 6 another attempt on the part of L'Éplattenier and his prime pupils to establish a regional centre for the creation and exhibition of applied art. This was Jeanneret's earliest attempt to synthesize his experience of Ema with a *parti* that had a more classical disposition; hence 5 the L-plan studios enclosing courtyards, emulating the standard Carthusian monastic cell type. These were ranged around the edge of a central top-lit exhibition hall that took the form of a glazed pyramid.

In April 1910 he went to Germany, where he visited Karlsruhe, Stuttgart and Ulm before settling for six months in Munich, where, once again, he found employment, this time in the office of the distinguished Deutsche Werkbund architect Theodor Fischer. In the interim, he devoted himself to urban research in the Bavarian State Library and somewhat fortuitously became an acquaintance of the Jura-born Nietzschean music critic and writer William Ritter. In June 1910 he received an official stipend from the school in La Chaux-de-Fonds to study the evolution of applied art in Germany, with an implicit focus on the development of the Deutsche Werkbund that had been established in 1907. This study would be published in 1912 under the title *Étude sur le Mouvement d'art décoratif en Allemagne*. In the course of documenting the movement he made two successive tours in Germany. The first, starting in June 1910, took him to Berlin, Halle, Weimar, Jena, Nuremberg and Augsburg; the second, starting in April 1911, took him to Heidelberg, Frankfurt, Mainz, Wiesbaden, Cologne, Hagen and Hamburg. His stay in Germany enabled him to become fluent in

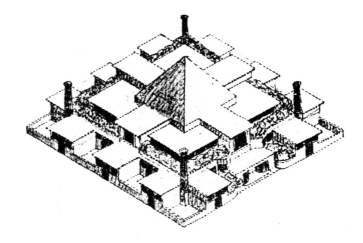

6. Project for the Ateliers d'Art Réunis in La Chaux-de-Fonds, Switzerland, 1909. Note that the individual artists' studios running around the perimeter at ground level are also arranged around garden courts.

German and this he put to good use when from mid-October 1910 to the end of March 1911 he worked in the office of Peter Behrens in Neubabelsberg near Berlin. While this employment led to his first encounter with Ludwig Mies van der Rohe, he was extremely disaffected with the five months he spent with Behrens: 'At Behrens's office', he wrote, 'one does not make pure architecture, only the façade: constructional heresies are evident everywhere ...'[5]

1910 was also the year in which Jeanneret first began to give serious consideration to the issue of town-planning, a theme to which he had again been introduced by L'Éplattenier. Inspired by the German theorist Camillo Sitte's *Der Städte-Bau nach seinen künstlerischen Grundsätzen* (City Planning According to Artistic Principles), which had appeared in French in 1902, L'Éplattenier proposed that he and Jeanneret co-author a book entitled *La Construction des villes* (p. 46). Once again his prodigy was launched into an overly ambitious piece of research; one which, while immediately helpful for L'Éplattenier who had to give an address on this very theme, did not come to fruition as a book until the publication of Le Corbusier's *Urbanisme* in 1925 (p.49).

At the end of his second tour, when Jeanneret had finally compiled enough material for his study of the Deutsche Werkbund, he suddenly left Germany for the Near East and Greece in the company of his new-found antiquarian friend August Klipstein. What he later called his *Voyage d'Orient* began in May 1911 and lasted for some five months, during which time he made over 300 drawings, took 500 photographs, and filled six exercise books with copious notes, excerpts from which were first published in the La Chaux-de-Fonds newspaper *Feuille d'Avis* in 1911.[6] When he finally got to Athens, Jeanneret was overwhelmed by the presence of the Acropolis. It was a spiritual encounter for which he had been prepared in advance by Ernest Renan's study, *Prière sur l'Acropole*, of 1894. That this experience had a lasting impact on his thought is indicated by the way the Acropolis reappears as a powerful image throughout his career. Thus we find him writing of the Erechtheion in 1922:

Emotion is born of unity of aim; of that unperturbed resolution that wrought its marble with the firm intention of achieving all that is most pure, most clarified, most economical. Every sacrifice, every cleansing had already been performed. The moment was reached when nothing more might be taken away, when nothing would be left but these closely knit and violent elements, sounding clear and tragic like brazen trumpets.[7]

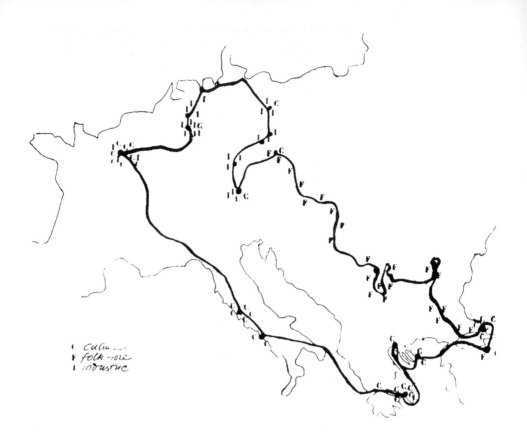

I Culin...
F folk-lore
I industrie

Renan was not alone among the authors who exercised an influence on Jeanneret at this time. He was equally impressed by Ruskin's *Seven Lamps of Architecture* of 1849 and in particular by Ruskin's theory that there were two distinctly different European cultures: the northern, practical and level-headed, and the southern, monastic and spiritual. The other writer to have an impact on him at this time was Henri Provensal, whose equally dialogical *L'Art de Demain* of 1904 argued that the task of art was the reconciliation of the material with the spiritual. For Provensal architecture was 'le drame plastique...de pleins et de vides, de jeux d'ombres et de lumières' – a text which found its paraphrase in Le Corbusier's 'Architecture is the masterly, correct and magnificent play of masses brought together in light.'[8]

However, neither of these luminaries had such a decisive and catalytic impact on Jeanneret as two relatively obscure Suisse-Romande intellectuals, the aforementioned William Ritter[9] and an artist named Alexandre Cingria-Vaneyre. Between them they shaped his entire outlook, not only nurturing his feeling for the vernacular but also seeding the neoclassical stance that he would adopt when he returned to La Chaux-de-Fonds in 1912, to begin his independent career as an architect. In this respect, the dominant influence was Cingria-Vaneyre, who claimed that classicism was the intrinsic cultural tradition of the Jura region, a thesis set forth in his book *Les Entretiens de la Villa du Rouet*, published in 1908. Ritter's influence took a more romantic form, serving not only to introduce Jeanneret to the Balkans and the Near East but also to further his penchant for the Orient and the spiritually evocative sites of the Greek world. Jeanneret became a particular disciple of Ritter in 1910, when he was given a signed copy of Ritter's novel *L'Entêtement slovaque* (Slovak Obstinacy). This was a fictitious but anthropologically accurate account of Slovak peasant life that predetermined Jeanneret's subsequent perception of Eastern Europe. As Paul Turner observed of his *Voyage d'Orient* (not published until 1965, the year of his death),

With the exception of the Parthenon and the mosques in Constantinople, everything he admires is anonymous folk-art...A large part of his account is devoted to descriptions of peasant villages (both in Eastern Europe and Turkey), their houses, their artifacts (pottery, silverwork, costumes, etc.), their rituals and celebrations and their life in general. In many passages, Jeanneret expresses the feeling that this peasant-culture is somehow superior to 'civilized' culture because it is universal and fundamental and, we sense, in touch with deep spiritual forces.[10]

7. Map of the *Voyage d'Orient* of 1911, drawn by Le Corbusier in 1925, showing a varying character of cultural development.
C culture
F folklore
I industry

8. Sketch of the Acropolis, Athens, 1911, reproduced in *Vers une architecture* in 1923.

Such sentiments were quite antithetical to the Socratic dialogue recounted in *Les Entretiens de la Villa du Rouet*, in which two Franco-Swiss art lovers argue that the true culture of the Suisse Romande is Mediterranean and hence, by definition, classic. Thus we must look to Cingria-Vaneyre as the ideological source for the calm geometric forms that would grace the Villa Jeanneret-Perret, designed by Jeanneret for his parents in 1912. Cingria also advocated the use of such earth colours as ivory, olive green and various shades of ochre. These earth colours should be combined, in his view, with white marble and roughcast rendering, approximating to a particular telluric range of tone and texture that would find an echo in Jeanneret's palette as a painter during his high Purist period of the 1920s.[11]

Both the Villa Jeanneret-Perret and the much grander Villa Favre-Jacot, built in La Locle at approximately the same time for the proprietor of the Zenith watch company, ring the changes on a number of crypto-classical tropes, some of them drawn from the work of Behrens. This could hardly be more ironic, given Cingria's anti-German disposition and Jeanneret's ambivalence towards Behrens. Behrensesque allusions are decidedly evident in the *Rundbogenstil* windows of the Villa Favre-Jacot, a work which, as Stanislaus von Moos has remarked, resembles Behrens's Goedecke House at Eppenhausen, Westphalia, of virtually the same date.[12] This was not the only Teutonic influence acting on Jeanneret at the time, however, as is suggested by the raised arises of the Villa Jeanneret-Perret, since these derived from the cable mouldings that emphasize every seam in Josef Hoffmann's Palais Stoclet, built in Brussels in 1911. At the same time the overhanging eaves of the villa, together with its banded windows, suggest an influence from farther afield, notably Frank Lloyd Wright, whose work Jeanneret would have known through the publication of Wright's Wasmuth volumes in Berlin in 1910.[13]

In 1912 L'Éplattenier established the Nouvelle Section de l'École d'Art, staffing his new industrial art school with three former pupils, Georges Aubert, Léon Perrin and Jeanneret himself, while for convenience Jeanneret opened his office nearby at 54 rue Numa-Droz in the following year. For the next two and a half years he would divide his time between teaching architecture and practising interior design, while supplementing his income with antique dealing, since after completing his parents' house and the Villa Favre-Jacot he did not receive another commission for a major work in La Chaux-de-Fonds until 1916. Then came two major

9. Villa Jeanneret-Perret, La Chaux-de-Fonds, Switzerland, 1912.

10. Josef Hoffmann: Palais Stoclet, Brussels, 1911: garden elevation.

10

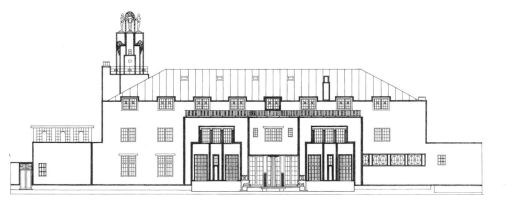

11. Villa Schwob, La Chaux-de-Fonds, Switzerland, 1916–17: living room.

12. Villa Schwob: street front.

commissions, the La Scala Cinema, based on a plan by Chapallaz, and the Villa Schwob, commissioned in April 1916 and completed early in 1917. 11–13

This luxurious house, austerely faced in precision brickwork and capped by a heavy stone cornice, was designed for the watch manufacturer Anatole Schwob, whose factory held the patents for Tavannes and Cyma watches. The classical ordering of this rather hermetic building is perhaps not immediately apparent; although its basic layout is derived from a square plan, its three-dimensional cubic form is subtly overlaid by a structural grid that subdivides it according to a Palladian $A_1 B$ A B A_1 rhythm, with a double-height central A bay and apsidal A_1 bays set to either side. This rhythmic scheme was fleshed out with stylistic tropes drawn from Jeanneret's early experience and schooling – above all the blank central Palladian panel[14] of the main façade and the overscaled cornice modelled in part on the houses of Auguste Perret and in part on the eaves of traditional Turkish houses, an idiosyncratic feature that led to the building being known locally as the 'Villa Turque'. The modulation of the front and back façades was indebted to Perret, while Hoffmann was patently a precedent for much of the interior, notably the balustrading of the first-floor mezzanine overlooking the double-height living room, the cabinets recessed into the walls of the mezzanine, and the living room chandelier. Both the cabinets and the chandelier reiterated the outline of the house in plan.

The pioneering use of a monolithic reinforced concrete frame throughout stemmed again from Perret, although Jeanneret's adoption of an all but beamless floor slab presaged the 'Dom-ino' beamless system that he had first attempted to patent in 1915. Jeanneret's obsession with such an ingenious system is evident 14

from his correspondence with his former school friend, the engineer Max Du Bois, who by 1915 had fully established himself in Paris as a technocratic entrepreneur.

The Villa Schwob made use of two techniques that had become the norm in the construction of watchmaking factories: a fireproof reinforced concrete structural frame, and double-glazing. This last had been dictated by the necessity in the horological industry to overcome the conflict between the need for protection against a severe climate and the need for large windows to provide light for the precision assembly of watches. The villa was equally sophisticated from the point of view of its central heating, since it was provided with a plenum hot-air system throughout, the ducts being cunningly integrated into its walls and floors.

From the formal standpoint one should also note that this was the first occasion on which Jeanneret employed the Golden Section, through the application of what he called *tracés régulateurs* 13 or 'regulating lines' with which to control the neoclassical deportment of the elevations.[15] The proportion of 1 : 1.618, as established by the diagonal of such a rectangle, was the main device used for modulating the façades, although he also seems to have used the arc of a circle to establish the projection of the lateral bays. This laconic, rather sombre, classical format was reinforced on the garden front by inset classical reliefs carved in stone by his colleague Léon Perrin. There thus emerged after considerable difficulty and a contentious relationship with the client the only work of quality to survive from Jeanneret's Swiss career as a specialist in reinforced concrete construction[16] – which, incidentally, was only one among a number of professional hats that he attempted to wear during his final years in La Chaux-de-Fonds.

13. Villa Schwob: garden front, demonstrating the application of *tracés régulateurs* (regulating lines).

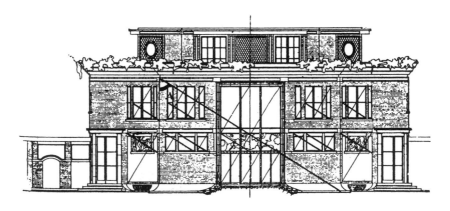

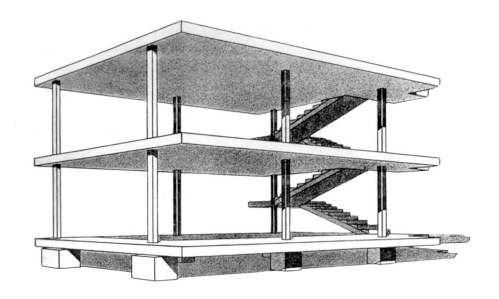

14. The Dom-ino system, 1915:
axonometric of the structure.

15. The Dom-ino system applied to
a courtyard block, 1915.

Chapter 2   Towards a New Architecture[1] 1915–1927

As an autodidact who had an unfailing sense for what should be the next step in his career, Jeanneret moved in January 1917 to Paris. There he became a consultant architect to Max Du Bois's Société d'Application du Béton Armé (SABA), for which he designed and realized a number of reinforced concrete buildings, including a water tower at Podensac (Gironde), an arsenal at Toulouse and a hydro-electric plant at L'Isle Jourdain. In the same year he was also commissioned to design workers' housing at a power plant under construction in Saintes (Charente-Maritime). From the time of his arrival in Paris, Du Bois seems to have employed him in a double capacity: in the first instance as a consultant-architect, and in the second as a partner-manager of the Alfortville brickworks to the southeast of the city, which had been established in part as a means of recycling clinker from the coal-burning generators of a power plant that Du Bois owned.[2] This clinker when mixed with cement was cast into the form of insulating blocks that Du Bois marketed under the name 'Brique Aéroscorie'. At the same time, Du Bois encouraged Jeanneret to establish a *bureau d'études*, a technical office, the Société d'Entreprises Industrielles et d'Études, operating under the acronym SEIE.

Veering away from his aspirations to become a high bourgeois architect, Jeanneret concentrated, at this stage of his development, on the rationalization of building production, particularly as it might be applied to low-cost housing. He had first addressed the issue in his Dom-ino studies of 1915, when he realized that the peri- 14, 15 od of reconstruction following the First World War would have to accord high priority to re-housing the population.[3] It was this that prompted him to take out patents on various systems of prefabricated concrete construction that he developed, and the same impulse also lies behind the conceit of devising patent names for his inventions, such as 'Dom-ino', which seems to have been derived from contracting and combining the words *domicile* and *innovation* – although it is characteristic of his penchant for double metaphors that the abstract representation of a typical Dom-ino structure in plan should also resemble a domino and be hypothetically capable of being assembled much like dominoes are during a game.

16. Le Corbusier and Pierre Jeanneret: Cité-Jardin Frugès, Pessac, 1924–26: view of 'skyscraper' blocks.

Given that the Dom-ino system already embodied the flat-slab, cantilevering principle of his famous *plan libre* or free plan of 1925–26, it is surprising to find that in its initial formation it was seen merely as a means to an end; that is to say, it appears to have been largely conceived as a flexible system of reinforced concrete framing that could be readily filled in with traditional masonry – as would indeed be the case in much of the housing that Le Corbusier/Jeanneret built in the early 1920s for the industrialist Henri Frugès. (By then, it should be noted, he had assumed the aristocratic-sounding sobriquet 'Le Corbusier' by which he would be known for the rest of his career: see p. 27.) Le Corbusier first tried out his Dom-ino system in the Maison du Tonkin, realized for Frugès in the centre of Bordeaux in 1924. This diminutive dwelling was accompanied by other works for Frugès at around the same time: two experimental houses built at Lège on the Atlantic coast, plus a large garden estate at Pessac (1924–26). Pessac was the first version of what Le Corbusier termed a 'cité jardin horizontale'. 16, 17 One should note here once again his polemical use of a 'patent' name for what was already by then a commonly received idea, namely the Anglo-Saxon garden suburb. At the same time, Pessac was also the occasion for his initial foray in polychromy, conceived somewhat after the 'dazzle' camouflage ships of the First World War. Of it he wrote in 1929:

We established a standard value: white elevations.
Where the rows of houses tended to fuse into an opaque mass, we camouflaged each house: the street facades are thus alternately brown and white. Where a lateral facade is white, the next one is pale green. The return end facade, whether the lateral is pale green or white, is dark brown. This tends to suppress the sense of mass and amplify the apparent surface area. Such polychromatic treatment is absolutely new. It provides an elemental architectural symphony of exceptional physiological power. The co-ordinated physiological sensations in terms of volume, surface, contour and colour, afford an intense lyricism.[4]

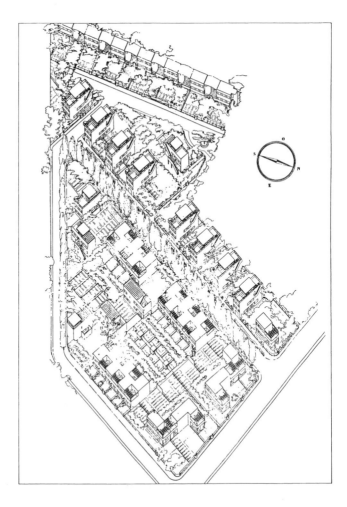

17. Le Corbusier and Pierre Jeanneret: Cité-Jardin Frugès, Pessac: axonometric.

A great deal of Le Corbusier/Jeanneret's energy over the years 1915–25 was spent in devising economical means of construction, and this led to a number of innovative structural systems, including a new way for constructing exterior walls out of hollow asbestos cement casings, the voids being filled with the rubble from war-damaged buildings. He first envisaged the system in his Maison Monol proposal of 1919. The patent name 'Monol', deriving from 'monolithic', was in fact misleading, since there would have been a decisive structural difference between the asbestos cement walls, filled with rubble, and the shell-vaults cast on top of corrugated asbestos, the curved form of the sheeting being used as permanent form-work. These vaults would have been supported by trimmer beams and free-standing cylindrical concrete columns.[5] Despite the ingenuity of such inventions, Jeanneret slowly came to recognize that untried building materials and methods were not readily marketable. He recounted his misadventure in this regard to Jean Petit:

I was not able to sell my products because they were too well suited to current needs. Everyday habit stood in my way. I had to balance myself constantly between two different impulses.
If I had been indifferent to the core within myself, I would have readily triumphed, but I sensed in my heart the way in which each one of us must live. Business is a cruel school. Ozenfant told me, Jeanneret, you must paint. I believed at one moment that I could do this in the afternoons, but my affairs caught up with me. I really had to get myself back into harness. One calls this the flux and re-flux of life and happily I soon began to find myself again.[6]

18. A sequence of single-storey Maison Monol units, 1919.

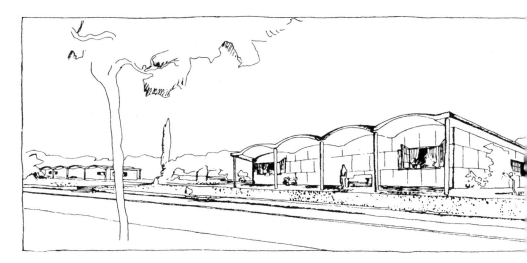

Le Corbusier is alluding here to the catalytic role played in his life
by the painter Amédée Ozenfant, whom he met through Perret during the last weeks of 1917 at a lunch that they took together on the
premises of the Association Art et Liberté. After meeting Ozenfant,
Jeanneret took to the habit of painting and writing at night while
continuing to work for SABA and the brickworks during the day. The
relationship between the two men was extremely fertile, for while
Jeanneret had much to gain from Ozenfant's cosmopolitan urbanity
and artistic sophistication, Ozenfant, in turn, was able to take advan-
tage of Jeanneret's architectonic outlook as a means of distancing
himself from the received line of the Cubist avant-garde. After a joint
vacation in Andernos, where Jeanneret learned the technique of oil
painting from Ozenfant, the two exhibited at the Galerie Thomas
and published their manifesto *Après le cubisme* on 15 October 1918.
Two years later they founded the magazine *L'Esprit Nouveau*, subti-
tled '*Revue internationale d'esthétique*', which they edited in collaboration with the Dadaist poet Paul Dermée, who remained an editor
for the first six issues. With the first issue, of 15 October 1920,
L'Esprit Nouveau declared its optimistic article of faith under the editorial premise, 'There is a new spirit, it is a spirit of construction and
synthesis guided by a clear conception.'[7] Ostensibly addressing
themselves to painters, musicians, writers, industrialists and engineers, the editors underplayed architecture in the first issue, save
for an article entitled 'Trois rappels à MM. les Architectes' (Three
Reminders for Architects), written jointly by Jeanneret and
Ozenfant under a pseudonym (see below). The same inaugural issue
carried an article entitled 'Sur la Plastique', in which they attempted
to deduce the syntax of Purism from first principles – a text signed
on this occasion with their actual names.

19

20

21

L'ESPRIT NOUVEAU

REVUE INTERNATIONALE D'ESTHÉTIQUE

PARAISSANT LE 15 DE CHAQUE MOIS   *DIRECTEUR : PAUL DERMÉE*

ESTHÉTIQUE   EXPÉRIMENTALE
PEINTURE   SCULPTURE   ARCHITECTURE
LITTÉRATURE   MUSIQUE
ESTHÉTIQUE DE L'INGÉNIEUR
LE THÉÂTRE LE MUSIC-HALL LE CINÉMA LE CIRQUE LES SPORTS
LE COSTUME   LE LIVRE   LE MEUBLE
ESTHÉTIQUE DE LA VIE MODERNE

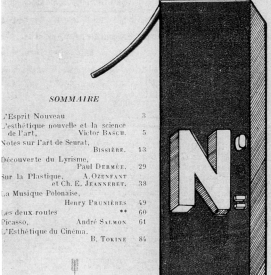

DANS CE NUMÉRO

50 photogravures et deux reproductions
aux trois couleurs,

SOMMAIRE

L'Esprit Nouveau   3
L'esthétique nouvelle et la science
de l'art,   Victor BASCH.   5
Notes sur l'art de Seurat,
    BISSIÈRE.   13
Découverte du Lyrisme,
    Paul DERMÉE.   29
Sur la Plastique,   A. OZENFANT
    et Ch. E. JEANNERET.   38
La Musique Polonaise,
    Henry PRUNIÈRES   49
Les deux routes   **   60
Picasso,   André SALMON   61
L'Esthétique du Cinéma,
    B. TOKINE   84

Trois rappels à MM. les Architectes,
    LE CORBUSIER-SAUGNIER.   91
Le Cirque, art nouveau,
    Céline ARNAULD.   97
Notes sur les revues 1914-1920,
    G. de LACAZE-DUTHIERS   99
Calligrammes *(Apollinaire)*,
    Louis ARAGON   103
Les Expositions (Picabia),
    G. RIBEMONT-DESSAIGNES   108
La littérature de langue espagnole
d'aujourd'hui,
    Vicente HUIDOBRO   111
La nouvelle poésie allemande,
    Ivan GOLL   113
Echos de l'Hôtel Drouot   116
    etc...   136

Voir au dos les avantages et les
primes réservés aux Abonnés.

PRIX NET : **6** francs français
POUR TOUS PAYS

ÉDITIONS DE L'ESPRIT NOUVEAU
SOCIÉTÉ ANONYME AU CAPITAL DE 100.000 FRANCS
13, QUAI DE CONTI
PARIS (VI⁰)

In that joint pseudonym of autumn 1920, Charles Édouard Jeanneret first addressed the world as 'Le Corbusier'. The piece was signed 'Le Corbusier-Saugnier', a fictive nom-de-plume derived from their family names. Where Ozenfant took his mother's maiden name, Jeanneret turned to that of his great-grandfather, a certain Monsieur Le Corbezier of Brussels, whose portrait had hung over the piano in Jeanneret's home during his youth.

With its arresting cover, designed by Le Corbusier's second 20 cousin Pierre Jeanneret (pp. 42–43) – a design in which the bold number of the issue was given equal weight with the title – *L'Esprit Nouveau* established a new genre of cultural journalism in terms of both content and graphics. Indulging in a proto-Surrealist adaptation of 19th-century playbill typefaces, it was simultaneously radical and conservative. Influenced by Apollinaire's 'Calligrammes' (reviewed in the first issue) and by F. T. Marinetti's equally graphic 'Words at Liberty' (*parole en libertà*), Le Corbusier's habitual exhortatory style, with his own polemical graphics, first appeared in the layout and editing of *L'Esprit Nouveau*. The Purist Manifesto, *Après le cubisme*, reworked as *Le Purisme*, would be featured in the fourth issue of the magazine in 1920. Arguing that the techno-scientific industrial character of the age demanded not the mechanical dynamism of the Italian Futurists but a deeper cultural response grounded in the universality of mathematics, they went on to distinguish between *primary* and *secondary* sensations, the one being induced by universal, Platonic forms, the other attaining its aesthetic effect by virtue of its significance within a specific cultural context.

There are secondary sensations, varying with the individual because they depend upon his cultural or hereditary capital...Primary sensations constitute the bases of the plastic language; these are the fixed words of the plastic language; it is a fixed, formal, explicit, universal language determining subjective reactions of an individual order which permit the erection on these raw foundations of a sensitive work, rich in emotion...An art that would be based only upon primary sensations, using uniquely primary elements, would be only a primary art, rich, it is true, in geometric aspects, but denuded of all sufficient human resonance: it would be an ornamental art.

An art that would be based only upon the use of secondary sensations (an art of allusions) would be an art without a plastic base.[8]

20. Pierre Jeanneret: cover design for *L'Esprit Nouveau*, 1920. Note, at the top of the right column of contents, the first appearance of the name 'Le Corbusier'.

This dialogical concept, combined with a belief in biological economy as the main principle behind natural selection, enabled them to transfer the concept of Darwinian evolution to the field of machine-made forms. At this juncture Purism went beyond being just a polemical aesthetic precept. In the very breadth of its discourse, it seems to have been posited as nothing less than a general theory of civilization. Thus iconographically and otherwise it was always more than just another avant-gardist line in the evolution of 20th-century art. A canonical canvas like Jeanneret's *Nature Morte à la Pile d'Assiettes* (Still-Life with a Stack of Plates) of 1920 was not only a demonstration of the interaction between primary and secondary forms: it was also intended to serve as an iconic evocation of a totally new way of life. Like the Cubist paintings from which it was derived, it represented a metropolitan civilization, in which the public realm of the café terrace was represented through a layering of architectonic planes and by overlapping plan and sectional representations of standard café tableware. In the centre of this canvas was the quasi-erotic symbol of two clay pipes interlocking about an empty glass. In imagistic terms, this was a characteristic Purist metaphor, part industrial, part folkloric. It was the focal point of an asymmetrical composition that was shifted off axis by a stack of plates and the pages of an open book. This last was a particularly ambiguous image in that it was left uncertain as to whether the ochre, shaded, curvaceous form occupying the centre of the picture was a book or a classical moulding.

The Purist *rappel à l'ordre*[9] extended forward and backward in time; forward towards the imminent industrialized future and backward towards the Greek world. Ozenfant wrote: 'the newness of our time re-establishes the tie with the Greek epoch'.[10] It also recalled Claude Perrault's 17th-century distinction between positive and arbitrary beauty. With typical Cartesian scepticism, Perrault had restricted the former to three attributes: symmetry, richness of materials, and precision of execution. The latter was dependent on local aesthetic convention, which for him included the five classical orders. In a parallel manner, Ozenfant and Le Corbusier wished to distinguish between the *primary* abstract character of architecture and the *secondary* attributes of ergonomic form, an interplay that both men saw as the inevitable dialectic of the machine age. The formal consequences of this interplay were made explicit by Le Corbusier in his book *Urbanisme* of 1925 when he wrote: 'We can say that the further human creations are removed from our immediate grasp, the more they tend to pure geometry; a violin or a chair, things which come into close contact with the body, are of a less pure geometry.'[11]

Almost all of *Vers une architecture*, published in book form in 1923 under Le Corbusier's name alone, was initially issued under the joint pseudonym 'Le Corbusier-Saugnier'. Only the last section, entitled 'Architecture ou révolution' (a title which he had once envisaged for the book as a whole), was credited to Le Corbusier. Elsewhere, when exhibiting conjointly as Purist painters, or writing on aesthetics, Le Corbusier and Ozenfant would assume their real names, although they would also use other pseudonyms such as Vauvrecy, Fayet, Paul Boulard (Le Corbusier) and Julian Caron (Ozenfant). Despite this close, almost 'incestuous' collaboration, the nineteenth number of *L'Esprit Nouveau*, appearing at the end of 1923, anticipated the eventual dissolution of their partnership, for thereafter Le Corbusier signed the pieces on architecture alone. Despite their estrangement, in the same issue Ozenfant wrote a generous appraisal of *Vers une architecture*, conceding credit for the text to Le Corbusier.

While *Vers une architecture* fails to sustain a tight, consequential argument, its importance as an overall primer in Purist aesthetic theory resides in the fact that here for the first time the fundamental split between engineering and architecture is set forth in dialectical terms. As Le Corbusier put it in a passage that heads each of the three sections dealing with architecture in the latter part of the book,

You employ stone, wood and concrete, and with these materials you build houses and palaces. That is construction. Ingenuity is at work.

But suddenly you touch my heart, you do me good, I am happy and I say: 'This is beautiful.' That is Architecture. Art enters in.

My house is practical. I thank you, as I might thank Railway engineers, or the Telephone service. You have not touched my heart.

But suppose that walls rise towards heaven in such a way that I am moved. I perceive your intentions. Your mood has been gentle, brutal, charming or noble. The stones you have erected tell me so. You fix me to the place and my eyes regard it. They behold something which expresses a thought. A thought which reveals itself without word or sound, but solely by means of shapes which stand in a certain relationship to one another. These shapes are such that they are clearly revealed in light. The relationships between them have not necessarily any reference to what is practical or descriptive. They are a mathematical creation of your mind. They are the language of Architecture. By the use of raw materials and starting from conditions more or less utilitarian, you have established certain relationships which have aroused my emotions.

This is Architecture.[12]

Silo à grain.

TROIS RAPPELS
A MESSIEURS LES ARCHITECTES

I

LE VOLUME

This lyrical tone is left behind as soon as he begins to address the rationalization of building production in the penultimate section of the book, entitled 'Maisons en série' (mass-production houses). In the final chapter, 'Architecture ou révolution', he touches on the idea of revolution, both technical and political. By the former, he clearly meant the industrial revolution, already achieved through the mass production of automobiles; by the latter, he presumably intended revolutionary socialism fermenting beneath the surface of society and due primarily, in his view, to the fact that the working class was ill-housed (see also p. 118):

The machinery of Society, profoundly out of gear, oscillates between an amelioration, of historical importance, and a catastrophe.

The primordial instinct of every human being is to assure himself of a shelter.

The various classes of workers in society to-day no longer have dwellings adapted to their needs; neither the artisan nor the intellectual.

It is a question of building which is at the root of the social unrest of to-day; architecture or revolution.[13]

The significance of *Vers une architecture* resides in the fact that for the first time the two sides of Le Corbusier's Purist vision – the Academic and the Machinist – were integrated at a programmatic level, sustained by the conviction, inherited from Adolf Loos, that the style of the modern era already existed. For Le Corbusier this was as manifest in the instrumental character of metropolitan life as it was in the sublime character of large-scale engineering works. The latter exemplified the Engineer's Aesthetic as this was already evident in skyscrapers, grain silos, cranes and bridges of the modern world – engineering structures that, together with newly mecha-nized means of transport, had been recognized as the technological elements of the new industrial age in the Deutsche Werkbund yearbooks of 1913 and 1914.

In *Vers une architecture,* Le Corbusier fused together two dis-tinctly different aspects of modern technology: on the one hand the German appraisal of the cultural significance of engineering form as this had been recognized by Walter Gropius and other Werkbund writers,[14] and on the other his own naïve experience in the field of prefabricated housing. To these two classes of production he brought two parallel complementary aesthetic perceptions. In the first instance, there was the proto-Dadaistic aura that accrued to large civil engineering works when these were set against the grandeur of nature, as one might find this, say, in Gustave Eiffel's

21

21. *Vers une architecture*, 1923: title page for the first of the 'Three Reminders to Architects', featuring a north American grain elevator.

22. Illustration from *Vers une architecture*, 1923: the transatlantic liner *Aquitania* compared to four Parisian monuments – Notre Dame, the Tour St-Jacques, the Arc de Triomphe, and the Opéra.

railway viaducts in the Massif Central, such as his Garabit Viaduct of 1884 which served as the key illustration to the title page of the chapter entitled 'The Engineer's Aesthetic and Architecture'. An equally sublime juxtaposition appears in the first section of the chapter 'Eyes Which Do Not See', where in a culled magazine image the liner *Aquitania*, with its capacity of 3,600 passengers, is displayed against four Parisian monuments, the cathedral of Notre Dame, the Tour St-Jacques, the Arc de Triomphe and the Opéra. Beneath this, he writes:

Architects live and move within the narrow limits of academic acquirements and in ignorance of new ways of building, and they are quite willing that their conceptions should remain as doves kissing one another. But our daring and masterly constructors of steamships produce palaces in comparison with which cathedrals are tiny things, and they throw them on the sea.[15]

In the second instance, there was the ongoing proliferation of standard, mass-produced objects which were seen by Le Corbusier and Ozenfant as a concatenation of *objets trouvés*, ranging in affective tone from the coldly hygienic to the sensuously utilitarian. They had in mind the partly machine-made, partly crafted straw hats, spats, shoes, cigarette cases, luggage, clothing, bidets, filing cabinets, dynamos, fans and other mechanistic accoutrements that frequently appeared as advertisements or as illustrations in the pages of *L'Esprit Nouveau*. With the discontinuation of the journal in 1925, these 'readymades'[16] were assembled as the anonymous lingua franca of the modern world in Le Corbusier's polemical *L'Art décoratif d'aujourd'hui* published in the same year.

Along with the Bauhausler László Moholy Nagy, Le Corbusier was one of the first propagandists of the modern movement to exploit the ceaseless proliferation of modern graphic and photographic images. He constantly mixed these images with his own projected work, thereby fusing the real with the ideal and vice versa. He even employed the technique of photomontage to imply the realization of works that were still only hypothetical, or alternatively, on occasion, to depict the buildings of others as though they were his own. Le Corbusier's consummate skill in juxtaposing word and image enabled him to substantiate one rhetorical claim after another. Especially, it helped to give conviction to his critique of the École des Beaux Arts and the fashionable Art Deco movement, which by the mid-1920s was the most appealing neo-modern alternative to Purism.

Above all, Le Corbusier was one of the first architects of the 20th century to set such store by the precise photographic record of his finished work. His realized buildings were invariably published as Purist set-pieces, pristine, empty, luminous spaces, removed from the quotidian contaminations of domesticity and the inevitable depredations of time, depicted without the furnishings of the occupant and often enhanced by certain objects that implied the elective affinities of Purism – a trilby hat casually placed on a hall table, a lay figure posed on a window sill, an electric fan, a coffee pot, a jug and a fish, these last four being posed together like a still-life on the table in the otherwise deserted kitchen.

23. Le Corbusier and Pierre Jeanneret: Villa Stein de Monzie, Garches, 1927: kitchen.

23

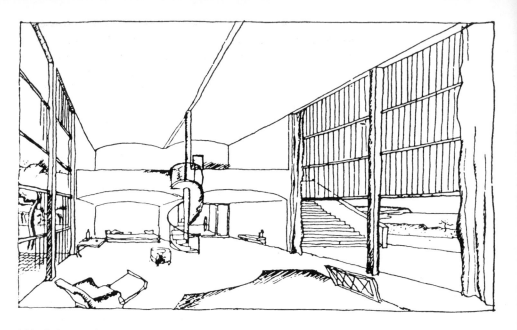

24. Le Corbusier and Pierre Jeanneret: 'Villa au bord de la mer', 1921.

25. Le Corbusier and Pierre Jeanneret: first version of the Maison Citrohan, 1920: perspective.

26. Le Corbusier and Pierre Jeanneret: first version of the Maison Citrohan: plans of the ground floor, mezzanine, and roof terrace.

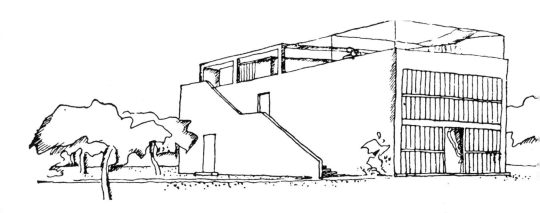

While the bulk of Le Corbusier's early project work as an independent architect in Paris consisted of prototypical low-cost workers' housing schemes of various kinds, the first esquisse for a bourgeois villa appeared in 1921 with his 'Villa au bord de la mer' 24 (house by the sea) for the couturier Paul Poiret. Among his housing schemes, the most innovative, from a constructional standpoint, were the various applications of the Dom-ino type-form to the 14, 15 accommodation of mass housing, and the Maison Monol proto- 18 type, the one contingent on an orthogonal concrete frame, the other on a concrete vault. However, the spatial breakthrough from which much of his future work would evolve came with the Maison Citrohan (1920) – the name being chosen in order to evoke the 25, 26 mass-production norms of a Citroën car.[17] This could hardly have been more misleading, however, since from a technical standpoint the house was somewhat retardataire. Its plan and sectional form were derived in part from the 19th-century artist's studio and in part from the megaron form of the Mediterranean vernacular. This last, typical of the islands of the Aegean and equally evident in North Africa, comprised two parallel load-bearing walls roofed by a primitive masonry vault and open at one end. It is the typical construction of the narrow-fronted, whitewashed peasant's house that one may still find in the Greek islands today. At the same time, the Maison Citrohan was also conceived as synthesizing other type-forms drawn from metropolitan culture: on the one hand, the typical small back-lot Parisian workshop, and on the other, the narrow-fronted café/restaurant. Le Corbusier's retrospective account of stumbling upon the latter as a kind of *objet trouvé* testifies to this:

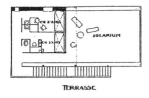

TERRASSE

ENTRESOL

REZ DE CHAUSSEE

We were in the habit of eating in a little coachmen's restaurant in the centre of Paris; there was the bar (the zinc), and the kitchen at the rear; a mezzanine cutting the height of the place in two; the big window opening onto the street. One fine day, we discovered this and we saw that a certain paradigm was in evidence here, namely, an architectural arrangement that could be adapted to the organization of a house.[18]

With the first Maison Citrohan the essential domestic themes of his architectural career are already established: the augmentation of a restricted floor area by a double-height volume; the exploitation of the flat roof as an elevated terrace; the combination of metal-framed, industrial glazing with a reinforced concrete frame and concrete block infill; an anomalous insistence on retaining such bourgeois amenities as a boudoir and a maid's room; and finally, the implicit paradox of positing this reduced, abstract

architecture as a classless, quasi-vernacular norm. In all of this the Viennese cultural debate of the turn of the century was more influential on Le Corbusier's early work than is perhaps sufficiently acknowledged. By 1920 he was evidently under the spell of Adolf Loos's opposition to Josef Hoffmann's compulsion to render the bourgeois dwelling as a 'total work of art', designing everything from the cutlery on the table to the ornamental pinnacles on the roof (cf. Hoffmann's Palais Stoclet, Brussels, 1911). Thus the stripped-down geometrical severity of the Citrohan House seems to have been a direct response to Loos's critical precept that 'a house should be rich within and banal without'.

One needs to remark here on Le Corbusier's habitual typological approach, exemplified in this instance by the way in which the first Citrohan House of 1920 was followed by a second, improved version exhibited as a model at the Salon d'Automne in 1922. The initial three-storey prototype was now raised on reinforced concrete pillars with garaging and services beneath, while the roof-top accommodation, that is to say the children's bedrooms (guest rooms in the first project) were now to be reached by an enclosed staircase extending from the raised living level to the roof. The standard Parisian workshop glazing was replaced by symmetrically composed large glass panes set in metal frames, while the overhanging roof slab and the balcony to the living room terrace were terminated with discreet cornices. One should hasten to add that the Citrohan House prototypes by no means exhausted the permutations that were to be derived from the original megaron form,

27. Le Corbusier and Pierre Jeanneret: second version of the Maison Citrohan, elevated on *pilotis*, 1922: model.

particularly as appears from the 'Maison d'artiste' of 1922 where an elevated single-storey living space is capped by a one-and-a-half-height monitor-lit studio, or the 'Maisons en série pour artisans' (mass-production craftsmen's houses) of 1924 where the initial primary volume is reduced to a half-cube. Above the square plan of this last, a ground-floor living level is ingeniously augmented by a triangular sleeping mezzanine with its balustrade and access stair aligning with the diagonal of the square. We should note in passing that Le Corbusier and Pierre Jeanneret would eventually realize a reduced version of their second Citrohan House at the Stuttgart Weissenhofsiedlung of 1927.

Along with its origin in European critical culture, the evolution of the Purist project depended upon a constant fertile interchange between architecture and painting, with Le Corbusier's architecture often being the three-dimensional equivalent of a Purist canvas and vice versa. This oscillation is particularly evident in two seminal pieces of the early 1920s: the Maison La Roche of 1923 and the Pavillon de l'Esprit Nouveau of 1925. The former originated with art in more than one sense, since Le Corbusier and Ozenfant had directly advised the young banker Raoul La Roche in his progressive acquisition of a series of Cubist and Purist pictures. As a consequence of this association Le Corbusier was commissioned to design a house to accommodate the collection, a project which was

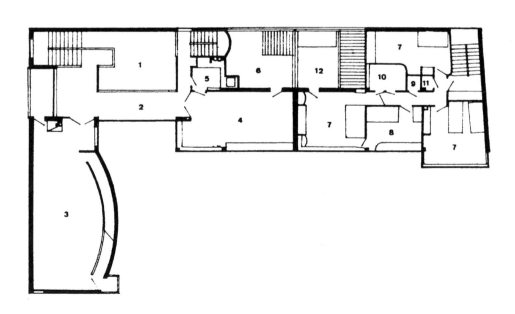

29. Le Corbusier and Pierre Jeanneret: Maison La Roche, Paris, 1923: general view, with the gallery wing on the left.

30. Le Corbusier and Pierre Jeanneret: first-floor plan of the Maison La Roche (left) and Maison Albert Jeanneret, Paris.
 1 void to entrance hall
 2 bridge
 3 picture gallery
 4 dining room
 5 servery
 6 yard
 7 bedroom;
 8 dressing room
 9 w.c.
 10 bathroom
 11 sluice

duly put in hand as part of an earlier independent proposal by the architect to build a small residential cluster in the Square du Docteur Blanche in the Auteuil district of Paris. However, as a result of an unforeseen reduction in the width of the site, this cul-de-sac set-piece was reduced to two three-storey houses. The first of these, on entering the street, was occupied by Le Corbusier's brother Albert Jeanneret and the latter's Swedish wife, Lotti Raaf. (By this date, the musical Albert was teaching dance and eurhythmics according to the Jaques-Dalcroze method.[19]) The second house, belonging to La Roche, ended the street with an art gallery standing on cylindrical concrete columns – the first incarnation of Le Corbusier's characteristic *pilotis*. With its three-storey entrance hall, double-height gallery and mezzanine library (this last being accessed by a steep ramp from the raised gallery), this was the larger and the more spatially elaborate house. However it was also the occasion for an unexpected confrontation between art and architecture, for in a letter to Le Corbusier in 1926 La Roche wrote:

Reading between the lines of your article in the Cahiers d'Art, *No. 3, I was aware of some criticisms levelled at me. Indeed you loyally warned me in advance of them. What can I say? No doubt you have reason for complaint if the impact of your walls, of whom I have been one of the chief admirers, is ruined … The house, once built, was so beautiful that on seeing it I cried:'It's almost a pity to put paintings in it!' Nevertheless, I did so. How could I have done otherwise? Do I not have certain obligations to my painters, of whom yourself are one? I commissioned from you 'a frame for my collection'. You provided me with 'a poem of walls'. Which of us two is most to blame?* [20]

31. Le Corbusier and Pierre Jeanneret: Maison La Roche: picture gallery and mezzanine library.

32. Le Corbusier and Pierre
Jeanneret: Pavillon de l'Esprit
Nouveau, Paris, 1925: interior,
with Purist furnishings.

33. Le Corbusier and Pierre
Jeanneret. Pavillon de l'Esprit
Nouveau: exterior.

The need to avoid this conflict between the 'walls' and the 'works' had already been touched on in the 'Manual of the Dwelling' section in *Vers une architecture*, where the reader is advised to exhibit only a few paintings at any one time. This precept would be demonstrated in the Pavillon de l'Esprit Nouveau, with its two exemplary Purist canvases by Fernand Léger and Le Corbusier discretely suspended on a large blank wall.

The Pavillon de l'Esprit Nouveau, located behind the Grand Palais in Paris (as a barely acknowledged counter-thesis to the Exposition des Arts Décoratifs of 1925), was posited as a proto-typical two-storey high-rise dwelling unit, created by combining the megaron form of the Maison Citrohan with the characteristic two-storey L-shaped monk's cell and garden of the standard Carthusian monastery. Lit by a light-well to the rear of the court, the duplex was built around an inset 'hanging garden' rather than being equipped with a balcony in the conventional sense. It is this singular feature that has remained a challenge for all residential high-rise construction ever since, perennially unrealizable it seems due to its volumetric extravagance. This hanging-garden type had already appeared in Le Corbusier's double-sided residential block of 1922, his 'Immeubles-Villas', enclosing a tennis court.

26

5

34

Notwithstanding the cultural trap of the 'total work of art', against which Adolf Loos warned in his 1900 parable 'The Story of a Poor Rich Man', Le Corbusier came near to a similar aesthetic closure by positing an ideal world of Purist objects that were supposedly redeemed from effete aestheticism by being *found* in the surrounding society rather than *designed*. As with the furnishing of the Jeanneret and La Roche houses, this was the essential cultural polemic of the Pavillon de l'Esprit Nouveau, which was equipped with Thonet bentwood chairs from Vienna, Maples leather-upholstered club armchairs from London, Parisian iron park furniture, standard café tableware. However 'readymade' these may have been in the Duchampian sense, they were to be unified as an ensemble by a Purist colour scheme: 'Polychromy: ceiling blue, left hand wall white, right hand wall lower part ochre, upper part white, storage units, yellow ochre.'[21]

It is difficult to overestimate the seminal role played by Le Corbusier's second cousin Pierre Jeanneret (1896–1967) during the first sixteen years of their joint practice in Paris at 35 rue de Sèvres. Pierre Jeanneret had been trained in architecture, sculpture and painting at the École des Beaux Arts in Geneva from 1913 to 1915. Thereafter he served as an architectural apprentice in Geneva

34. Le Corbusier and Pierre Jeanneret: 'Immeubles-Villas', 1922: perspective and typical floor plan.

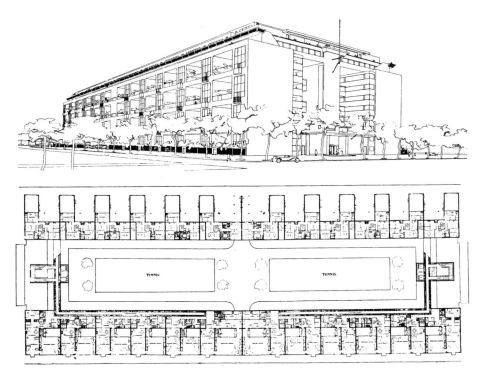

before working for Perret Frères in Paris in the early 1920s. The two cousins began their professional association at the end of 1923 with the inauguration of 'Atelier 35S' (named from the house number plus the 'S' of rue de Sèvres). Pierre Jeanneret was already assisting his cousin part-time during the years he was with Auguste Perret, when he acquired the technical expertise that would prove crucial to the subsequent realizations of the partnership. In this complementary, and at times difficult, association, it is clear that Pierre Jeanneret was the pivotal figure who was constantly present in the studio.[22] He took full responsibility for the everyday production and supervision of the work, while his volatile cousin was always on the move, or even when not travelling was invariably engaged to some degree with his other intellectual activities. Nevertheless Le Corbusier remained responsible for the genesis of the basic concept in most instances, while Jeanneret was limited in large part to the task of evolving and perfecting the form, both spatially and technically. Of their relationship Le Corbusier wrote towards the end of his life (evoking perhaps, at the same time, the ambivalence that he had felt for his mountaineering father): 'I am the sea and he is the mountain and as everyone knows these two can never meet.'[23] There was nonetheless an indissoluble bond between them which, even after it had been forcibly disrupted by the Second World War, was restored in 1951 when Pierre Jeanneret became the site architect for the building of Chandigarh in India.

Le Corbusier and Pierre Jeanneret's Ozenfant atelier of 1926 transformed the second Citrohan House prototype into an irregularly configured cubic studio space under which the rest of the dwelling was rather incommodiously crammed. The main volume was a double-height painter's studio. It was lit by large glazed walls on two adjacent sides and by a saw-tooth factory rooflight above a flat studio lay-light in obscured glass. This privileged Purist space, flooded with light, could hardly have been more different from the cramped sleeping quarters of the single-storey space beneath. The idea of a *promenade architecturale* (p. 79) seems to have been tentatively broached in this work in a carefully contrived sequence of small-scale moves that were intended to accentuate the experience of the space, from the corkscrew compression of the spiral access stairs, both within and without, to the tubular steel companion ladders that afforded a more liberated, if precarious, means of access to the library and mezzanine at the narrow end of the studio.[24] This distorted megaron on an awkward urban site was patently designed to cater to the spiritual needs of the 'artist/monk', as the new ideal, metropolitan man.[25]

35, 36
27

Le Corbusier's work entered a period of unparalleled creativity in the first half of the 1920s that culminated in the realization of three diminutive canonical pieces: the Ozenfant studio, the Maison La Roche, and the Maison Cook. The latter (see pp. 73–77), realized in 1926, combined in a compelling way both the classical and the vernacular strains of the European domestic tradition (cf. Adolf Loos) and at the same time inflected this synthesis with elements drawn from the new industrial world, with metal furnishings, radiators, fenestration and balustrading. Moreover, the use of flat-slab, concrete-framed, cantilevered construction enabled Le Corbusier to happen upon the free plan (*plan libre*) which hitherto had always remained latent in his work but was never actively expressed. Here it was employed not only to liberate the façade from any load-bearing function but also to reconcile in plan and section the interlocking proportions of the square and the Golden Section which modulate the volumetric and surface displacement throughout.

35, 36
28–31
59–62

Chapter 3   The City of Tomorrow¹ 1910–1933

As we have seen, the young Édouard Jeanneret first became concerned with issues of urban design in 1910 when at the instigation of L'Éplattenier he began to research the theme of city form in general, in preparation for their proposed book *La Construction des villes*. Jeanneret modelled his initial studies on Camillo Sitte's *City Planning According to Artistic Principles* of 1889, published in French in 1902 as *L'Art des bâtir les villes* (The Art of Building Cities). This led him away from the rationalist city-planning tradition as he would have known it from the gridded format of La Chaux-de-Fonds with its parallel streets laid out on a slope to receive the sun. The notebooks of the study tours that he made in Germany in 1910 and 1911, when he was ostensibly documenting the achievements of the Deutsche Werkbund, show that he devoted an equal, if not greater, amount of time to the study of urban form.² The focus for his research was the medieval German town, but he also gave considerable space to analysing contemporary developments, as he encountered these in Werner Hegemann's exhibition of city-building staged in Berlin in 1910. There he seems to have become aware of the contemporary work of such pioneer urbanists as the Germans Theodor Fischer, Ludwig Hoffmann and Fritz Schumacher and the Dutch architect/town-planner Hendrik Petrus Berlage, whose 1908 plan for the The Hague was included in the exhibition. He was equally influenced by Raymond Unwin's *Town Planning in Practice* of 1910 and through that he made a study of Unwin's work in Hampstead. As far as the garden city movement in Germany is concerned, he paid particular attention to Paul Mebes's work in Berlin-Zehlendorf and Richard Riemerschmid's garden city of Hellerau outside Dresden, where in 1910 Jaques-Dalcroze had been invited to establish his eurhythmic institute.

Jeanneret's growing familiarity with the European garden city tradition found a certain fulfilment in the garden city that he designed for Arnold Beck in La Chaux-de-Fonds in 1914,³ but in the same year, with the beginning of his Dom-ino studies, he started to renounce his Sittesque manner in favour of a more normative approach to urban design as we find this in his *villes-pilotis* of 1915. That vision of a multi-storey urban fabric raised on piles seems to have been directly influenced by Eugène Hénard's *Études sur les transformations de Paris 1903-1909* (Studies on the Transformations of Paris) that he had found during his research in the Bibliothèque Nationale.[4] One of his earliest proposals for the typological rationalization of city-form, the *rue à redents* or 'street with set-backs' of 1920, is clearly drawn from this source, with the set-backs providing for green space in depth on either side of the typical Haussmannian boulevard. (Hénard was critical of the Haussmannian street; his term 'boulevard à redents' seems to have been derived from the zig-zag fortification system perfected by Vauban at the end of the 17th century.) To this critique Le Corbusier would add his radical proposal for a city of towers, the *ville-tours* of 1920, which we must recognize as the beginning of his heroic attempt to rationalize the received form of the American skyscraper.

Le Corbusier entered a period of unparalleled creativity in the early 1920s, culminating as far as his ideal urban dwelling unit was concerned in the Pavillon de l'Esprit Nouveau of 1925. First formulated in 1922, the double-height Esprit Nouveau cell, with its suspended terrace, would serve as the normative dwelling for all of Le Corbusier's high-rise housing projects until 1930. He initially conceived of it in relation to two different paradigms: on the one hand the unit derived from the Carthusian monastic cell; on the other the Baroque palace, as this had been appropriated by the Utopian Socialist Charles Fourier as a new vehicle for collective living (p. 150). In his *Le Nouveau Monde industriel et sociétaire* (The New Industrial World) of 1829, Fourier had argued that if only we would relinquish the individual family house we could all live as grandly as Louis XIV had done in a palace at Versailles. This totally new kind of utopian collective dwelling was updated a generation later by the

37

32, 33

5

37. *Rue à redents* or 'street with set-backs', 1920.

engineer Henry Jules Borie in his 'Aérodomes' project for Paris of 1865. Employing the same prefabricated iron-framed greenhouse technology as Joseph Paxton had developed for the London Crystal Palace of 1851, Borie's Aérodomes would have consisted of vast ferro-vitreous residential blocks, superimposed at random over the still somewhat medieval fabric of the city.

Taking Borie's scale as his own, Le Corbusier rendered the twelve-storey perimeter blocks of his 'Ville Contemporaine' of 1922 as though they were diminutive Aérodomes. Each *bloc à cellules* comprised six floors of superimposed duplexes or maisonnettes arranged around the four sides of a garden court. This was patently meant as a critique of the standard courtyard housing block commonly deployed in the expansion of continental European metropolises from 1890 onwards (cf. Berlage's plans for Amsterdam South of 1900–1917 and The Hague of 1908). Unlike the standard perimeter block which tended to be scantily planted, the *bloc à cellules* was proposed as a 'green' urban form, suitable for dense inner-city development. Within the interstices of his city Le Corbusier also used the same block section in castellated plan formation to create what he called his *blocs à redents*.

First exhibited at the Salon d'Automne of 1922, the 'Ville Contemporaine pour trois millions d'habitants' (contemporary city for three million people) was projected as a dense metropolis

38
38–4

38. Le Corbusier and Pierre Jeanneret: Ville Contemporaine, 1922: axonometric of *bloc à cellules*.

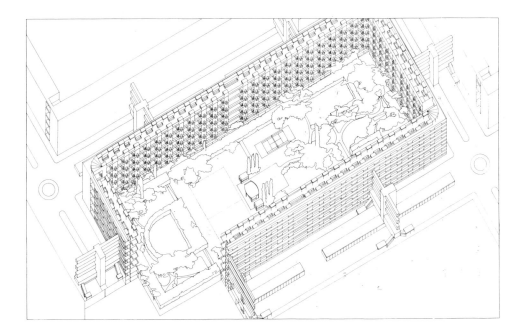

39. Le Corbusier and Pierre Jeanneret: Ville Contemporaine, 1922: panoramic view of the centre from a café terrace.

of apartment blocks and office towers, with workers' garden cities (cf. Pessac) being sited, along with light industry, beyond an encircling green belt. This green belt served to isolate the urban élite from the suburban proletariat while providing relief to the density of the built-up area. The city as a whole, patterned in plan like an oriental carpet and four times the area of Manhattan, consisted of the aforementioned perimeter blocks plus twenty-four sixty-storey cruciform office towers in the centre. The overall double-square plan was shown surrounded by open fields and penetrated by a picturesque park conceived along the lines of Central Park in Manhattan. The cruciform glass towers were reminiscent in their serrated plan-form of the stepped temples of Angkor, and as such they seem to have been posited as the secular equivalent of the religious buildings that had always occupied the centres of traditional cities, signified by the spires of the cathedral in the west and the pagoda in the east. This recognition of the interdependence of the monumental religious structure and urban form had first been set forth as a critical thesis in Bruno Taut's canonical text *Die Stadtkrone* (The City-Crown) of 1919, although whether Le Corbusier had read that we do not know.[5]

This latent theocratic aspect was not lost on the Communist newspaper *L'Humanité*, which regarded the entire project as reactionary, a judgment that was partially confirmed by the publication in 1925 of Le Corbusier's book *Urbanisme* (translated as *The City of Tomorrow*), particularly since the last full image was an engraving of Louis XIV supervising the construction of the Invalides in Paris. Left-wing criticism was hardly to be assuaged by Le Corbusier's disclaimer that this image was not to be seen as propaganda for the French Fascist Party, Georges Valois' Action Française.

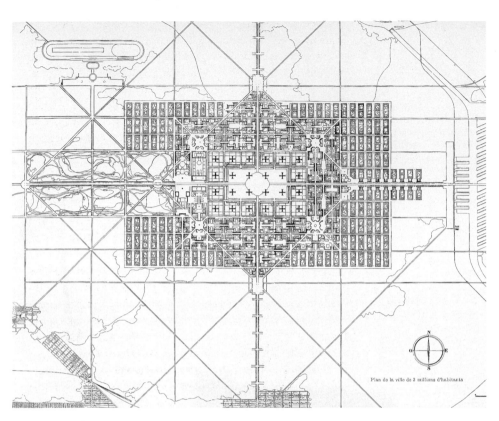

Plan de la ville de 3 millions d'habitants

As we have already remarked, the residential fabric of the Ville Contemporaine was made up of two different block types, the perimeter *bloc à cellules* which we have already discussed and the *bloc à redents*, borrowed from Hénard, where the same prototypical housing fabric advances and retreats symmetrically about the straight line of a street corridor. Where the *bloc à cellules* when arranged almost around the periphery of the Ville Contemporaine conveyed the impression of a permeable wall, the *bloc à redents* implied a wall-less, open city, a vision that would be more fully projected in 1930 as 'la Ville Radieuse' (the Radiant City), where the residential fabric is made up exclusively of *blocs à redents* elevated on *pilotis* above the surface of a continuous park. The anti-street polemic of this more mature vision was made explicit in 1929 in an essay on the street that Le Corbusier wrote for the French Syndicalist newspaper *L'Intransigeant*.[6]

In the midst of the skyscrapers of the Ville Contemporaine, there was a central transportation interchange integrating multi-level road, rail and metro systems. The roof of this megastructure was equipped with a landing strip, thereby replicating, as Reyner Banham put it, the Futurist Antonio Sant'Elia's suicidal proposition 'of asking aircraft to land between the ranks of tall buildings'.[7]

Rivalling Tony Garnier's Cité Industrielle of 1917 with its repertoire of modern urban types, Le Corbusier's Ville Contemporaine was more typologically developed than any other utopian city projected in the 1920s and early 1930s. At the same time, it was caught between the poles of utopia and dystopia, for like Ludwig Hilberseimer's 'Hochhausstadt' (skyscraper city) of 1924 it was an authoritarian machine city rather than the idyllic industrial city

suggested by the open plan and liberative institutional form of Garnier's Cité Industrielle. The detailed development of the Ville Contemporaine seems to have heightened the dystopian dimension in that the typical residential block was to have been built above five subterranean levels, plus a sidewalk set one floor below the lowest duplex dwelling. These various underground levels were conceived as accommodating different categories of transport and service, including the existing Paris Metro system lying just below ground level. This multi-level elaboration was once again derived from Hénard, this time from his 'Rue Future', first publicly presented at the RIBA Town Planning conference held in London in 1910.[8]

Only when we examine Le Corbusier's perimeter blocks in detail do the inhuman aspects of the proposition become fully manifest: as the perspective indicates, the entire street system would have been virtually devoid of movement. Except for the need to gain access to cars parked on the median strip, there would have been little cause for pedestrians to venture forth into the open. All the vehicular and human traffic crowding the Haussmannian metropolis would have been channelled out of the street, either into subterranean *autoroutes* or into the single-loaded corridors that were elevated well into the air in order to provide pedestrian access to the dwelling units every other floor.

The inhuman, hermetic character of this format was surely one of the factors that caused Le Corbusier to abandon it in favour of the *bloc à redents* that became his normative housing block type after 1922. The shift was already apparent in the diorama attached to the Pavillon de l'Esprit Nouveau of 1925, where the Ville Contemporaine was exhibited opposite Le Corbusier's Plan Voisin, a scheme for the radical rebuilding of the centre of Paris sponsored by the aircraft manufacturer Voisin.

43. Le Corbusier and Pierre Jeanneret: Ville Contemporaine, 1922: section of bridge link between blocks and multi-level street system.
VS double-height living space
VJ hanging garden
S roof garden
C corridor
A raised walkway
N pavement
M roadway
P freight route
R enclosed courtyard
Z pedestrian underpass

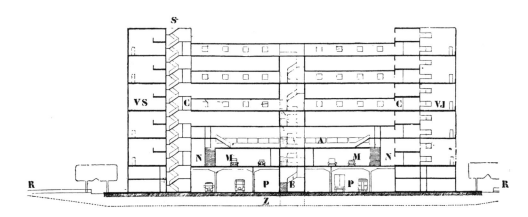

44. Le Corbusier and Pierre
Jeanneret: Plan Voisin for Paris,
1922–25: aerial view of model.
The Seine, with the Ile de la Cité,
appears bottom right.

Le Corbusier came to modify the generic parameters of his
contemporary city through responding to a request for advice that
he received from the Soviet government in May 1930. This covered
a wide spectrum of issues, ranging from general planning strategies
to more specific questions as to optimum residential forms for
future urban development. Responding to the challenge of de-
urbanization as this had been recommended in the Communist
Manifesto of 1848, Soviet architects and urbanists were uncertain
as to whether one should 'decant' Moscow through a series of
decentralizing garden cities or, on the contrary, consolidate its
existing tentacular form. Le Corbusier's reply to the questionnaire
led, in effect, to the reformulation of his generic city plan as the
'Ville Radieuse' or Radiant City, displayed on seventeen panels at
the third Congrès International d'Architecture Moderne staged in
Brussels in 1930.

Unlike the Ville Contemporaine, the Ville Radieuse was not
planned about a central cluster of cruciform skyscrapers. Instead,
the business district, comprising fourteen cruciform towers, was
shifted towards the north, corresponding, one should note, to
the centre of divine power in traditional Chinese city planning.
Le Corbusier had already cited Peking as an exemplary model in

45

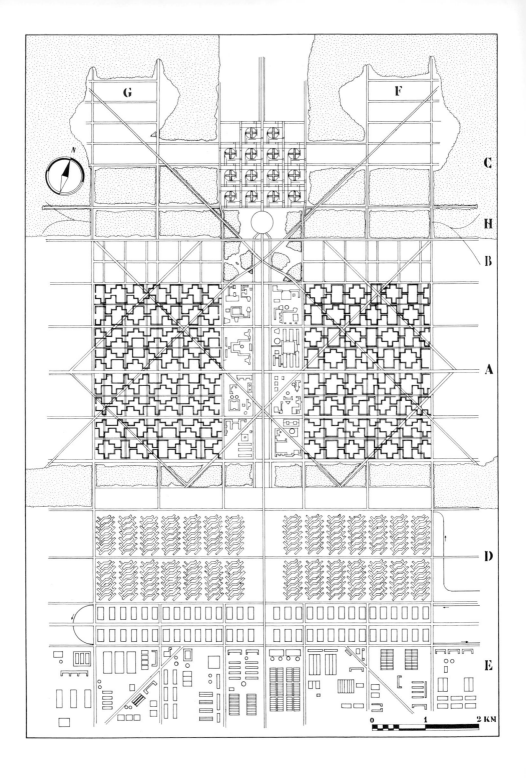

Urbanisme. Here, in lieu of the Forbidden City, the business centre was to be situated along with the government and university buildings in an isolated green zone. Below this, the Ville Radieuse was organized into parallel zones comprising a transportation zone providing for rail and air transit, a residential zone made up of *blocs à redents*, a green zone, a light industry zone, a zone dedicated to warehousing and freight, and a heavy industry zone. All were capable of lateral expansion, theoretically allowing each to develop independently as in Garnier's Cité Industrielle. In this respect he was convinced that the Ville Radieuse was a marked improvement upon the Ville Contemporaine: 'Any concentrically designed city (all cities created in the past on ground plans determined by "donkey tracks"; also my own 1922 project for a modern city of 3 million inhabitants) makes regular, organic development impossible: a biological defect.'[9] Despite the processal, linear character of its organization, Le Corbusier still imposed over the infinitely expandable Ville Radieuse the trace of an anthropomorphic ideogram reminiscent of Leonardo da Vinci's spread-eagled man. Thus the cluster of cruciform towers was seen as the 'head' of the city, while the cultural core on the central axis was seen as the 'heart,' with the residential 'lungs' situated to either side.

With the exception of the perimeter blocks of the Ville Contemporaine, both of Le Corbusier's ideal cities employed the same typology, namely the cruciform office tower which, as we have seen, first appeared in his *villes-tours* of 1920, and the residential block with set-backs, elevated above continuous parkscape. Panels 1–12 of the Ville Radieuse display focused on the infinitely variable formations of the *à redents* block system plus the way in which each segment of the orthogonal block pattern, meandering in plan, could be served at strategic intervals by multi-storey parking garages which like the orthogonal road network and the housing itself were elevated above ground level.

Where the *bloc à redents* was an implicit critique of the Haussmannian city, the cruciform tower, with its outer curtain wall castellated in plan, was conceived as an alternative to the American skyscraper which had only just evolved into its characteristic pinnacled form with Cass Gilbert's Woolworth Building of 1913. However, as Francesco Passanti has pointed out, Le Corbusier's cruciform high-rise may have had another precedent, Louis Sullivan's Fraternity Temple, projected for Chicago in 1891.[10]

Le Corbusier remained obsessed with skyscrapers throughout the next decade, so that by the time of his 1935 publication *La Ville Radieuse* he would directly compare the vertically set-back

45. Le Corbusier and Pierre Jeanneret: Ville Radieuse, 1930: plan.
A residential band interspersed with cultural centres
B hotels, embassies
C green band with business centre
D light industry
E heavy industry
F, G satellite cities for government institutions or universities
H airport

American skyscraper to his own cruciform skyscraper, clad from top to bottom in the sheer face of a vertical curtain wall. But this was not the only merit of his alternative high-rise form, for he believed that flat-roofed skyscrapers all rising to the same height would be capable of creating a virtual horizontal plane hovering some sixty storeys above the city parallel to the ground. Of this rationalized or Cartesian skyscraper he wrote:

In opposition to New York, to Chicago, we offer the Cartesian skyscraper – translucent, cleancut, gleamingly elegant against the sky of the Ile-de-France.

In place of the porcupine and Dante's inferno, we propose an organized, serene, forceful, airy, ordered entity. From below, it could be sublime. From the air (we are all now learning to look at cities from above), it will be a symbol of the spirit…

Instead of New York (magnificent and milling clamour of the machine age giant in its adolescence), I propose the Cartesian city: I propose the era of horizontal skyscrapers…Paris, city of the straight line and the horizontal (man does live on a horizontal plane), follows that line in its style of architecture.[11]

However, it was nonetheless typical of his method that once he became aware of the limitations of a type, he would improve on it. Thus while the Ville Radieuse of 1930 still featured the cruciform skyscraper of 1922, once he realized its heliothermic limitations he opted for a sun-inflected high-rise form with a Y-shaped plan. This was to be the final form of his Cartesian high-rise, and in a footnote to his Antwerp Plan of 1933 we find him writing:

During these past few years, I have reworked the design of the cross-plan skyscraper and evolved a more living form with the same static safety margin: a form dictated by sunlight… There are no longer any offices facing north. And this new form is infinitely more full of life.[12]

A visit to Latin America in 1929 (see Chapter 6) made Le Corbusier acutely aware of the need to avoid over-exposure to low-angle evening sun, and the consideration led him to adopt a southwest-northeast orientation for his *blocs à redents* in the Ville Radieuse. For this he depended on Justin Pidoux's heliothermic method as set forth in his book *La Science des plans des villes* (The Science of Town Plans) of 1928.[13]

The first edition of *La Ville Radieuse* not only outlines the basic thesis of the Radiant City but also goes on to document the various town-planning schemes that Le Corbusier had recently designed, including the reorganization of the Porte Maillot in Paris of 1930; studies for Geneva in Switzerland, Oued Ouchaia in Algeria, and the Plan Macia for Barcelona, dating from 1932; and a plan for the left bank of the River Scheldt in Antwerp, designed with Huib Hoste and Paul Otlet, and two projects for Stockholm, all dating from 1933.

46. Le Corbusier and Pierre Jeanneret: Cartesian skyscraper, proposed for Antwerp, Belgium, in 1933: model.

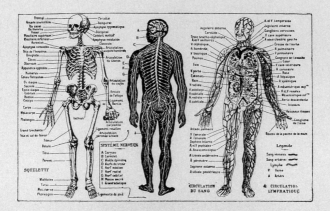

BESOINS-TYPES

MEUBLES-TYPES

C'est ici que l'on quitte les royaumes angoissants de la fantaisie et de l'incongru, et que l'on peut reprendre possession d'un code aux articles rassurants. Le poète déchoit, c'est vrai ; il chute

Chapter 4 Decorative Art Today 1925–1937

Between 1925 and 1928 Le Corbusier and Pierre Jeanneret's attitude to furniture was transformed, as they modified their critique
of the *Gesamtkunstwerk* or total work of art that they had initially
adopted at the time of the 1925 Exposition des Arts Décoratifs.
The shift began around 1927, the year in which the young interior
decorator Charlotte Perriand exhibited her 'Bar sous le Toit'
(bar under the roof) at the Salon de la Société des Artistes
Décorateurs. The spectacular success of this set-piece, fabricated
out of tubular steel and shiny folded metal, led to her being invited
to join Atelier 35S. Profoundly influenced by her reading of *Vers une
architecture* and *L'Art Décoratif d'aujourd'hui*, Perriand was impressed   47
by Le Corbusier's distinction between *besoins-types* (type-needs),
meubles-types (type-furniture), and what he called *objets-membres
humains*, 'human-limb objects'. Following this conceptual lead, she
helped to create a range of furniture that was closer to the idea
of equipment than to any previous notion of furnishing. As Le
Corbusier put it in 1925, 'The human-limb objects are type-objects,
responding to type-needs: chairs to sit on, tables to work at, devices
to give light, machines to write with (yes indeed), racks to file things
in.'[1] In a footnote, he accounted in Darwinian terms for the universal acceptance of Thonet bentwood chairs and for his own particu-   28
lar adoption of anonymous English club furniture, upholstered in
leather. Almost as a prescription for the furnishing of the Maison La
Roche and the Pavillon de l'Esprit Nouveau, he wrote:

*Having established this hierarchy – that is, this channelling of our
attention only to those things worthy of it – there remains all around us
that group of tools which we call furniture. During the long and
scrupulous process of development in the factory, the Thonet chair
gradually takes on its final weight and thickness, and assumes a format
that allows good connections; this process of perfecting by almost
imperceptible steps is the same as that to which an engine is subjected,
whose poetry is to run well – and cheaply. The Maples arm chair
[Maples was a London shop known for traditional furnishing], which is
attuned to our movements and quick to respond to them, assumes an
ever more distinctive profile. The stenographer's desk becomes daily
more convenient in the battle of the marketplace...*[2]

47. Chapter title page in *L'Art
Décoratif d'aujourd'hui*, Paris, 1925.

Evidently such objects paralleled Adolf Loos's injunction, in his essay 'Die Abschaffung der Möbel' (The Suppression of Furniture), to the effect that 'The walls of a building belong to the architect. There he rules at will. And as with the walls so with any furniture that is not movable.' When it comes to the movable pieces, on the other hand, 'everyone may buy these for himself according to his own taste and inclination.'[3] Elsewhere, in his essay *Cultural Degeneracy* of 1908, Loos insisted, contrary to the applied-art ambitions of the Deutsche Werkbund, that 'the style of our time already exists', and this seems to have chimed with Le Corbusier's vision of industry as an evolutionary demiurge, thereby justifying his preference for standard Parisian cast-iron park chairs and mass-produced office furniture on the grounds that both were examples of anonymous equipment:

Decorative art is an inexact and wordy phrase by which we denote the totality of human-limb objects. These respond with some precision to certain clearly established needs. They are extensions of our limbs and are adapted to human functions that are type-functions. Type-needs, type-functions, therefore type-objects and type-furniture. The human-limb object is a docile servant. A good servant is discreet and self-effacing, in order to leave his master free.

Certainly, works of decorative art are tools, beautiful tools.

And long live the good taste manifested by choice, subtlety, proportion and harmony![4]

That all of this was Loosian was directly acknowledged in the next chapter: 'It seems justified to affirm: *The more cultivated a people becomes, the more decoration disappears* (surely it was Loos who put it so neatly).'[5] Moreover if we examine the development of his attitude towards furnishings over the previous five years, dating from his Maison Monol project of 1919, one senses the continual influence of Vienna and thus ultimately of Loos.

This critical influence was again evident in the penultimate illustration of *L'Art Décoratif d'aujourd'hui*, where he inserted, without explanation, a map of his *Voyage d'Orient* of 1911, annotated with the letters C, F and I, so as to indicate the relative interplay between the dominant cultural values coexisting at the time. Thus where Berlin and the Ruhr were perceived as being the province of I (industry) with the addition of some C (culture), Paris, Rome and Athens were seen as being totally permeated by C, and the Balkans largely dominated by F (folklore). All of this was evidently related to Loos's perception that men live at the same time in different periods of history, as this had been set

Pour nos aises, pour faciliter notre travail, pour éviter la fatigue, pour nous restaurer, en un mot pour *libérer notre esprit* et nous isoler du fatras qui encombre notre vie et risque de tuer

PÈSE-LETTRES
n°893 FORCE 500 Gr

PINCE A RELIER
SANS ATTACHES

CHAISE DACTYLO
N° 2375

TRIEUR OR'MO

Ceci est froid et brutal, mais c'est juste et vrai ; ce sont là les bases (Ormo).

forth in his essay 'Ornament and Crime' of 1908, which Le Corbusier had republished in French, in *L'Esprit Nouveau* No. 2. Loos wrote:

> *I suffer the ornament of the Kefir, that of the Persian, that of the Slovak farmer's wife, the ornaments of my cobbler, because they all have no other means of expressing their full potential. We have our culture which has taken over from ornament. After a day's trouble and pain, we go to hear Beethoven or Wagner. My cobbler cannot do that… Primitive men had to differentiate themselves by various colours, modern man needs his clothes as a mask. His individuality is so strong it can no longer be expressed in items of clothing. The lack of ornament is a sign of intellectual power. Modern man uses the ornament of past and foreign cultures at his discretion. His own inventions are concentrated on other things.[6]*

48. Found image as an illustration in *L'Art Décoratif d'aujourd'hui*, 1925, showing patent office furniture by Ormo, including a typist's swivelling chair. The caption comments: 'This is cold and brutal, but right and true: here are the basic elements'.

In the last analysis *L'Art Décoratif d'aujourd'hui* was basically an elaboration of the same disjunctive cultural perception, although now qualified by two interesting corollaries. The first of these implied that the gulf between culture, folklore and industry may be bridged by the geometric impulse underlying all cultural form, that is, by the latent universal drive towards purification irrespective of technique. Le Corbusier characterized this convergence by drawing the reader's attention to the similarity between the habitual whitewash seasonally applied to Mediterranean dwellings and the lead-based white enamel paint of industrial civilization. He saw these two finishes – *le lait de chaux* (whitewash) and *la loi du Ripolin* (the rule of Ripolin, a commercial paint) – as a common purifying radiance uniting the vernacular of the Aegean with the Purist plasticity of the industrial north. The second corollary turned on a certain Dadaist frisson that could be seen as emanating from industrial form, as in say the Brown-Boveri dynamo that appears as a cryptic coda in the final chapter of *Vers une architecture*. Such objects, occurring even on a smaller scale, such as a hole punch or a ventilator cowl, could also be seen as introducing a similar sense of poetic estrangement, comparable to that which had already been identified by Marcel Duchamp in his initial 'readymade', the *Bottle Dryer* of 1914.

When Charlotte Perriand joined Atelier 35S in 1927 this critical stance was modified in favour of a more normative approach, which led to a range of chromium-plated tubular steel and leather furniture that has long been associated with the name of Le Corbusier alone. The line first appeared in the furnishing of two works: a refurbishing of the Maison La Roche, and a three-storey pavilion built in 1928 for his American clients Henry and Barbara Church in the gardens of their existing classical villa in Ville d'Avray, outside Paris. Perriand seems to have taken the lead in both these works, her hand being patently evident in the built-in units lining one wall of the library in the Church annexe.

While Le Corbusier and Pierre Jeanneret evidently participated in the design of the free-standing furniture pieces of the late 1920s, Perriand dealt with all the interior design commissions during the decade when she remained with the atelier, from 1927 to 1937. The first three classic pieces – the *siège grand confort* (large club armchair), the *petit fauteuil à dossier basculant* (little armchair with tilting back), and the *chaise longue* – were already present as an ensemble in the 1928 furnishing of the Maison La Roche and the Ville d'Avray library. However, the full range would not appear until the luxurious Purist interior that Perriand designed for the Salon d'Automne in 1929, a glistening glass-and-steel-panelled assembly enriched by a fur bedcover and a free-standing cylindrical shower stall.

The most seminal aspect in all this was the idea of demountable, movable, light-weight storage walls made up of *casiers* (units, or cupboards). This nomadic strategy had already been tried out in prototypical form in the Pavillon de l'Esprit Nouveau, where they

49. Le Corbusier, Pierre Jeanneret and Charlotte Perriand: model bedroom (foreground) and bathroom exhibited at the Salon d'Automne, Paris, 1929.

also served as the half-height partitions by which the interior was subtly divided. In the display apartment mocked up for the Salon d'Automne all the *casiers*, aside from being space dividers, were modular, modifiable and interchangeable. Modelled after the Innovation travelling trunk, the Le Corbusier/Perriand *casiers standards* (free-standing units) were permutable elements that were hypothetically capable of being assembled in such a way as to meet the storage needs in any dwelling. While Le Corbusier and Jeanneret developed an open, light-weight, transformable apartment behind an equally transformable ferro-vitreous façade, as this appears in their Immeuble Clarté built for Edmond Wanner in Geneva in 1931–33, Perriand demonstrated the flexibility of the *casiers standards* in the various exhibitions that she designed in the first half of the 1930s. The free-standing furniture elements that animated these various arrangements were the aforementioned pieces of the Atelier 35S line – the large club armchair, the little armchair with tilting back, the chaise longue, the *siège tournant* or swivelling dining chair, and finally the glass-topped *table-tube d'avion*. The latter was so named because the elliptical tube used for its legs

50. Le Corbusier, Pierre Jeanneret
and Charlotte Perriand: living room
exhibited at the Salon d'Automne,
Paris, 1929. *Casiers standards*
serve as space dividers. In the
foreground, examples of the *siège
tournant* or swivelling dining chair
surround a glass-topped *table-tube
d'avion*; beyond are a *siège grand
confort* and a *petit fauteuil à dossier
basculant.*

51. Le Corbusier, Pierre Jeanneret
and Charlotte Perriand: sofa and
armchair versions of the *siège grand
confort*, Salon d'Automne, Paris,
1929.

52. Le Corbusier, Pierre Jeanneret
and Charlotte Perriaud: 'small
armchair with tilting back',
Salon d'Automne, Paris, 1929.

was of the same section as the wing-stays in biplane construction.
The other industrial referent was the framing in chromium tube,
which surely derived from the standard bicycle frame. This explains
why they attempted (unsuccessfully) to persuade the bicycle
manufacturer Peugeot to mass-produce the pieces.

It is interesting to note how each of these furniture types
had a traditional origin and how each implied a different posture.
Thus the *siège tournant*, upholstered in leather, was based on the traditional typist's chair, whereas the *siège grand confort* was derived from
the Maples club armchair, although all the components were articulated in such a way as to render it 'nomadic'. It consisted of a
chromium-plated tubular steel frame plus an undersheet and five
removable leather cushions – two for the seat, one for each arm, and
one for the back. Its enclosed cubic shape insisted on a frontal,
Egyptian posture, an archaic stance that seems to have been associated with the male figure. It also came in a wider version, which was pre-
disposed towards a more relaxed, asymmetrical, feminine posture.
The *petit fauteuil à dossier basculant* was based on the traditional
British campaign chair, which has solid wooden cylindrical legs

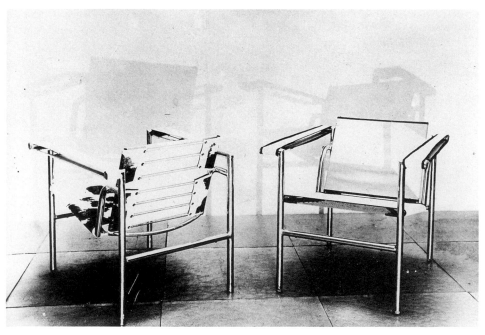

connected through socketed joints to cylindrical wooden framing, and is furnished with leather straps serving as armrests and a removable canvas seat and back. Le Corbusier transformed this folding wooden assembly into a fixed frame of welded chromium-plated tubular steel from which were suspended the indispensable leather or pony skin seat, back and armrests. Thus although the furniture was undoubtedly light-weight the nomadic demountability was more virtual than actual.

The most complex set-piece was the chaise longue, associated once again with the female figure. Aside from its lightly upholstered, removable lining of leather or pony skin and its leather bolster attached by straps, this could be disassembled into two basic pieces: the cradle on which the chair rested and the chromium-plated steel frame of the chair itself. This last comprised two chords – an undulating upper chord conforming to the line of the body, and a lower chord which by virtue of being a smooth arc of a circle provided a simple means for adjusting the inclination of the chair; that is, the circle could be freely rotated within the cradle. Taken together, the two chords reiterated the Purist thesis that the more intimate the contact between an object and the body, the more it reflects our human form, whereas the more distant the relationship, the more the object tends towards abstraction. This opposition may be seen as paralleling the original Purist distinction between *secondary* and *primary* sensations, where the secondary, the inner chord, conforms to the morphology of the body and the

53. Le Corbusier, Pierre Jeanneret and Charlotte Perriand: drawing of the chaise longue, 1929, showing the relationship between the outer, circular (Platonic), and inner (anthropomorphic) tubular frame supporting the chair.

54. Le Corbusier, Pierre Jeanneret and Charlotte Perriand: chaise longue, Salon d'Automne, Paris, 1929. The reclining figure is Charlotte Perriand.

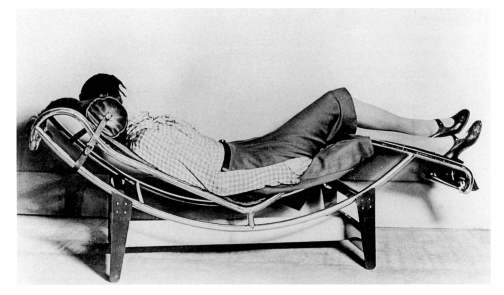

55. Study for the first 'muralnomad' tapestry, designed for manufacture by Marie Cuttoli, 1936.

primary, the outer chord, corresponds to the circular arc. This dialogical play between the organic and the geometrical was enriched in this instance by a metaphorical and tactile opposition between different materials, that is to say between the dull pliability of the leather and the hard brilliance of the tubular steel. And where the latter was essentially the result of an industrial process, the former evoked a pre-industrial, even pre-agricultural civilization, returning us once again to the nomadic theme.

Of this last, Le Corbusier remarked in 1960: 'We have become "nomads" living in houses which will be equipped with communal services; we will change our apartments according to the evolution of our families; from time to time we will change our neighbourhood as well.'[7] By then, he had been preoccupied with the design of objects for a nomadic existence for more than a quarter of a century. In 1936 he turned to tapestry as the quintessential nomadic artwork,[8] designing his first 'muralnomad' for Marie Cuttoli.

As Le Corbusier's ideological stance shifted towards the vernacular in the early 1930s so the character of the interior

55

furnishings designed by Atelier 35S began to change. This was particularly evident in the 'Sportsman's Gymnasium and Study' displayed at the Brussels exhibition of 1935. While the Purist *siège tournant* was still in evidence, there was otherwise not a single trace of chromium-plated tubular steel. Both the free-standing storage cabinet and the slate desktop were supported on cantilevered cast-iron frames with tubular iron legs cast integrally with the circular iron bases. Perriand began to introduce a totally new palette at this juncture, with a preference for dark, matt materials such as slate and cast iron. The doors of the cabinet were incised with a perspective from *La Ville Radieuse* and with sketches used by Le Corbusier to illustrate his Buenos Aires lectures of 1929. These images were made by the same engraving techniques as those employed in the manufacture of printer's blocks.

Instead of the *petit fauteuil à dossier basculant*, Perriand employed a standard piece of rustic furniture, framed in turned wood with a woven straw seat and back. Similarly, the storage unit was no longer a repetitive modular system. It was a well-proportioned free-standing, self-sufficient, multi-purpose cabinet carried on tubular cast-iron supports. Perriand wrote: 'I wished to show that one could work honestly with any material, taking into consideration the situation, the means of production and the needs.'[9] With this, the heroic project of equipping the machine age with standard furniture was being relinquished in favour of varying pieces of quite different scale and character. Thus the Purist thesis began to turn away from the utopian promise of the machine, just as Le Corbusier began to focus his artistic attention on what he

56. Le Corbusier, Pierre Jeanneret and Charlotte Perriand: model cast-iron 'drop-in' bathroom designed for Jacob Delafon, Paris World Exhibition, 1937.

termed 'objets à réaction poétique', the poetically evocative objects that had already become the quasi-figurative substance of his painting (p. 204).

The bathroom module that Le Corbusier, Jeanneret and Perriand designed for the Paris World Exposition of 1937, a proto-typical prefabricated unit made by the sanitary engineering firm Jacob Delafon, marked a momentary return to their former machinist eloquence. Cast in one piece out of iron, it was intended to be dropped into any given structural fabric from above. As such it was presumably intended for upgrading sanitation in existing buildings. The ideal Purist economy was once again in evidence here, for the WC was devised so as to double as a bidet, while an equally elegant handbasin and shower were integrated into the cast-iron shell. This prototype was enriched by a particular cross-cultural sensitivity, in that the WC could be used either in the bourgeois sitting position on a cantilevered hinged seat or squatting, without a seat, à la turque. The entire inner surface of the unit was finished in white enamel, while a wooden slatted floor facilitated drainage and cleaning. In an unexpected way this brilliant piece of industrial design would have a lasting influence on Le Corbusier's practice, for from now on he began to regard the sanitary core as a potential metaphor for the polymorphous character of the human body.

Chapter 5   A House, A Palace 1923–1929

Le Corbusier's 'Four Compositions' published in 1929 crown a
period of intense creativity during which he evolved an entirely new
form of middle-class residence, as this had been intimated in the
'Manual of Dwelling' published as part of *Vers une architecture*.[1] This
development was consciously inscribed within the dichotomous
legacy of the Western domestic tradition. Like Adolf Loos, Le
Corbusier found himself caught between two rival typologies: on
the one hand the irregular, asymmetrical Arts and Crafts tradition
of the yeoman house, with its L- or U-shaped plan; on the other, the
regular, symmetrical prism, stemming from Palladio, as that had
been tentatively broached in the Villa Schwob. As in Loos's Villa
Moissi projected for the Venice Lido in 1922, Le Corbusier sought to
reconcile these two traditions by fusing them into a new synthetic
unity, that is into an elided spatial form which he called *le plan libre*,
the free plan.[2]

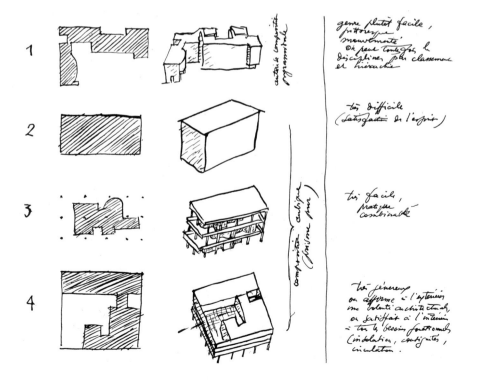

The Four Compositions were first formulated during a series of lectures that he gave in Buenos Aires in the autumn of 1929. They were published a year later in his *Précisions sur un état présent de l'architecture et de l'urbanisme* (*Precisions on the Present State of Architecture and City Planning*). In the fifth lecture, dealing with the plan of the modern house, he wrote:

We, Pierre Jeanneret and I, have built quite a lot of houses. Studying our own production, I manage to discern the general intention that determined the tendency of our work…up to now we have worked on four distinct types of plans, each expressing characteristic intellectual preoccupations.

The first type shows each organ rising up next to its neighbour, in accordance with an organic reasoning: 'the inside takes its ease, and pushes out to form diverse projections.' This principle leads to a 'pyramidal' composition, which can become busy if one doesn't watch out.

The second type shows the compression of organs within a rigid envelope, absolutely pure. A difficult problem, perhaps a spiritual delight; spending spiritual energy within self-imposed limitations.

The third type furnishes, with a visible framework (skeleton structure), a simple envelope, clear, transparent as a network; it allows for the creation of useful volumes of rooms different on each floor in form and quantity. An ingenious type appropriate to certain climates; such compositions are easy, full of possibilities.

The fourth type attains on the outside the pure form of the second type; inside, it has the advantages, the characteristics of the first and the third. A very pure type, very ample, also full of possibilities.[3]

While not all of these types were at the same level of differentiation, it is clear that the first corresponded to the house that he built in Paris in 1923 for La Roche, while the fourth was the Villa Savoye, as completed at Poissy in 1929. Most of Le Corbusier's Purist residences of the 1920s range between these two poles, both chronologically and conceptually, although the second and third compositions in the series – the Villa Stein de Monzie completed at Garches in 1928 and the Villa Baizeau, realized in modified form at Carthage, Tunisia, in 1927 – were particularly complex syntheses. The first of the Four Compositions was patently a Purist adaptation of a typical Arts and Crafts L-shaped house, complete with a minstrels' gallery overlooking the entry hall, while the last, the Villa Savoye, was essentially the same plan dropped into a single-storey open tray, raised one floor above the ground.

57. 'Four Compositions', 1929. There is an evident division between the irregular additive form of the first composition, based on the Maison La Roche, and the other three, all established within the frame of cubic form.

29, 30
67
63

Within this general schema, the Maison Cook of 1926 came to 59–62 synthesize Le Corbusier's 'Five Points of a New Architecture', first published in that year (*Les Cinq Points d'une architecture nouvelle*): (1) the *pilotis*, (2) the *toit-jardin*, (3) the *plan libre*, (4) the *fenêtre en longueur* and (5) the *façade libre*. The underlying classical affinity of this seemingly objective formulation is suggested by the fact that a sixth point, calling for the elimination of the cornice, was suppressed.[4] These points were also a tactical ellipsis conceived as a means by which to reconcile the twin poles of the European domestic tradition – the regular, symmetrical, aristocratic palazzo, and the asymmetrical peasant farmhouse.

Irrespective of this polarity, we may interpret Le Corbusier's residential work during this period as pursuing three distinct lines of typological development: first, the *megaron* type, stemming from the Maison Citrohan (1922) and developing into the Ozenfant 27 studio, Paris (1926), the Maison Guiette, Antwerp (1926), and 35 finally the ingenious Maison Canneel, projected for Brussels (1929); second, the irregular Arts and Crafts type, extending from the Maison La Roche (1923) through the Lipchitz-Miestschaninoff 30 double house in Boulogne-sur-Seine (1924) to culminate in the double-fronted, two-storey annexe for the Church family at Ville d'Avray (1928); and third, the prismatic type, evolving from the Maison Plainex, Paris (1924–27), and the design for the Villa Meyer (1925), to culminate in the Maison Cook at Boulogne-sur-Seine 59–61 (1926) and the Villa Stein de Monzie at Garches (1928). Needless to 63 say none of these paradigms was developed in isolation, as one may judge from the Maison Plainex and the Church annexe, both of which displayed symmetrical masses that were basically cubic and classical. In a similar way, the volumetric hierarchy of the Maison Citrohan and the Pavillon de l'Esprit Nouveau were combined, as we have seen, at a higher level of resolution in the Maison Cook.

In the last analysis four designs stand out as canonical amid the various residences projected during the period: they are the Villa Meyer, regrettably never built; the Maison Cook; the Villa Stein de Monzie; and the Villa Savoye. Of these four it is the *avant-projet* for the Villa Meyer that establishes the Virgilian theme for the other 58 three, as we may judge from the evocative letter that the architects sent to their client together with a drawing showing the view the house would have of the 18th-century garden 'ruin' of the Folie St-James next door: 'This project, Madame, has not been created from a gesture made by the rushed pencil of an office draughtsman. It has been slowly developed, nurtured during perfectly calm days before an extremely classic site.'[5]

The Villa Meyer was seminal in that it fully integrated a radical element that had hitherto only been used in a rhetorical manner, namely a system of ramped access running through part of the building. This mode of access had first been broached by Le Corbusier in the Maison La Roche of 1923. It would thereafter appear in a different 31 ent form in two successive designs for the Villa Meyer: first as a free-standing ramp tower and then as a ramp running against a party wall. For Le Corbusier the ramp was the quintessence of what he regarded as an Arab approach to architecture: 'Arab architecture affords us an invaluable lesson. It understands what it means to walk on one's feet since it is through walking and shifting one's position that one sees the architectural order unfold. It is the counter principle to Baroque architecture, which is conceived on paper about a fixed theoretical point. I prefer the lesson of Arab architecture.'[6]

Removed from the monumental scale of the Villa Meyer, the Maison Cook, built in Boulogne-sur-Seine in 1926 for American 59–62 clients, synthesized with great subtlety and economy the divergent trajectories of Le Corbusier's thought in the mid-1920s. Its double-height living space, situated at the top of a four-storey 62 mass, reinterpreted the volume of the Pavillon de l'Esprit Nouveau, 32 while the third-floor mezzanine library, overlooking the living space, recalled the position of the minstrels' gallery in the hall of a Gothic Revival house. At the same time, the axiality of the double-height living space was given a classical inflection by virtue of a semi-circular, inverted apse at one end of the volume and a narrow balcony on axis, overlooking the garden, at the other.

58. Le Corbusier and Pierre Jeanneret: Villa Meyer, Paris, second project, 1925: view from the garden terrace overlooking the Virgilian landscape of the Folie St-James.

59. Le Corbusier and Pierre Jeanneret: Maison Cook, Boulogne-sur-Seine, 1926: street front, exemplifying the Five Points of a New Architecture – the roof garden, free façade, *fenêtre en longueur*, free plan, and *pilotis*.

60. Le Corbusier and Pierre Jeanneret: Maison Cook: plans of the ground floor, first floor, second floor, and (top) mezzanine library with roof garden.

61. Le Corbusier and Pierre Jeanneret: Maison Cook: axonometric, showing the second and third floor levels, mezzanine library and roof garden.

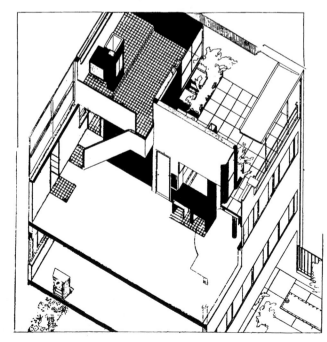

Moreover, as the photographs of the interior indicate, the house attempted to synthesize the cultural range of the Purist sensibility, in that various aspects of contemporary civilization were alluded to. Thus, while the classical was evoked as I have intimated, the vernacular announced itself through the furnishing of the floors with kelims. By a similar token, the world of industry was made manifest though the exposed radiators and naked light bulbs, and above all through the smooth sliding action of the metal-framed horizontal windows – the *fenêtre en longueur* that Le Corbusier would characterize in his Five Points as *l'élément mécanique-type de la maison* – the typical mechanical element of the house.[7]

With the Five Points as they are demonstrated in the Maison Cook, the representational façade is reduced to a taut asymmetrical machine-like membrane, while an essential touchstone of the

63. Le Corbusier and Pierre
Jeanneret: Villa Stein de Monzie,
Garches, 1928: garden front.

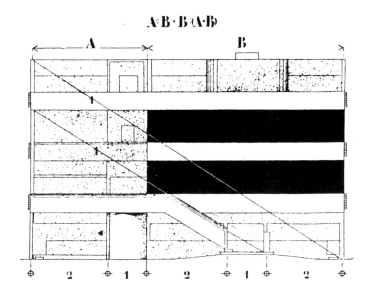

64. Le Corbusier and Pierre
Jeanneret: Villa Stein de Monzie:
tracés régulateurs (regulating lines)
on the principle of the Golden
Section applied to the garden
façade. Note the manipulation
of the ground surface.

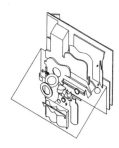

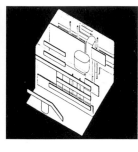

65. Comparative axonometric analyses of the spatial layering in Le Corbusier's painting *Nature morte à la pile d'assiettes* (see fig. 28) and the Villa Stein de Monzie (drawn by Bernard Hoesli).

classical, namely the peristyle, reappears beneath the house in the form of *pilotis* and in the free-standing columns of the free interior. The so-called 'free façade' was now no longer a tectonically articulated skin, as in Auguste Perret's Notre-Dame du Raincy of 1922, but rather a non-load-bearing membrane. For Le Corbusier it seems to have been analogous to the stretched fabric of an aircraft. As we have seen, an equally distinctive feature of this membrane was the machinist *fenêtre en longueur* rather than the traditional humanist *porte-fenêtre* favoured by Perret.[8] This transposition between different typological values attained its apotheosis in the roof garden, where the area occupied by the house reappears as the 'bridge of a ship' floating above a sea of trees. This was, in fact, an elevated terrace which, with the *pilotis*, jointly denied the house both its pitched roof and its traditional anchorage in the ground.

The question as to whether the Purist villa was to be seen as an industrial product or a hand-crafted artifact attains its most contradictory formulation in the Villa Stein de Monzie and the Villa Savoye. In both instances the machine appearance ('the impression is of naked polished steel', as Le Corbusier wrote of the entablature of the Parthenon in *Vers une architecture*) was achieved through the application of stucco, which, significantly enough, was the one material which Perret tried to avoid throughout his practice. While this revetment was antipathetic to the tradition of Structural Rationalism, it was by no means unsympathetic to the neo-Palladianism which had indirectly informed these works.

59, 62

63

68

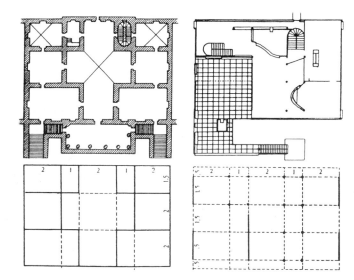

66. Plan and structural grid of the Villa Stein de Monzie (right) compared to those of Palladio's Villa Malcontenta of c.1560.

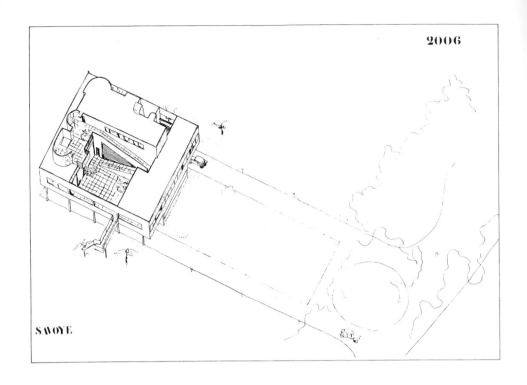

2006

SAVOYE

67. Le Corbusier and Pierre Jeanneret: Villa Savoye, Poissy, 1929: axonometric of the penultimate scheme. Note the driveway that approaches the house and then runs under it on three sides (cf. III. 69).

68. Le Corbusier and Pierre Jeanneret: Villa Savoye: view from the living room towards the elevated patio, with a ramp to the sun terrace on the roof.

69. Le Corbusier and Pierre Jeanneret: Villa Savoye: axonometric of the ground floor (drawn by John Pettit West III). A driveway runs between the recessed ground floor and surrounding *pilotis*, and a garage is provided to the right of the axial entrance. The hall leads to a ramp up to the first floor and the roof.

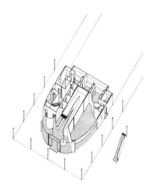

Along these lines, convincing parallels would be drawn between these villas and their respective 16th-century prototypes in the Veneto, above all by the critic Colin Rowe, who compared the Villa Stein de Monzie at Garches to the Villa Malcontenta and the Villa Savoye to the Villa Capra. Of Garches and Malcontenta he wrote:

66

In both cases six 'transverse' lines of support in rhythmically alternating single and double bays are established; but the rhythm of the parallel lines of support, as a result of Le Corbusier's use of the cantilever, differs slightly. At the villa at Garches, it is ½ : 1 ½ : 1 ½ : ½ and at Malcontenta 2 : 2 : 1½. In plan, Le Corbusier thus obtains a sort of compression for his central bay and interest seems transferred to his outer bays, which are augmented by the extra half unit of the cantilever; while Palladio secures a dominance for his central division, and a progression towards his portico, which focuses interest there. In both cases the projecting element, terrace or portico, occupies 1½ units in depth.[9]

Rowe went on to point out that the square plan, elliptical entry and central ramp of the Villa Savoye could be read as a displaced reference to the centralized, bi-axial, cruciform plan of the Villa Capra. There, however, the similarity ends, with Palladio insisting on centrality and Le Corbusier asserting within the confines of the square plan the asymmetrical qualities of rotation and peripheral dispersal. Moreover, as opposed to the Palladian symmetrically arranged load-bearing wall, Le Corbusier's 'free façade' was conceived as an asymmetrical, non-loadbearing luminous screen upon which the *tracés régulateurs* of the Golden Section inscribed their harmonic unifying rhythm. In Le Corbusier's view, it was this agency as much as anything else that was capable of bestowing upon a house the nobility of a palace, just as the convenience of a functional plan would enable a palace to become a house.

64

Both the *avant-projet* of the Villa Stein de Monzie (1926) and the Villa Savoye as built exemplify the concept of the 'architectural promenade', conceived as a topographic itinerary in which the floor planes, bent upwards to form ramps and stairs, are fused with the walls so as to create the illusion that the subject is literally 'walking up the walls', a device that served to induce a dynamic if somewhat idiosyncratic perception of space. At the same time, as Colin Rowe and Robert Slutzky have remarked, the planar order of the prismatic envelope established the frontal layering of the internal volume, and this striated spatiality was related to the shallow space of Cubist painting and thus to the early Purist canvases of Le Corbusier and Ozenfant.[10]

67–69

65

79

70. Le Corbusier and Pierre Jeanneret: project for the League of Nations building, Geneva, 1927: lake front elevation. The secretariat is on the left, the assembly on the right.

71. Le Corbusier and Pierre Jeanneret: project for the League of Nations building: axonometric.

72. Analysis of the planar layering implicit in the League of Nations site plan (after Colin Rowe and Robert Slutzky). The axial approach to the assembly building from the land is at the top.

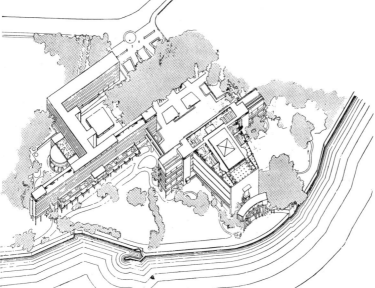

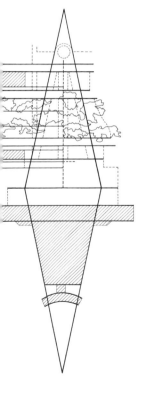

With their 1927 entry to the international competition for the Société des Nations or League of Nations headquarters in Geneva, Le Corbusier and Pierre Jeanneret produced their first design for a large and complex public structure. Their attention had hitherto been focused on the 'house' and on the concomitant simplicity of its compact prismatic form. Now they addressed themselves to the necessary complexity of the 'palace' as a large, institutional structure. The competition's conditions stipulated two separate buildings, one for the secretariat and one for the assembly, and this seems to have prompted the architects to take an 'elementarist' approach to the design; that is to say, they adopted a procedure in which the aggregate elements of the programme were first assembled and then manipulated in order to generate a series of alternative compositions. This approach was an extension of the elementarist method professed at the turn of the century by the Beaux-Arts theoretician Julien Guadet, who would have come to Le Corbusier's notice via Guadet's renowned pupils Tony Garnier and Auguste Perret. That Le Corbusier adopted this stratagem when dealing with large complexes is borne out by his preliminary studies for his entry to the Palace of the Soviets competition of 1931–32. There, under eight alternative layouts, we read: 'The various stages of the project, wherein one sees the organs, already independent from one another, gradually assume their reciprocal places to lead to a synthetic solution.'[11]

We find a similar remark appended to an alternative scheme for his League of Nations entry, published in his book *Une Maison, un palais* (A House, A Palace) of 1928. Under a symmetrical, and evidently more functional, layout we find the caption: 'an alternative proposition employing the same compositional elements'.[12] The asymmetrical organization finally adopted testifies to a conflict between the circulatory convenience of a symmetrical parti and the rhetorical necessity of maintaining a visually unobstructed axial approach to the representational façade of the main assembly.

This competition had the effect of returning Le Corbusier to the French Graeco-Gothic tradition from which his Purist architecture had been indirectly derived. I am alluding to the evolution of Jesuit architectural theory in France, beginning in the early 18th century with the writings in which the Abbé de Cordemoy sought to combine Gothic (organic) intercolumniation with Greek (prismatic) trabeated form.[13] This is evident from the classical format adopted for the overall organization of the League of Nations design, from the symmetrical A B A B A arrangement of the assembly building to the facing of the entire complex in coursed ashlar and

steel-framed plate glass. That the assembly building was organized
as a 'classically rational' machine is evident from the interaction of
two distinctly different architectonic value systems. On the one
hand there was a hierarchical enfilade drawn from the classical tradition, comprising elements labelled on the plan as a 'peristyle'
(portico), a 'scala regia' (grand staircase), and a 'salle des pas
perdus' (the large foyer running under and around the auditorium),
while on the other there was a structurally hierarchical steel-
framed skeleton carrying the roof of the hall. That Le Corbusier was
conscious of the way in which he was continuing the structural
rationalist tradition in France is suggested by the caricature of himself and Auguste Perret, respectively standing and sitting, that he
depicted under the portico of the assembly building. Many other
features point to the conscious fusion of these two French

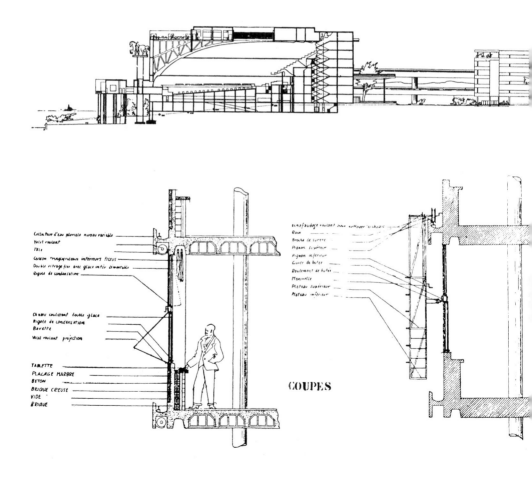

traditions, among them the organization of the library after the nine-square format of Henri Labrouste's Bibliothèque Nationale, Paris, of 1868. To this we may add the overall A B A B A cross-axial structure of the secretariat wing and an elaborate *promenade architecturale* within the assembly building, leading through the *salle des pas perdus* to the secretary general's suite, situated on axis, overlooking the lake. Other equally classical tropes may be readily identified, including the monumental sculptural group above the secretary general's pavilion backing on to the assembly hall, comprising a lion and an eagle flanking a centrally placed horse and man derived from the classical *Dioscuri* (for its symbolism see below, pp. 200–201). This sculptural group stressed the axial structure of the assembly hall and paralleled the classical allusion of the concrete cornice of the secretariat building with its suspended pedal-driven cleaning cradle (the *passerelle bicyclette*). While that feature hardly amounted to a classical profile, it could be nonetheless construed as a surrogate moulding. This Purist/Classic synthesis reached its apotheosis in the proposed illumination of the assembly hall, which was envisaged as being naturally lit through translucent double-glazed walls during the day and artificially illuminated by floodlights between the two layers of glass at night. Had it been built, this particular arrangement would surely have been readable as a metaphor for enlightened world governance – the assembly being visibly in session by the side of the lake at night with its light radiating out into the world!

Le Corbusier regarded his League of Nations site layout as a *conception paysagiste*, a phrase evoking both the English Picturesque and German Romantic Classicism. This hybrid landscape intention seems to be confirmed by the combination of a classical axial approach with irregular dense clusters of trees in the English Picturesque tradition. However, the principles by which the building would have been integrated into the site went well beyond the scope of any landscape tradition, for as Rowe and Slutzky have pointed out, Le Corbusier's proposal established a series of parallel planes and slots that ran perpendicular to the main east-west, perspectival approach.[14] Thus on approaching the assembly building on axis through its monumental forecourt the visitor would have had to pass through a series of layers which, either real or virtual, thick or thin, built or planted, granite or green, would have had the effect of deflecting the eye to lateral views of the lake and the attendant foliage.

The League of Nations competition became the *cause célèbre* of European modern architecture at the end of the 1920s. The jury,

173

74

71

72

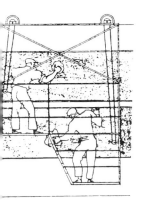

VUE DE L'ECHAFAUDAGE ROULANT

chosen in a diplomatically appropriate manner, consisted of nine distinguished architects among whom one could count a sizable number of proto-modernists, including Karl Moser (Switzerland), Josef Hoffmann (Vienna), H. P. Berlage (Holland), and Victor Horta (Belgium), the latter soon to revert to academicism. Admittedly, the other five members were of a conservative cast: Charles Lemaresquier (France), a Beaux-Arts architect to the letter; John Burnet (England); the Nordic Classicist Ivar Tengbom (Sweden); A. Muggia (Italy); and C. Gato (Spain). The verdict given after three weeks of deliberation was that of the 377 entries the jury could find none deserving of the first prize. Instead, they offered nine equal prizes, in three different categories, one of which went to the scheme submitted by Atelier 35S. It would seem that internal disagreement had been such that each of the nine members of the jury had voted for a different design. To add insult to injury, Lemaresquier successfully petitioned to have the Le Corbusier and Jeanneret scheme disqualified on the grounds that, contrary to the competition conditions, their plans had been printed, rather than submitted to the jury as ink drawings. This came after Horta had already indicated publicly that their scheme had been generally favoured for its exceptional economy.

The international uproar that followed was not alleviated by the appointment of the Comité des Cinq, a group of five non-aligned diplomats, who in December 1927 selected among the *ex æquo* 'winners' the Franco-Swiss team of Nénot and Flégenheimer to work on the final commission, in collaboration with C. Broggi (Italy), C. Lefèvre (France) and G. Vago (of Italo-Hungarian origin). Le Corbusier's response to this *débâcle* was to petition the League of Nations in February 1928 and to elicit the support of the French delegate to the League, Aristide Briand, in a vain effort to overturn the decision of the diplomatic committee.[15]

It is clear that the shambles of the League of Nations competition had a catalytic effect on the plans for the creation of an international organization of modern architects that had been in the minds of a number of Swiss architects for some time. The key patron of this organization was Madame Hélène de Mandrot-Revillod, who had long since acquired a reputation as a major supporter of the arts, operating alternately, summer and winter, from her château of La Sarraz near Lausanne and her apartment in Paris. Accordingly, between 25 and 29 June 1928 the inaugural meeting of the 'Congrès Internationaux d'Architecture Moderne' (CIAM) was held at the château, leading to the 1928 'La Sarraz Declaration' signed by twenty-four architects from seven countries

— six each from France and Switzerland, three each from Germany and Holland, two from Italy, two from Spain, and one each from Austria and Belgium. This initial conference was already the occasion for a stand-off between Le Corbusier and the left-wing Swiss avant-garde (specifically the members of the German-speaking ABC Gruppe), but all the same unanimity prevailed due to a convergence between Le Corbusier's utopian socialist views and the more materialist line of the left.

Madame de Mandrot herself favoured the Le Corbusier faction, particularly since that group was still involved in the furore over the League of Nations competition. The Geneva authorities had now shifted the site away from the Parc de l'Ariane, a move which necessitated her permission since she was one of the executive lessors of the new site. She refused to grant the lease until those competitors who had been set aside initially were allowed to enter a second competition, with a new brief enlarged to include a world library.[16]

Despite the fact that the second competition turned out to be little more than another political manipulation, Le Corbusier remained active in Geneva, projecting for a terrain adjacent to the League of Nations his remarkable 'Cité Mondiale' and 'Mundaneum' of 1929, designed for the Belgian philanthropist Paul Otlet. The Mundaneum was to be the intellectual centre of the Cité Mondiale, and within it the ideological and architectural centrepiece was to have been the 'Musée Mondial', conceived as a spiralling tripartite ramp built up into a pyramidal form, where visitors would move along three parallel aisles, the first devoted to cultural objects, the second to the historical epoch, and the third to the geographic and geological attributes of the place. In this museum — influenced, it would seem, by Le Play's scheme for the World Exposition in Paris of 1867 — visitors would have gained access to the crown of the pyramid by means of inclined lifts, similar to those installed in the Eiffel Tower. Starting at the apex with the prehistoric origins of the species, they would then have worked their way down through the saga of human history.[17]

Over the next five years, Le Corbusier's designs for public institutions would become increasingly symmetrical. In this respect his

76

75

75. Le Corbusier and Pierre Jeanneret: Musée Mondial, 1929: section.

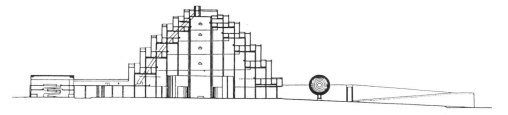

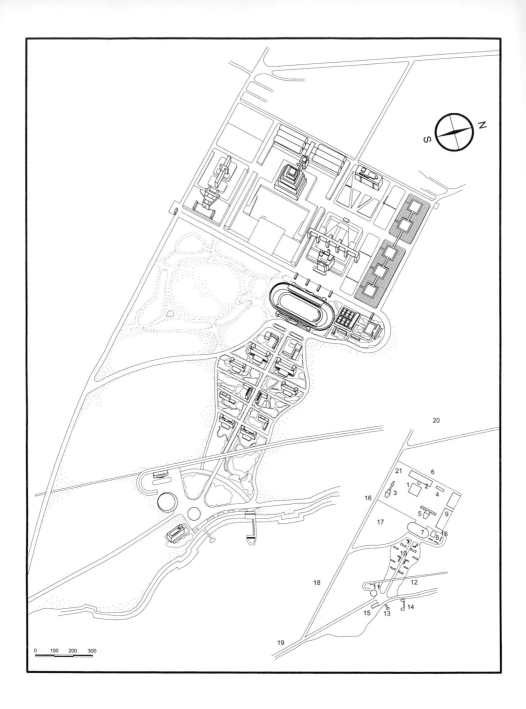

first League of Nations scheme was a watershed, not only in terms of his own development but also in terms of his relation to the modern movement. Le Corbusier's subsequent drive to combine his functionalist approach with a classical sense of hierarchy would soon bring him into conflict with the socialist architects of the international avant-garde. Thus the left-wing Czechoslovak critic Karel Teige, who had initially rallied behind Le Corbusier in the debate over the League of Nations competition, subsequently attacked him in *Stavba* in 1929 not only for the monumentality of the Musée Mondial but also for the formalism of the entire layout:

According to Le Corbusier, architecture as art believes that its mission begins where construction ends, namely with the rational solution and the products of the engineer. It aspires to eternity while the engineer responds to actuality… If we have occupied ourselves so carefully with the Mundaneum project, it is because we believe this work, whose author is a leading and foremost representative of modern architecture, should serve as a warning to its author and to modern architecture generally. The Mundaneum illustrates the fiasco of aesthetic theories and traditional prejudices, of all the dangers of the slogan 'house—palace,' and thus of utilitarian architecture with an artistic 'addition' or 'dominant'. From here it is possible to go all the way to full academicism and classicism, or, on the other hand, to return to the solid reality of the starting point demonstrated so precisely by the motto, the 'house as a machine for living in', and from there once again to work towards a scientific, technical, industrial architecture. Between these two poles, there is space only for half-baked projects and compromised solutions. [18]

Despite his caustic response, entitled 'Défense de l'architecture', published first in Czech translation in the magazine *Musaion* in 1931 and then in French in *L'Architecture d'Aujourd'hui* in 1933, Le Corbusier would shift his architectural expression towards the left-wing, Constructivist line with his entry for the Palace of the Soviets competition of 1931.

76. Le Corbusier and Pierre Jeanneret: Cité Mondiale for Paul Otlet, 1929: axonometric.

 1 Musée Mondial, at the centre of the Mundaneum
 2 halls of modern times
 3 international associations
 4 library
 5 university
 6 *cité universitaire* (student housing)
 7 stadium
 8 sports centre
 9 exhibitions
10 hotels and residences
11 railway station
12 highway from Geneva to Lausanne, Bern and Zurich
13 harbour
14 marina
15 International Labour Office (existing)
16 lightbhouses
17 botanical and mineralogical gardens (extension to the Parc de l'Ariane)
18 highway to France
19 Quai Wilson linking the Cité Mondiale to Geneva
20 sites for airport and broadcasting station
21 reserved site

Chapter 6 World Architect: Czechoslovakia, Russia, Brazil, North Africa, North America, France and Switzerland 1928–1936

Among the peripatetic pioneers of the modern movement Le Corbusier is the sole figure who would project himself at a global scale, not only through the world-wide circulation of the magazine *L'Esprit Nouveau* but also through his incessant globe-trotting, which began with his first visit to Moscow in October 1928 and continued, more or less without a break, until 1936, the date of his last voyage outside France before the Second World War. The single year 1929 would see him pass from one world to another, as he went from supervising the initial stages of the Centrosoyuz building in Moscow in June, to embark three months later for South America, where he had been invited to give lectures in Buenos Aires, Montevideo and Rio de Janeiro. This tour, lasting just over two months from late September to early December, had an enormous impact on his psyche, heightening and transforming that 'oceanic' aspect of his vision. I have in mind not only the literal sense of the ocean that one may readily associate with a long sea voyage, but also Sigmund Freud's use of the term to allude to a mystical sense of oneness with the universe, suggested to him as a primary source of spirituality by the writer Romain Rolland.[1]

En route to Russia Le Corbusier first went to Czechoslovakia, where he was warmly received between 1 and 6 October by the Czech avant-garde – above all by the poet Vitěslav Nezval, the architect Jaromír Krejcar, and the poet/typographer and cultural critic Karel Teige. The modern movement was already well established in Prague, above all because of the polemical activities of Teige and Nezval who had founded the avant-garde Devětsil movement in 1920. This initiative had been immediately substantiated by Krejcar's precocious production as an architect, most notably his Vančura Villa at Zbraslav near Prague of 1923 and his structurally rationalist Olympic Building, completed in the centre of Prague in 1926. Subject to the influence of *L'Esprit Nouveau*, Teige had grounded much of his 'Constructivist-Poetist' thesis in Purism, and as a result he was at first one of Le Corbusier's strongest supporters, writing a glowing review of *Vers une architecture* when it first appeared. However, Devětsil ultimately occupied a position halfway between Russian Constructivism and Purism, for while Purism had advanced itself as the spontaneous consummation of machinist civilization, it was too committed to high art values to satisfy the more open Czech acceptance of the poetics of modern life in all its aspects. Consciously occupying a space between poetry and painting, Nezval's project of 'the world as poetry' depended upon the incorporation of subtle strands coming from Dadaism and Magical Realism in painting.[2] Despite these cultural nuances and their affinity for Constructivism, the left-wing Czech architects remained dependent on Le Corbusier for much of their method and a good deal of their syntax.

The rival position in this regard, in terms of both theory and practice, was the international Neue Sachlichkeit movement that asserted itself as a socio-economic, functionalist alternative to Le Corbusier's bourgeois formalism. The dialogical thesis of *Vers une architecture*, namely the necessary interplay between 'the engineer's aesthetic' and 'architecture', sat ill with the Constructivists' utilitarian hard line, although evidently, as Le Corbusier insisted, they too would eventually have to confront the inevitability of some kind of *a priori* composition. In 1928 this functionalist vs. formalist conflict had yet to come to a head, and Le Corbusier was able to learn a good deal from the technically precocious Czechs. He admired above all their pioneering demonstration of curtain-wall construction as evident in the then newly completed International Fair Building built in Prague to the designs of Oldrich Tyl and Josef Fuchs.

Going on by train via Warsaw, Le Corbusier was equally warmly received in Moscow on 10 October by Andrei Burov, Nikolai Kolli and Alexander Vesnin and other prominent members of the

77. Le Corbusier in Moscow in 1928 with members of the OSA group. He is surrounded by the Vesnin brothers – from left to right, Viktor, Leonid and Alexander – and by the (beardless) Andrei Burov.

Association of Contemporary Architects (OSA) founded in 1925 by Vesnin and Moisei Ginzburg. While Le Corbusier extolled the virtues of his 1925 Plan Voisin for Paris in his public lectures, he also strongly criticized any notion of totally demolishing the existing fabric of Moscow, above all its historic monuments. He wrote in his lecture notes:

It is a criminal mistake to resuscitate things from the past, for the result is not living organisms but papier mâché ghosts. But it is essential to preserve the testimony of works that in their time were 'contemporary', that they might serve as a lesson and provoke admiration among people of quality.[3]

Le Corbusier approached the Soviet Union as though it were the only truly modern nation that now possessed the political and techno-economic means to transcend the demise of vernacular culture through the unequivocal adoption of a scientific, machine-age civilization, with all that this entailed. As in Czechoslovakia, his reception had been prepared in advance by the wide diffusion of the magazine *L'Esprit Nouveau*. This was especially the case in Russia, since from the ninth issue onwards the publication continually featured articles that were sympathetic to the Soviet Union, going so far in May 1922 as to make an international appeal for economic aid for the young socialist state.[4] By the mid-1920s Le Corbusier had already established contact with both El Lissitzky[5] and Moisei Ginzburg, the latter doing him the honour of echoing aspects of *Vers une architecture* in his own *Stil i Epokha* (Style and Epoch) of 1924, a book which in many respects was a Constructivist gloss on the initial Corbusian thesis. Where both men saw the aeroplane and the grain elevator as being indicative of the forms that modern architecture should adopt, they differed most decidedly over the seminal role to be played by wooden construction, with Ginzburg featuring such primitive Constructivist works as Konstantin Melnikov's all-timber Makhorka Pavilion of 1923. At the same time, Le Corbusier's work was well received by avant-gardist artists who in other respects were rather distant from him. One thinks of the Suprematist painter Kasimir Malevich, who praised his model dwellings in the Stuttgart Weissenhofsiedlung of 1927 largely on ergonomic grounds.[6]

The influential OSA magazine *Sovrememaia Arkhitektura* (Contemporary Architecture), edited by Ginzburg, followed Le Corbusier's work assiduously from its very first issue of 1926, according particular acclaim to the books *Urbanisme* and *L'Art Décoratif d'aujourd'hui* soon after they were published in 1925.

Thus by the time Le Corbusier arrived in Moscow in 1928 he was already a celebrity, to be feted as much by the cultural establishment as by the architectural avant-garde. Anatoly Lunacharsky, the People's Commissar for Education, attended his main lecture given at the Polytechnical Museum; also present was Olga Kameneva, Trotsky's sister, who was president of VOKS, the Soviet institution expressly created for the purposes of cultural exchange.[7] Such contacts enabled him to meet other leading Soviet architects and intellectuals, including the theatrical director Vsevolod Meyerhold and the cinéaste Sergei Eisenstein – for whom Burov had designed a Purist model farm, prominently featured in Eisenstein's film *The General Line*, released in 1929.

The design for the headquarters of the Centrosoyuz, or Central Union of Consumer Co-operatives, was determined through three successive competitions, the first being an all-Russian open competition, won by B. M. Velikovsky. For reasons that remain obscure a second, limited competition was organized to which, in addition to the Centrosoyuz's own architects, the following participants were invited: Max Taut from Berlin, Thomas Tait of the well-established British firm of Burnet Tait & Lorne, and Le Corbusier and Pierre Jeanneret from Paris. Having received the initial brief in May 1928, Le Corbusier submitted his first scheme in July. The project was very warmly received by the authorities and Le Corbusier was invited to participate in yet a third competition along with Peter Behrens and eight different Russian teams. During his time in Moscow, from 10 to 30 October, he was able to rethink his initial design on the spot, introducing *pilotis* beneath the office wings and making other modifications resulting in his second scheme, submitted on 20 October. Such was the enthusiasm with which this second project was received that most of the Soviet participants considered Le Corbusier should be awarded the commission – if for no other reason than to establish the prestige of modern architecture in the Soviet Union. Already aware of the latent forces of conservative reaction, the Soviet architectural avant-garde seems to have felt that the realization of such a project would serve to advance the cause of modern architecture in the Soviet Union as 'a clear and effective representation of the architectural ideas of today'.[8]

In his two successive revisions of this proposal, the last dating from January 1929, Le Corbusier constantly rearranged virtually the same typological elements as he had employed in his League of Nations proposal of 1927, only now the auditorium was much smaller and assumed a more organic, elliptical shape, while the

78

71

78. Le Corbusier and Pierre
Jeanneret: second project for the
Centrosoyuz, Moscow, 1928:
model.

79. Le Corbusier and Pierre
Jeanneret: Centrosoyuz, Moscow,
1928–35: general view, with the
auditorium on the left.

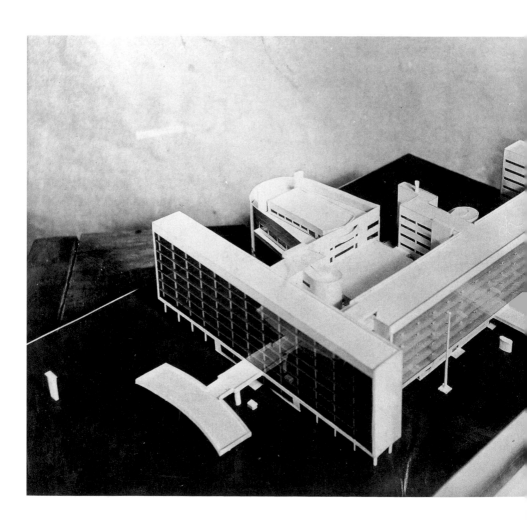

bureaucratic wings began to evolve into a characteristic prismatic form that was totally glazed on one face and opaque on the other, save for a series of square windows illuminating the access corridor. This was exactly the 'glazed versus opaque' paradigm that would inform the dormitory slab of the Pavillon Suisse realized in Paris in 1932, and the same alternating elevational format would be encountered in the residential slabs projected for the Ville Radieuse in 1930. The process was typical of Le Corbusier's 'elemental' method, in which a given prototype comes to be adapted through different projects or even through different versions of the same project. Here was the indispensable economy of his approach: it allowed him to produce an enormous volume of work over a relatively short period of time.

In the first sketches for the Centrosoyuz building, the elements of the original League of Nations proposal were loosely distributed about the perimeter of the site, almost in anticipation of the *à redents* slabs that would later make up the generic residential fabric of the Ville Radieuse. In the second entry the whole asymmetrical complex, consisting of two wings of different lengths and widths, was raised up on *pilotis*, creating an extensive and freely planned foyer beneath. This development, consistent with his 'Five Points of a New Architecture' of 1926, introduced into the Corbusian civic repertoire a particularly fluid approach towards circulation, made evident here in an elaborate system of ramps that ostensibly permitted alternative summer and winter access to the 1,000-seat auditorium on the first floor. Le Corbusier characterized the complex in aphoristic terms as 'une maison sans escaliers', a house without stairs. Of the final version of the Centrosoyuz building he remarked:

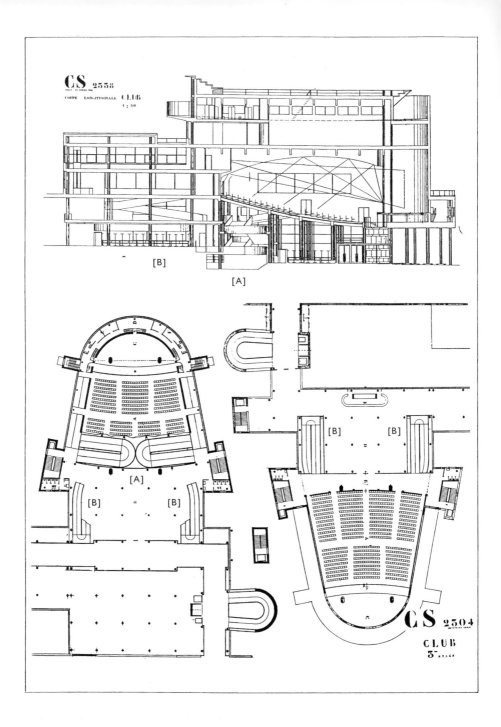

CS 2558
COUPE LONGITUDINALE CLUB
1 : 50

[B]

[A]

[A]

[B]   [B]

[B]   [B]

CS 2504

CLUB
3ᵉ ÉTAGE

It is necessary to regulate the crowds entering and leaving all at the same time. A sort of forum is needed at those hours for people whose galoshes and furs are full of snow in winter: an efficient set of cloakrooms and the circulation around them are needed ... A set of pilotis covers the site entirely, or almost. These pilotis carry the office building, which starts only at the second floor. Under it one circulates freely, outdoors or in rooms opening onto a big space, fed by two entrances and creating the 'forum' suggested above. The elevators leave from this forum, as do the 'paternosters' (cabins on a continuous cable) and immense helicoidal ramps, instead of staircases, allowing a more rapid flow. Doors are opened where useful, under the buildings, in front of them, far from them. Light is captured at will. The analysis is quite clear; such a building has two aspects. The first, an arrival in disorder, on a vast horizontal plane on ground level: it is a lake. The second aspect that of stable motionless work, sheltered from noise and coming and going, everyone at his place and controllable: whereas it is rivers, means of communication, that lead to offices.

Circulation is a word I have applied unceasingly in Moscow to explain myself, so often that it finished by making some representatives to the Supreme Soviet nervous. I maintained my point of view. A second outrageous fundamental proposition: architecture is circulation. Think it over, it condemns academic methods and consecrates the principle of 'pilotis'.[9]

It was perhaps just this kind of rhetoric that eventually served to distance him both from the later Socialist Realist line (embodied in Anatole Lunacharsky's slogan 'pillars for the people') and even from the otherwise sympathetic Constructivist wing of the OSA group, which continued to support him, despite the fact that his *pilotis* could be construed as having classical connotations. The main thrust of the left-wing criticism directed at Le Corbusier both during and after the erection of the Centrosoyuz building in the 1930s was that his architecture was not class-based and hence not sufficiently 'materialist' – or, to put it in the terms of the parallel critique made by Friedrich Engels of Fourier's Utopian Socialism, its social implications were felt to be utopian and idealistic rather than analytical and scientific.

Aside from Le Corbusier and Pierre Jeanneret, two other figures must be credited for the completion of the Centrosoyuz building in 1935: the first was Isidor Liubimov, who fortunately continued to be the client of the building even when it became the Ministry of Light Industry (Narkomlegprom) in 1932; the second was the Russian architect Nikolai Kolli, who assisted in the

80. Le Corbusier and Pierre Jeanneret: Centrosoyuz, Moscow, 1928–35: the auditorium wing. The section and the plans of the second and third floors (positioned nose-to-tail for graphic purposes) show the relationship between the multi-level foyers, cloakrooms, and means of ramp access to the auditorium. Entrances at either end lead to halls with cloakrooms at the lowest level; from there the audience passes via wide ramps (A) to the first-floor foyer, and thence via a second set of ramps (B) to the auditorium itself.

development of Le Corbusier's design from its final resolution in Paris in 1929 to the topping-out in Moscow six years later. The fact that the Centrosoyuz was realized at all is nothing short of a miracle, particularly since Le Corbusier was forbidden from overseeing the job after his final visit to the Soviet Union in March 1930.

This prohibition did not entirely end Le Corbusier's relations with the Soviets, however, for in May 1930 he was invited by Sergei Gorny, administrator for the greater Moscow area, to submit his recommendations for a hypothetical reorganization of the capital city. This took the form of his *Réponse à Moscou* (Reply to Moscow), sent to Kolli on 5 July after six weeks' work in Paris. The document was a radical reformulation of his Plan Voisin for Paris of 1925 and, at the same time, a repudiation of A.V. Shchusev's 1923 proposals for the expansion of Moscow as a garden city. Le Corbusier's *Réponse à Moscou* was exhibited in the West as the seventeen panels of the 'Ville Radieuse' (VR) at the Brussels CIAM Congress of 1930. As hypothetically applied to Moscow, the Radiant City model proposed that the existing residential fabric would be demolished and replaced by *blocs à redents* in the midst of parkscape.

Taking the average for Moscow at 15 square meters [161½ sq. ft] of real living space per inhabitant, it is possible to achieve a density of 1,000 inhabitants per hectare in the 'green city'.

The consequence of this prodigious increase in density is that it solves the public transport crisis, repudiates the mistaken, reactionary

81. Le Corbusier and Pierre Jeanneret: Palace of the Soviets, Moscow, 1931: model, from *L'Architecture vivante*, Autumn–Winter 1932.

and slovenly principle of garden cities on the outskirts of the city and,
by building high-density green cities, eliminates the problem of
suburban transport.[10]

This prescription reflected the critique he had levelled earlier in the year at Ginzburg and Mikhail Barshch's Green City proposal of 1930, with its aim of decanting the population of Moscow into ribbon-like bachelor apartments paralleled by a highway. The units, elevated as a continuous band on *pilotis* along the length of an un-interrupted green zone, were to have been served at intervals by bus stops, sports arenas and workers' clubs. Le Corbusier respond-ed to this Soviet de-urbanization model with the argument that one should urbanize town and country to an equal degree. Where the young Russians believed that, following the precepts of the 1848 Communist Manifesto, one should forcibly redistribute the urban populace over the countryside, Le Corbusier remained convinced that the generic city should be rebuilt as continuous parkscape while maintaining the same high density throughout the region.

In 1931, in the company of three Russian teams led by the archi-tects Ivan Zholtovsky, Boris Iofan and German Krasin and along with eight other foreign firms, Le Corbusier and Pierre Jeanneret were invited to submit an entry for the Palace of the Soviets com-petition. The brief required no less than two separate large audito-riums – one seating 15,000, the other seating 6,000 – plus four smaller ones arranged in pairs, two having a capacity of 500 each and two of 200 each. The League of Nations by comparison would have been assembled around one large auditorium accommodating 2,500 people, and where its relatively modest brief envisaged parking for no more than 100 cars, in the Palace of the Soviets project parking was to be provided for some 500 cars in the under-croft of the auditoriums. As Le Corbusier put it with a certain irony: 'Bolshevism means everything at its biggest.' The complex had to be capable of accommodating the mass pageantry of the Soviet state, irrespective of whether it was Vsevolod Meyerhold's bio-mechanical stage or Nikolai Evreinov's tattoo-like theatrical-ization of everyday life. Le Corbusier's Palace of the Soviets used the device of the inclined plane, first hinted at in the extensive ramps of the Centrosoyuz, as a means to facilitate circulation throughout the foyer of the large auditorium and, at the same time, as a device for providing continuous access between the parking in the podium and the auditorium above. Le Corbusier described this arrangement as a 'classification machine' in which the various class-es of users, while aware of each other, follow precise routes which

I.
81–83

lead them automatically to their appointed destination. He likened these inclined planes to mountain tracks, *routes de montagne*.[11] Similar inclined circulation also occurred for the smaller of the two main auditoriums, in the form of totally glazed access ramps attached to the side elevations. At the same time, the exposed and suspended roof structures of the axial auditoriums were dramatically expressed as a Constructivist trope on the Moscow skyline. This was particularly true of the parabolic arch sailing above the large auditorium, fancifully envisaged as the dematerialized equivalent of a dome in the comparison that Le Corbusier drew between his Palace of the Soviets entry and the cathedral complex at Pisa.

Borrowing its expressive structure from the engineer Eugène Freyssinet's use of a concrete parabolic arch for his airship hangars built at Orly in 1921, Le Corbusier's proposal for the Palace of the Soviets was a megastructural *tour de force*, to such an extent that its machine-like instrumentality caused it to be rejected by the otherwise appreciative Soviet authorities who, influenced by the emerging Socialist Realist line, favoured a more traditional approach towards monumental form. This transitional moment no doubt accounts for the simplified, quasi-Beaux-Arts, quasi-Constructivist syntax adopted by Boris Iofan's winning design. Le Corbusier would again be defeated by the academicism that had denied him the first prize in the League of Nations competition.

Aside from its dramatic structural syntax, Le Corbusier's design for the Palace of the Soviets seems to have been distinguished by three characteristics that served to put it in a class apart: first, its axial, symmetrical composition; second (in contrast to his Centrosoyuz and League of Nations proposals), its relative indifference to

82. Le Corbusier and Pierre Jeanneret: Palace of the Soviets, Moscow, 1931. Perspective of cloakrooms and entry foyer. The ramp on the right leads up to the main hall; the opening in the centre, to the forum below the hall.

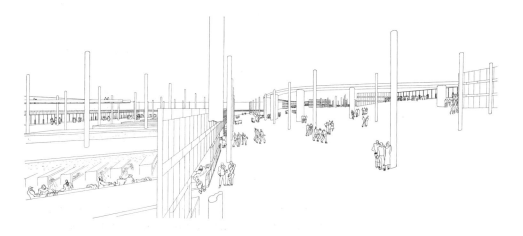

83. Le Corbusier and Pierre Jeanneret: Palace of the Soviets: perspective, showing crowds flocking on the ramps during a May Day parade.

the context, although this was mitigated by the way its profile was related to the spires of the Kremlin; and third, its highly ingenious use of warped surfaces and ramps as the principal device for handling the large numbers involved. Of the latter he wrote:

Large hall for 15,000 people. General entrance: the audience comes in through a 120-metre [394 ft] wide frontage of continuous doors; they are then filtered through the cloakrooms and from there they gradually ascend to the main hall, or from the middle they move towards the forum which is under the main hall. The entire operation, from outdoors right through to the seats in the hall, takes place without the use of a single step, on a continuous, concave, inclined plane.[12]

82

Le Corbusier's commitment to the needs of a mass society, both technically and ideologically, was evident from a perspective that depicted the May Day parade entering the raised podium behind the 15,000-seat hall. This space was able to accommodate some 50,000 people assembled before an orator whose voice would have been amplified by a double acoustic reflector, a device that was both a technical instrument and a metaphor for Soviet ideology, that is to say for the mass rallies and political speeches that were such an essential aspect of the young socialist state.[13]

83

As it happened, the Palace of the Soviets would turn out to be the last parliamentary structure to be designed by Le Corbusier until his 1947 proposal for the United Nations Headquarters in New York.

Despite Le Corbusier's incessant travelling between 1928 and 1936, the early 1930s turned out to be a particularly productive period for Atelier 35S. It was during these exceptionally fertile years that he and Pierre Jeanneret were finally able to synthesize the interplay between 'the engineer's aesthetic' and 'architecture' in a truly convincing way, that is to say to reconcile modern productive technique with the abstraction of Neo-Humanist form. During the first decade of their practice, they had been caught between a Purist preoccupation with plastic form, as set forth in the 'Three Reminders to Architects' of *Vers une architecture,* and the Fordist ideal of rationalized building production, as articulated in the penultimate chapter of the same book ostensibly concerned with prefabricated housing. Such serial production was by definition incompatible with a form of construction that was wet and largely cast in place on site, as in the Purist villas of the 1920s. While these villas assured the 'correct and magnificent play of masses brought together in light', prefabrication, by virtue of the tolerances required, favoured dry assembly and this tended towards some kind of tessellated, light-weight, modular fabric such as Le Corbusier and Pierre Jeanneret encountered in developing the fully glazed membranes of their Cartesian curtain-walled buildings of the early 1930s.

In his single-minded effort to create a new architecture, Le Corbusier seems to have been divided between a drive to conceive of programmatic forms appropriate to the epoch and the application of relatively untested industrial techniques that ought, in theory, to have been capable of realizing such forms. This gap between form and technique was particularly evident in the case of the workers' housing that he realized at Pessac for Henri Frugès. In this instance, Le Corbusier and Pierre Jeanneret seem to have posited an unconventional technology that neither they nor Frugès were capable of mastering, for what was possible in the case of building expensive bourgeois villas close to the capital city could not be easily carried through in the provinces for the production of low-cost housing, particularly with unskilled labour. In the early 1920s, as Brian Brace Taylor observes, Le Corbusier's will-to-form and will-to-technique were often mutually counterproductive:

16, 1

From the very outset, it may be said that Le Corbusier pushed ahead
as he invariably did with other clients with his own personal conception
of what constituted development research; he insisted on the client
(Frugès) purchasing sophisticated machinery (compressors, etc.)
for producing granite cement panels, and on ordering custom-made
metal framing for doors and windows. The result was disastrous both
financially and functionally.

We confront here a tactic to which Le Corbusier resorted
repeatedly in subsequent years of 'forging ahead' with what he
considered to be 'scientific research' leading to real progress in the
industrialization of building techniques... [14]

In a word, Le Corbusier and Pierre Jeanneret constantly over-
reached themselves technically. Where the architectural practice of
Auguste and Gustave Perret was linked with the family contracting
firm, Atelier 35S suffered from the lack not only of internal expertise but also of technical consultants who would have enabled them
to bring their ambitious projects to a successful conclusion.

In the early 1930s Le Corbusier and Pierre Jeanneret attempted
to realize their technocratic vision in four major works: the 84–88
Immeuble Clarté in Geneva, and the Cité de Refuge (a hostel for
the Salvation Army), the Pavillon Suisse of the Cité Universitaire,
and a block of apartments at the Porte Molitor in Paris. In each
instance, ferro-vitreous fenestration, plate glass, glass blocks, ashlar
and ceramic tiles were woven across the surfaces of variously
steel-framed and concrete-framed structures, as though these
membranes were variations on the curtain-wall façades devised
for the *à redents* blocks of the Ville Radieuse.

Le Corbusier's preoccupation with the curtain wall at this time,
as it appeared in both the Centrosoyuz and the Cité de Refuge, was 79, 88
accompanied by a conviction as to the necessity of central air-
conditioning. That such advanced technology was clearly beyond
the capacity of either the building industry or the engineering
profession in the early 1930s may well account for his subsequent
loss of faith in the manifest destiny of the machine age. Central air-
conditioning was virtually unknown in France at the time — a
technological limitation that was hardly helped by his postulation
of a system that he called *respiration exacte*, whereby a building was
supposed to be heated and cooled by tempered air being distributed throughout via an all-enveloping plenum, integral with its
outer skin. These 'neutralizing walls', as he called them, were to be
made up of an inner and an outer glass membrane, with an air-space
in between, constituting a jacket through which either warmed or

cooled air would be passed according to the season of the year. The application of such a system to the Cité de Refuge proved impossible on grounds of cost, and the building had to make do with a single skin of glass and a more conventional blower system for heating. Unfortunately, Atelier 35S failed to foresee the 'greenhouse' effect that would necessarily result from the provision of an unshielded curtain-wall façade facing south in high summer. A similar techno-economic impasse was encountered during the belated realization of the Centrosoyuz building, where, with the assistance of Kolli, an unsuccessful attempt was made to install an organic air-conditioning system integral with the floor structure and the double glazing of the building.[15]

Switzerland finally yielded a 'captain of industry' who was able to translate the technical aspirations of Le Corbusier and Pierre Jeanneret into a substantial reality, in the form of a building that to this day remains one of the most progressive achievements of their pre-war career. I am alluding to the Immeuble Clarté, Geneva (1931–33), a nine-storey block of some forty-nine dwellings of differing size and section, built in just over a year by Edmond Wanner who was both client and contractor. Since Wanner owned a metal fabricating company, he was able to calculate and rapidly erect an exposed structural frame in electrically arc-welded steel, together with sophisticated metal fittings for the entire building including sliding windows, roller sun blinds, roller shutters and continuous metal balconies, lined with wooden slats. In the main, save for secondary wooden joists, brick partitions, plasterwork, and mechanical services, the dry assembly of the structure only called for two trades, glaziers and metalworkers. Well protected against the sun through mechanical blinds and shutters, with smooth-sliding windows mounted on ball-bearings, and double-glazed against the cold, this building with its dematerialized skin was, in many respects, a 'hi-tech' structure *avant la lettre*.[16] A further technical breakthrough in the Immeuble Clarté was the application of glass stair treads on a steel substructure that enabled zenithal light to filter down the stair shaft from the roof.

Without Wanner's direct input, Le Corbusier and Pierre Jeanneret would apply similar levels of sophistication to two other technically successful works that were built over the same period – the Pavillon Suisse in the Cité Universitaire (1930–32), elevated off the ground on a reinforced concrete platform, and an apartment building in the rue Nungesser-et-Coli near the Porte Molitor (1933), on top of which Le Corbusier had his own penthouse. Like Pierre Chareau's Maison de Verre, which Le Corbusier had

84

85, 86

87

84. Le Corbusier and Pierre Jeanneret: Immeuble Clarté, Geneva, 1931–33. Note the glass lenses used in the end wall.

85. Le Corbusier and Pierre Jeanneret: Pavillon Suisse, Cité Universitaire, Paris, 1930–32.

86. Le Corbusier and Pierre Jeanneret. Pavillon Suisse: plans of the ground floor and a typical floor. From the projecting ground-floor foyer, the elevated four-storey dormitory slab is reached by means of a stair and lift tower.

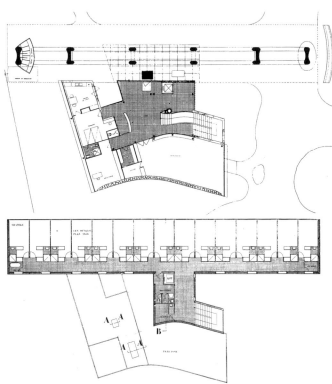

87. Le Corbusier and Pierre Jeanneret: apartment building in the rue Nungesser-et-Coli, near the Porte Molitor, Paris, 1933: perspective.

88. Le Corbusier and Pierre Jeanneret: Cité de Refuge, Paris, 1929–33: model. Note the prisms in front of the slab.

witnessed under construction in Paris during the early 1930s, the seven-storey Porte Molitor building was equipped with steel fenestration, sliding plate-glass windows and glass lenses. Similar lenses, in fact, would be used on the ground floor and end walls of the Immeuble Clarté.

All these buildings were remarkable achievements at other levels, inasmuch as they were contextual interventions: with the exception of the Pavillon Suisse, they were densely planned structures inserted into tight urban sites. This was particularly true of the Cité de Refugé, where a series of modulated Platonic forms – an open-sided cube, a cylinder and a parallelipiped – were set in front of a curtain-walled slab block, providing for a portico, a reception hall and an auditorium amongst other amenities. Aside from their 'hi-tech' character, all four structures manifested elaborate architectural promenades on their ground floors, providing ingenious spatial sequences leading in each instance from the main entry to the various systems of vertical and horizontal circulation.

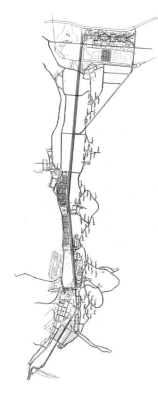

89. Le Corbusier and Pierre Jeanneret: plan of Zlín, Czechoslovakia, for Baťa, 1935.

Le Corbusier's contact with Eastern Europe from the late 1920s on served as a crucial stimulus for his achievements of the early 1930s, so that despite certain misunderstandings he still garnered from the experience a number of models that he would hardly have encountered had it not been for his visit to Czechoslovakia and his contact with the Soviet Union. Most important of these perhaps were the 'linear city' thesis advanced by N. A. Miliutin in his book *Sotzgorod* (Socialist Towns) of 1930, and the prototypical commune as this was realized in Moscow in 1929 by Moisei Ginzburg and Ignati Milinis in their Narkomfin apartment block.) Miliutin's banded linear city model was evidently the basis for Le Corbusier's 1935 design for the expansion of the Baťa shoe company town of Zlín in Czechoslovakia, a commission which he received at the invitation of the Baťa house architect František Gahura. While this plan was never adopted, like his other studies for the Baťa corporation, including a whole series of standard shops, Le Corbusier nonetheless felt that he had found in Jan Baťa his ideal 'captain of industry' as he had evoked this type in *Vers une architecture* – a figure to stand alongside Kees van der Leeuw, the Dutch patron of the Van Nelle factory in Rotterdam, to whom he would pay homage in his book *La Ville Radieuse*.

Le Corbusier's experience in Latin America, which followed his initial visit to Eastern Europe and lasted from 27 September to 7 December 1929, was a personal epiphany, as is evident from the sketches that he made during the trip and from a series of erotic drawings from the same period, including a number of images of

90. Le Corbusier and Josephine Baker on the liner *Lutetia*, returning from Latin America, 1929.

Josephine Baker, with whom he seemingly had a close relationship during his return voyage on the S.S. *Lutetia*.[17] He appears to have associated the female form with the undulating character of the Brazilian landscape and vice versa, with a profound effect on his entire personality, for soon after his return he married Yvonne Gallis, whom he had known since the early 1920s. It would be difficult to imagine a more contrasting figure than this dressmaker from Monaco, with her dark complexion and Latin temperament, her anarchic disposition and eccentric sense of humour. Throughout their married life, she remained in the background; a perennially supportive figure consciously excluded from the limelight.

Meanwhile, his trips over the South American continent by plane (piloted by the pioneer aviators Jean Mermoz and Antoine de Saint-Exupéry) caused him to imagine vast megastructural extensions, integrated into the volcanic terrain at an unprecedented scale. São Paulo, Montevideo and Rio de Janeiro were all rendered as viaduct cities that extended over the landscape with an Olympian force. Under this rubric Le Corbusier envisaged an expansion scheme for Rio in the form of a coastal highway, some 6 kilometres (3¾ miles) in length, elevated 100 metres (328 ft) above the ground and carrying beneath its roadbed some fifteen residential floors. Among the antecedents for this proposal we may cite Giacomo Mattè-Trucco's Fiat factory, Turin (1920–23), with its rooftop racing-car test track, which Le Corbusier had featured positively in *Vers une architecture*.

91. Sketch for expanding Rio de Janeiro, Brazil, as a continuous road town, 1929, from *La Ville Radieuse*.

107

92. Le Corbusier and Pierre Jeanneret:
Plan Obus or 'Plan A' for Algiers, 1930:
photomontage.

93. Le Corbusier and Pierre Jeanneret:
Plan Obus: perspective, from *La Ville Radieuse*.

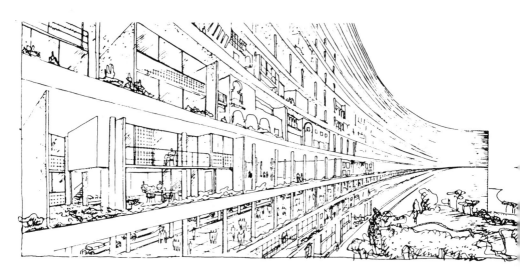

This 'roadtown' esquisse gave rise to a whole series of plans developed for Algiers during the years 1931–42. The first of these, the 'Plan Obus' or 'Plan A' of 1932, projected a similar megastructure to that of Rio running for the entire length of an equally spectacular corniche. This project was seemingly given the name 'Obus' because of the way in which its parabolic plan form resembled the trajectory of a shell.[18] With six floors beneath its road surface and twelve above, Le Corbusier's 'viaduct city' now came into its own, since each floor, set some 5 metres ($16\frac{1}{2}$ ft) apart, constituted an artificial site on which individual owners would have been free to erect two-storey dwellings in any style they saw fit. This provision of a pluralistic infrastructure for individual appropriation was destined to find further currency some twenty-five years later among the architectural avant-garde of the 1950s and 1960s.[19]

92, 93
91

The organic plan configurations created for the cities of Rio de Janeiro and Algiers were related to certain transformations occurring in the expressive structure of Le Corbusier's painting, which after 1926 had begun to gravitate from Purist abstraction towards sensuously figurative compositions, featuring the introduction of what he called 'objets à réaction poétique', that is to say evocative objects such as shells, crystals and driftwood. The female nude first appears in his painting in 1929, and the sensuous, heavy manner in which such figures are rendered lends a certain substance to his claim that, like Delacroix, he had rediscovered the essence of female beauty in the casbah of Algiers.[20] (This was hardly the first time that an experience of the exotic had had a fundamental impact on his consciousness.) In the Plan Obus it was particularly manifest in the arabesque layout of the *à redents* blocks of the Fort l'Empereur hill overlooking the harbour, a figure which in plan was suggestive of Kufic script. This complex, together with the detached skyscraper of the business centre, effectively terminated the serpentine block running along the corniche. Of this simultaneous reference to Arabic script and the female form Mary McLeod has remarked:

Previously restricted to a scale close to the human body, bathroom walls, furniture, bottles painted in sombre purist tones, the curve is now best perceived like the bends in the Amazon from the air. The long viaduct of the Obus ... sweeps gracefully along the coast; the five redents of Fort l'Empereur, supplanting the carefully configured rectilinear set backs of the Ville Radieuse, bend in response to winds, sun, and views to the broad horizons. Enormous objects, grouped in a kind of frozen dance on the Kabyle Hills, they evoke the forms of his robust Algerian women.[21]

The Plan Obus was his last urban proposal of overwhelming grandeur. Here, his involvement with the potential of the viaduct city spent itself in one final, passionate testament to the splendour of the Mediterranean coast. As Manfredo Tafuri has argued, this motopian megastructure was permeated by a profound feeling of pathos, stemming from the fissure that had opened up between the rootless character of modern technology and the rooted harmony of pre-industrial culture, expressed by the confrontation between the Plan Obus and the existing casbah of Algiers.[22] In the event, Le Corbusier's hypothetical reconciliation between a supposedly liberative modern technology and the aggregative forms of a pre-industrial world could not be brought about, and from now on his approach would be more circumspect, while his urban paradigms would gradually assume a less idealized character.

His subsequent encounter with North Africa in the early 1930s assumed an equally romantic and yet in some ways more realistic cast, particularly when he flew over the Atlas Mountains in 1933 in order to overview the land-locked cities of the M'Zab. Of this con- 9 frontation between the Purist flying machine and the sequestered harmony of a pre-industrial world he wrote:

The Mozabites, persecuted heretics, driven in exile from Islam, arrived at length in territory so far off and so terribly barren that they were left alone. They were no longer hunted down, for it was assumed that hunger and thirst would finish the work of destruction. This was a thousand years ago. They made the seven cities of the M'zab and the seven oases... Durafour, steering his little plane, pointed out two specks on the horizon, 'There are the cities! You will see!' Then, like a falcon, he swooped several times upon one of the towns, coming round in a spiral, dived, just clearing the roofs, and went off in a spiral in the other direction... Thus I was able to discover the principal towns of the M'zab. The airplane had revealed everything to us, and what it had revealed provided a great lesson. Behind the walls of the streets were laughing houses, each opening with three ample arcades on an exquisite garden...[23]

As with the Russian Suprematist painter Kasimir Malevich, the direct experience of flight totally transformed Le Corbusier's sensibility. The revelation stemmed not only from an aerial experience of the sublime but also from what he perceived as an apocalyptic image of the earth from the air. This Archimedean point,[24] with respect to a sudden awareness of vast cosmic forces and their cyclical capacity for destruction and recreation (see pp. 203–4), made Le Corbusier increasingly aware of the fragility of the species in relation to the promise and the pathos of the machine. 'From the plane there is no pleasure,' he later observed, 'but a concentrated, mournful meditation.'[25] Le Corbusier's outlook would become further divided as the years advanced, not only between the First and Third Worlds, in an economic and cultural sense, but also between the liberative promise of the machine and the fragile beauty of traditional cultures that he saw as perishing before the impact of industrialization. He had first become aware of this during his 'Voyage d'Orient' of 1911, when he already perceived the erosive effect that the railway had had on the Balkans in the second half of the 19th century, since the iron road bore with it the virus of industrial kitsch that would prove fatal to the authenticity of the vernacular culture.[26]

Le Corbusier first visited the United States in October 1935, at the invitation of the Museum of Modern Art in New York, which had organized a travelling exhibition of his work in conjunction with a lecture tour. He approached North America with considerable ambivalence. He admired the American skyscraper for its evident mastery of steel-frame construction, and American technology for its capacity to realize such megastructures. At the same time, he despised the cultural decadence of the Beaux-Arts manner and had nothing but contempt for the typical stone-clad high-rise building executed in one historical pastiche or another, be it Gothic Revival or Neo-Renaissance. The press conference that he gave after his crossing on the S.S. *Normandie*, in which he

94. Composite sketches of Ghardaia in the M'zab, North Africa, from *La Ville Radieuse*. At the top, above the view in silhouette, he notes: 'the aeroplane discovers the secrets of the desert cities'; below right, he shows four courtyard houses flanked by streets, and comments: 'life is within…pale blue arcades, exuberant vegetation'; below left, he draws a street, with the comment: 'the *mute* street, without traffic'.

had the temerity to declare that the skyscrapers were too small and that Manhattan was a 'fairy catastrophe', hardly endeared him to the American public. Nevertheless he was duly impressed by the panorama of the city at night and by the general precision and grandeur with which Americans were able to build, admiring in particular the metal detailing of Howe and Lescaze's PFSF Building in Philadelphia. Although he was equally charmed by the utopian campuses of America, he was also disconcerted by the naïve, over-enthusiastic response that he elicited in such places as Vassar, Cranbrook and Princeton. While he envied the technocratic aspects of Manhattan – the high-speed elevators, the gridded city, the flawless air-conditioning, the ramped access to the trains in Grand Central Station – he was appalled by the unplanned congestion, by the slums of Harlem, and above all by the continual commuting, back and forth, between suburbia and the city centre. In an article written for *The American Architect* in 1936 he wrote:

Manhattan is so antagonistic to the fundamental needs of the human heart that the one idea of everybody is to escape. To get out. To avoid wasting one's own life and that of one's family in that hard implacable atmosphere. To see the sky. To live where there are trees and to look out on grass. To escape forever from the noise and racket of the city.

This dream of the million has been realised. Millions of city dwellers have moved out to the country. They arrive and settle down and in so doing they cause the destruction of the country. The result is a vast, sprawling built-up area encircling the city – the suburbs. All that

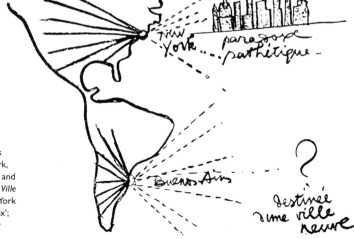

95. Sketch comparing Buenos Aires, Argentina, to New York, and the respective land mass and sea lanes they serve, from *La Ville Radieuse*. The image of New York is captioned 'pathetic paradox'; Buenos Aires is free to enjoy the 'destiny of a new city'.

remains is the dream – the dream of being free, the dream of being master of one's destiny.

This suburban development makes necessary the hours spent daily in the metros, buses and pullmans and causes the destruction of that communal life which is the very marrow of a nation. Yet all this only makes a life of very little real freedom – front doors side by side on the edge of the roads, windows overlooking each other, neighboring roofs shutting out the sky, and an occasional tree which has survived this onslaught. (I am still speaking here of those masses who have not succeeded in doing very well for themselves and who are the vast proportion of the populations of New York and Chicago.)[27]

Despite his contacts with people of influence and power, including the young Nelson Rockefeller, he left the United States empty-handed as far as commissions were concerned, save for a rather tentative yet intriguing project for a college president's house somewhere near Chicago. Of Le Corbusier's first North American foray Stanislaus von Moos has written:

The New Deal had no use for a Colbert from the Old World; it ascribed more importance to good technicians and managers. Le Corbusier's New York proved to be yet another crusade that ended in disaster, for it was based on a tragic misconception of the possible role of the architect in an advanced industrialized society governed by liberalism and big money.[28]

His bitter-sweet memories in this regard were rapidly transposed into yet another book, *Quand les cathédrales étaient blanches* (When the Cathedrals Were White), published in 1937 with the audacious subtitle *Voyage au pays des timides* (Journey to the Land of the Timid).

In 1936, less than a year after his return from the United States, he was again invited to Brazil, this time to work with Lucio Costa and his team on the design of two major works in Rio de Janeiro: the Cité Universitaire – planned as a variation of the Cité Mondiale, complete with the first horizontal version of its pyramidal museum (his 'Musée à croissance illimitée' or museum of unlimited growth) and the Ministry of Education. In this last, realized in 1943, he managed to be instrumental in putting his invention of the *brise-soleil* or sun-breaker into practice. In addition to Costa, the local collaborators on both these projects comprised the architects Oscar Niemeyer, Alfonso Reidy, Carlos Leao, Jorge Moreira and Hermani Vasconcelos and the engineer Emilio Baumgart.

96

96. Oscar Niemeyer, Lucio Costa et al.,
in association with Le Corbusier:
Ministry of Education, Rio de Janeiro,
Brazil, 1936–43. The *brise-soleil* or
sun-breakers, introduced here, are
adjustable.

As Jean-Pierre Giordani has remarked, Le Corbusier's time in Brazil was in all probability the happiest of his life, for here he felt, for the first time perhaps, that his vision of modernity could be realized on a grand scale and in a manner that was totally in keeping with the climate, the landscape, and the life of the people. [29] This affinity was reflected in the wide following that he seems to have engendered throughout Latin America, a following that was particularly evident in the case of Brazil, in the neo-Corbusian practice pursued by such architects as Costa, Niemeyer, Reidy and Moreira, and others such as the team of Marcello and Milton Roberto, who first turned to the use of the vertical *brise-soleil* in their ABI Press Association building erected in Rio in 1936.

Le Corbusier's particular sympathy for Brazil, which he visited for the last time in 1962 while working on his project for the French Embassy in Brasilia (p. 220), is evident in the brief homage to Niemeyer that he made shortly before his own death:

Oscar works with his heart, with optimism. I have often thought of him during the construction of Brasilia, a city that now exists. Niemeyer has managed his task well. He has gone through with it. He is in the front line of combat. Like Lucio Costa, he is a fellow fighter, a faithful friend. I can excuse him his inaccuracy; it is Brazilian and one excuses everything about Brazil, generous and welcoming land. [30]

97. Le Corbusier and Pierre Jeanneret: the principle of the sun-breaker (here fixed), demonstrated in a section of an office block projected for Algiers, 1938.

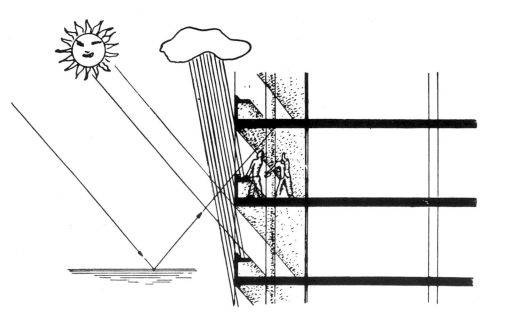

Chapter 7 The Politics of the Unpolitical: Le Corbusier and Saint-Simonian Technocracy 1923–1947

Throughout the 1920s Le Corbusier hoped to be able to transform the existing urban fabric through applying the principles of scientific management to building production, and it was this pre-occupation that first prompted him to become involved with Ernest Mercier's reformist movement, Redressement Français. Mary McLeod explains:

For Le Corbusier, Mercier, the managing director of France's leading utilities company and later president of the Compagnie Française des Pétroles, was representative of a new élite that envisioned leading France, with men 'capiteaux et généraux.' In the midst of the critical financial crisis of 1925, Mercier decided to initiate a movement for general reform that would enlist the 'directing classes' of the nation. Called the Redressement Français, it sought to overhaul the Third Republic along technocrat lines though a dynamic economy predicated on mass production and a government headed by experts...Mercier embraced the Taylorized belief in enlightened industrial production as a weapon against social injustice and indeed hoped for a victory of Ford over Marx... [1]

The reorganization of the productive forces along these lines was widely regarded as the key to the modernization of French society in the aftermath of the First World War. Figures as diverse as Georges Benoît-Lévy, Hyacinthe Dubreuil, Lucien Romier, Henri Sellier, Albert Thomas, and above all Raoul Dautry believed to an equal degree in the necessity of achieving a planned economy. In one way or another all these men were committed to a wide application of Frederick Winslow Taylor's managerial theories, not only to the rationalization of industrial production but also to the refor-mation of society and the amelioration of the urban environment (see Taylor's *The Principles of Scientific Management*, 1911). Thus Benoît-Lévy, a lawyer-cum-social reformer and author of *La Cité Jardin* (The Garden City, 1904), believed like Le Corbusier in the application of Taylorist principles to the production of housing. Dubreuil was a leader of the CGT trades union, a mechanic by trade, and therefore, like Taylor, an advocate of applying the organized, ergonomic division of labour to every sphere of life, from household management to industrial production, from the distribution of goods to the rational planning of the environment. Sellier was the secretary of the HBM (*habitations à bon marché*) low-cost housing organization and a syndicalist specializing in housing reform. Thomas was the director of the Bureau International du Travail (International Labour Office) at Geneva. Romier was a radical economist, close to Dautry, and a spokesman for Redressement Français. Dautry, like Mercier, was a graduate of the École Polytechnique employed by the French railway systems. He was engaged in the rationalization of the national rail network, first from 1918 as engineer to the Chemins de Fer du Nord and then from 1928 as director-general of the Chemins de Fer de l'État. Following the First World War he had been occupied with the construction of a large number of garden cities for railway workers, and this brought him into contact with leading architects of the 1920s including Henri Sauvage and Louis Süe. As a result of this activity, he presided over the urbanistic section of Redressement Français and in that capacity in 1928 he heard Le Corbusier lecture on two occasions, first on the theme of modernizing Paris and then on the Taylorization of building production. In the very same year, he helped to draft the Loi Loucheur that was ostensibly destined to facilitate the construction of low-cost dwellings throughout France. This legislation, which eventually became the basis for the HLM (*habitations à loyer modéré*) scheme, had its origins in the efforts of the minister, Louis Loucheur, to initiate a national reconstruction programme after the First World War.

Like the rest of this élite whom he so much admired, Le Corbusier remained a Saint-Simonian at heart, and while he was not a political animal in the strict sense of the term his writings nonetheless evince a certain political position. Believing in technocratic leadership and in some form of collective decision-making, which he characterized in the early 1930s as 'government by *métier*', that is a hierarchical form of government, effected through the

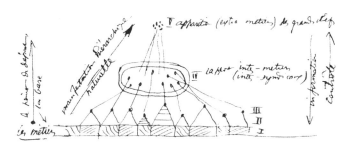

98. Sketch illustrating the syndicalist theory of governance through the election of trades union representatives (I, II, III), who meet with the technocratic élite (V) at the inter-union council (IV).

liberal professions and the trades unions, Le Corbusier favoured the democratic process only in so far as it would assist the 'captains of industry' in their modernization of society. The social crisis confronting France after the war was thus overtly alluded to in the last chapter of *Vers une architecture* (p. 31), wherein under the slogan 'Architecture ou révolution' he wrote:

Disturbed by the reactions which play upon him from every quarter, the man of to-day is conscious, on the one hand, of a new world which is forming itself regularly, logically and clearly, which produces in a straightforward way things which are useful and usable, and on the other hand he finds himself, to his surprise, living in an old and hostile environment. This framework is his lodging; his town, his street, his house or his flat rise up against him useless, hinder him from following the same path in his leisure that he pursues in his work...

There reigns a great disagreement between the modern state of mind, which is an admonition to us, and the stifling accumulation of age-long detritus.

The problem is one of adaptation, in which the realities of our life are in question.

Society is filled with a violent desire for something which it may obtain or not. Everything lies in that: everything depends on the effort made and the attention paid to these alarming symptoms.

Architecture or Revolution.

Revolution can be avoided.[2]

From this we can see that in 1923 Le Corbusier thought revolution could be judiciously avoided through the provision of housing on the part of the state and the industrialization of building production. Six years later, following the Wall Street crash of 1929, the political situation had become increasingly unstable and a worldwide economic crisis was beginning to take hold, so much so that by the time Le Corbusier met the Syndicalist lawyer Philippe Lamour[3] in 1930 he was convinced of the need for radical action. However, despite the Swiss anti-modernist architect Alexander von Senger's accusation that Le Corbusier was the 'Trojan Horse of Bolshevism', he was hardly a radical of the left.[4]

It is true that Syndicalism advocated the nationalization of industry through the strategy of the general strike, even if it had already passed its zenith as an influential working-class movement by 1931, when Lamour, Jeanne Walter and Hubert Lagardelle[5] inaugurated their Syndicalist magazine *Plans*, with Le Corbusier, the engineer François de Pierrefeu[6] and Dr Pierre Winter[7] acting as contributing editors. The first issue, in January, had leading articles by Lamour on the interdependence of modernization and economic federalism and by Lagardelle on the capacity of Syndicalism to overcome the weaknesses of democracy, accompanied by pieces from Winter on the importance of sport, from de Pierrefeu on the need to limit property rights, and from Le Corbusier, whose essay 'Invite à l'action' would later form a chapter in his book *La Ville Radieuse*. Just as the magazine *L'Esprit Nouveau* was the proving ground for the text of *Vers une architecture*, so *Plans* first published material that was to be embodied, in a different sequence, in the fourth section of *La Ville Radieuse*.

Some of Le Corbusier's essays in *Plans* did not reappear in the book: most notable among the omissions is his pacifist essay, 'La Guerre? Mieux vaut construire', which appeared in the sixth issue, published in 1931 under the subtitle *La Guerre est possible*. In that issue Lamour argued for a European customs union, under the challenging title 'Faites l'Europe, sinon faites la guerre', while elsewhere in the same issue Le Corbusier contributed the argument that the total mobilization so essential to the conduct of modern war ought now to be applied to the construction of peace. Exhortatory and telegrammatic as usual, the way in which he formulates the issue reveals a great deal about his Manichean habit of mind. He asks whether the powers that be have any conception at all of what is conducive to human happiness, and in a sequence of rhetorical questions he points out that it is not money or the escapist pleasures of Hollywood that really afford men happiness, but rather the feeling that they are acting together to transform the world; the same feeling, in fact, that may be negatively induced by inflaming nationalistic passion for the waging of war and destruction. Playing with the metaphor of the human species as an acrobat on a high-wire, he writes of tipping the balancing pole ever so slightly in one direction rather than another, towards the good rather than the bad. He advocates in somewhat simplistic moralistic terms mobilization towards peace rather than war:

The mobilisation of the land, the people and the means of production in order to realise the plan. Happiness is in this imperceptible inclination of the balancing pole towards active production. Equipment: the word of command, armaments, machines and circulation, discipline? EXACTLY THE SAME AS FOR THE WAGING OF WAR.

One asks oneself in disbelief, 'can it really be so easy?' a simple decision of the spirit … to decide to build instead of entering into destruction.[8]

He would advance a similar polemic in the apodictic phrases emblazoned on the exhibition panels of his 1937 Pavillon des Temps Nouveaux at the Porte Maillot, Paris, and in the subsequent expansion of these arguments, published in book form in 1938 under the title, *Des Canons, des munitions? Merci! Des Logis… S.V.P.*, wherein he formulated the issue as one of choosing between annihilation and the provision of public housing. Once again, he advocated a kind of pacifist mobilization, set forth in the slogan 'La mobilization du sol, des gens et de la production pour réaliser le plan' (the commandeering of the land, of the population and of the means of production in order to realize the plan).

Influenced by the radical arguments advanced by Georges Sorel in his *Réflexions sur la violence* of 1908, both Lamour and Lagardelle had been associated prior to the 1930s with right-wing, national socialist organizations, above all with George Valois' proto-fascist Faisceau des Protecteurs et Combattants, founded in 1925.[9] While Dr Winter had also been involved with Valois' organization, the editors of *Plans* tended to be technocratic and reformist rather

99. Cover design for *Des Canons, des munitions? Merci! Des Logis… S.V.P.*, 1938.

than politically radical in the revolutionary sense. This was as true of Le Corbusier as of François de Pierrefeu, who as director of the Entreprises des Grands Travaux Hydrauliques would later sponsor Le Corbusier's plans for Algiers (1931–42) and Nemours (1935). Close throughout his life to the neo-Saint-Simonian Catholic right, de Pierrefeu was so impressed by the work and thought of Le Corbusier and Pierre Jeanneret that he wrote the first definitive monograph on their work.[10]

In the early 1930s the editors of *Plans* were interested in being politically effective at a regional level. They formed a group known as the 'Cercle des Amis de *Plans*' which functioned as a federation for French regional organizations, committed to the establishment of *natural* rather than *artificial* national boundaries. Much of this thought would reappear in *La Ville Radieuse*, as we may judge from the chapter entitled 'Les Graphiques expriment' ('Truth from Diagrams'). He had first written this chapter for the magazine *Préludes*, the successor to *Plans*, which he edited with de Pierrefeu and Lagardelle between 1933 and 1935.[11] Aside from arguing for the determination of regional frontiers in terms of land formation and corresponding differences in climate, the text also recapitulated the ideal Syndicalist model of governance, with the various trade unions influencing decisions from below and an elected technocratic élite governing from above. At the same time, with France already subject to the threat of another war, Le Corbusier suggested how the pending conflict might be averted first by modifying national boundaries along ecological lines and second by decentralizing all forms of government.

Préludes, like *Plans*, was only one among a number of polemical journals that surfaced during the politically nonconformist period of the 1930s that preceded the electoral compromise of Léon Blum's Popular Front. Responding to the continuing economic depression and to the corresponding rise of totalitarianism in Europe, and thus being able, *faute de mieux*, to combine within a single administration the hitherto mutually antagonistic Communist, Socialist and Radical representatives, the Popular Front, which lasted with and without Blum's leadership from 1936 until October 1938, temporarily overcame the excessive factionalism that had previously plagued post-war political life in France.

Following Blum's rise to power, Le Corbusier was involved in a number of projects that in one way or another reflected the mediatory policies of the Popular Front: there were self-generated commissions such as the 100,000-seat stadium projected for Vincennes and the Pavillon des Temps Nouveaux of 1937, and a

100

100. Le Corbusier and Pierre Jeanneret: 100,000-seat stadium
projected for Vincennes, 1937: model.

101. Le Corbusier and Pierre Jeanneret:
projected monument to Paul Vaillant-Couturier, 1937.

request to participate in competitions such as the design of a
monument to the memory of the late Communist mayor of
Villejuif, Paul Vaillant-Couturier, a competition which Corbusier
would have won had it not been for the opposition of Léon
Moussinac.[12] This, the first monument of his career, introduced the
theme of the open hand, a motif which would reappear in a different
form after the Second World War in the open hand designed for the
Capitol in Chandigarh.

While Le Corbusier moved to the left during the time of the
Popular Front, his ultimate political views in the late 1930s favoured
some form of national socialism, a position that eventually led to
the dissolution of the partnership with his cousin. As was to be the
case for many people, a close alliance was ended over the single
issue of the Vichy government, when after the German invasion of
France in June 1940, a face-saving compromise was evolved in July
with the formation of the non-parliamentary government of the
'État Français' under the leadership of Marshal Pétain. Each went
his own way, Le Corbusier aligning himself with Vichy and Pierre
Jeanneret moving to Grenoble, where, with Denise Cresswell,
Georges Blanchon and André Masson, he founded a design/
research unit known as 'Le Bureau Central de Construction'
(BCC). That Jeanneret continued to work with Jean Prouvé during
this period testifies to the particularly close relationship between
the two men, given Prouvé's later association with the Resistance
during the occupation of France.[13] Meanwhile Le Corbusier and
de Pierrefeu consolidated their views in a policy statement on
environmental design entitled *La Maison des hommes*, written in
Vichy in the summer of 1941 and published in the following year.

This book, the only significant work to come from Le
Corbusier's hand during his Vichy adventure, was of consequence at
two distinct levels. In the first instance, it categorically repudiated
the moribund academicism of the French architectural profession,
going so far as to advocate a return to the medieval guild system. In
the second, it argued for revolution from above, the Third Republic
being seen as the epitome of parliamentary decadence.[14] Anti-
capitalist, anti-consumerist and anti-media, de Pierrefeu made
their position clear when he wrote:

*the capitalist system found itself forced, by its own diabolical urge,
continually to expand – to impose, not upon savages but upon
countries already crammed with goods, this general surfeit known as
over-consumption.*

With exceptional ecological awareness given the date, he continued:

The dogma today is the utter waste of a cosmic reserve, *irreplaceable and given us but once. Whereas productive energy ought to have assured a perfect technique without harm to our terrestrial domain through the use of our water cycle, of a revenue that, renewed annually, the sun puts at our disposal; the gathering of waters flowing over the earth.*[15]

However much he may have inexplicably ignored the achievements of the American Tennessee Valley Authority with its regional network of hydroelectric dams, de Pierrefeu's concept of the *domaine bâti*, the built realm, presupposed the planned transformation of entire regions wherein the culture of architecture should extend to every terrestrial component, whether it be a building, a bridge, a dam or a viaduct.

La Maison des hommes makes it clear that the architect and the engineer had influenced each other for so long that many of their views were interchangeable. Le Corbusier limited himself to commenting on de Pierrefeu's essay in a series of sketches, accompanied by extended captions. Although he may have taken issue with the bigotry that crops up here and there in de Pierrefeu's text, the two men seem to have had similar views when it came to the modernization of society. In short, the Syndicalist, national-socialist, decentralized line is set forth here for one last time – the ideal of achieving some kind of socio-political homeostatic balance between the region and the state and thus between regional autarchy and technocratic central control. Significantly enough, given the times, the Syndicalist idea of government by *métier*, as it was sketched out in *La Ville Radieuse*, seems now to have been conveniently dropped.[16]

Four synthetic diagrams from *La Maison des hommes* are particularly revealing not only because of their ideological implications but also for the way in which they testify to the cosmic and dialogical character of Le Corbusier's world view. In one of these, the Vichy government is rendered as a tree, representing the hypothetical, hierarchical structure of the French state, with its roots descending into the soil of the region and thus into the traditional values of region, family, agriculture and craft; the whole is overseen and governed from above by the *doctrine générale*.[17] Another, more universal, diagram draws our attention to the natural twenty-four-hour solar cycle, while yet another is given over to the first incarnation of Le Corbusier's image of a single head, divided between the

102. Hypothetical syndicalist model of the French state, from *La Maison des hommes*, 1942. The state, envisaged as a tree, is seen as growing out of the 'universal man' and the history of the French people; its roots are regional culture, family life, agriculture, craftsmanship and industry. The branches are financial and constructional techniques, law, corporation, and *doctrine générale*. The latter is applied to the built realm, explained to public opinion, and established by law, and culminates in administration, whereby the law is applied.

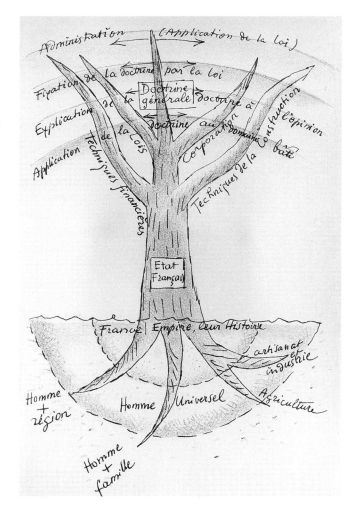

103. Sketch of the twenty-four-hour cycle, represented as a metabolic dialogical rhythm, from *La Maison des hommes*, 1942.

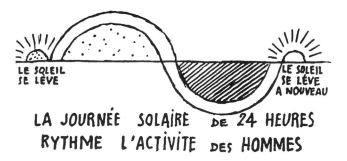

beatific radiance of Apollo and the ferocious torment of Medusa, 104
thereby hinting, however obliquely, at the play between light and
dark forces that seems to have preoccupied Le Corbusier throughout his life. For his part de Pierrefeu seems to have conceived of this
duality as a perennial conflict between rationality and irrationality,
prompting him to end his essay with the words: 'to think in terms of
reason only petrifies the world'.[18] In a parallel diagrammatic syn- 105
thesis, which would later serve as the symbol of the ASCORAL
group (see below), Le Corbusier diagrammed and colour-coded
the respective roles to be played by the architect (blue) and the
engineer (red) in relation to the generic building task. He elected to
characterize this split as a division of labour between *l'homme spir-
ituel* and *l'homme économique*, that is to say between the spiritual
and economic aspects of human motivation. Le Corbusier saw that
first one and then the other aspect became dominant in the
process of construction, depending on the nature of the sub-set
under consideration at the time.

Constituted in Paris at Le Corbusier's initiative in May 1943, the
Association des Constructeurs pour la Rénovation Architecturale

104. Sketch of the Apollo/Medusa
image, signifying a dialogical
balance between opposing forces,
from *La Maison des hommes*, 1942.

(Association of Constructors for the Renewal of Architecture) or ASCORAL was the means by which Le Corbusier redeemed himself from the futile compromise of his association with the Vichy government.[19] While this entailed distancing himself from his former Vichy colleagues, above all from de Pierrefeu and the brilliant stage designer André Boll,[20] he nonetheless still adhered to the *planisme* of the Saint-Simonian line. In this he was assisted by a number of former associates including the 'intellectual peasant' Norbert Bézard, who throughout the 1930s had been advocating the strategy of agrarian reform as embodied in Le Corbusier's generic 'Ferme Radieuse' or 'Radiant Farm' proposal of 1934. He was joined by other technocratic figures of the same generation, men such as Hyacinthe Dubreuil and Urbain Cassan, who had been Dautry's top engineering assistants throughout the 1920s and '30s, and the distinguished architect Marcel Lods of Beaudoin et Lods. Around this core of veterans from the inter-war era stood the first echelons of the younger generation who would assist him in re-opening the studio at 35 rue de Sèvres, including Roger Aujame and Gérald Harding. Where Le Corbusier's atelier ended and

106, 107

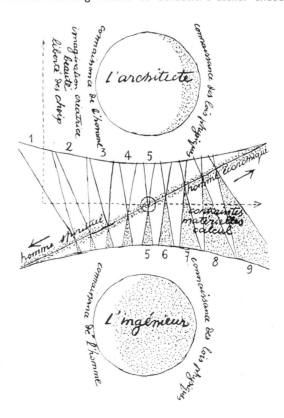

105. Sketch of the dialogical relationship obtaining between the architect and the engineer, from *La Maison des hommes*, 1942. The vertical axis indicates that where the architect has a better understanding of man, the engineer is better acquainted with the laws of physics. The horizonatal axis expresses the same interaction in terms of spirituality and economy.

ASCORAL began was left deliberately vague. This was not the only ambiguity that attended its constitution and activity: in part an architect's office, in part a research centre, and in part, however quixotically, an institution for the generation of public policy, ASCORAL could be perceived as being active on an extremely broad front and hence as displaying a comprehensive technical capacity that would put it in a prime position to build on a grand scale at the end of the war. Moreover, even under wartime conditions Le Corbusier persisted with his perennial cultivation of the 'captains of industry', soliciting financial assistance from the glass cartel of Saint-Gobain and the oil company Sinco.

Prior to its transformation into the French wing of CIAM at the Sixth CIAM Congress held at Bridgwater in England in 1947, ASCORAL's ideological position seems to have been based on the book *Les Trois Établissements humains*, written during the Occupation with the assistance of Aujame, Bézard, Harding and Dubreuil, amongst others, and published in 1945. Perhaps the most impressive thing about *The Three Human Establishments* is the comprehensiveness of its vision, for it set forth once and for all an environmental synthesis in which it was impossible to separate radical architectural form from an equally radical restructuring of society as a whole. Among its many paradoxes, however, was the way in which it quietly adopted as its own the long-standing Marxist aspiration for the creation of a unified, de-urbanized proletariat, comprised to an equal degree of peasants and workers, inextricably mixed together. This populace was conceived as forming the fundamental basis of a new society, to be accommodated in linear cities laid out in the rural landscape and made up of Le Corbusier's Radiant Farms and 'Green Factories'. At the same time, there was something mediatory about this vision of mixed production that veered, however unconsciously, towards a world view that was revisionist and existential rather than militantly radical. The new man and new way of life now seemed to be more down-to-earth and realistic against the green fields and the grey light that emanated from Le Corbusier's post-war *béton brut*. Cast from rough timber formwork, his concrete walls seemed to express a coming to terms with the harsh realities of life and perhaps a certain tragic and redeeming acceptance of things as they are. This was the pre-consumerist, homeostatic mediatory moment that confronted Europe at the end of the Second World War.

127
106,
107

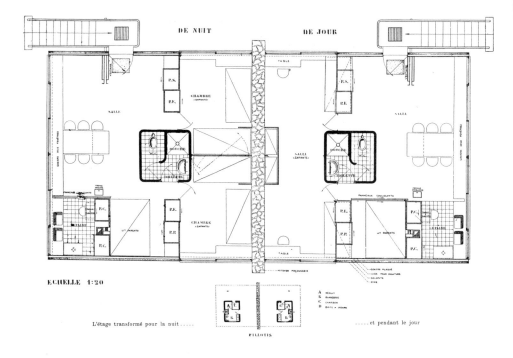

ECHELLE 4:20

L'étage transformé pour la nuit.....   .....et pendant le jour

108. Le Corbusier and Pierre Jeanneret: Maison Loucheur project, 1929: first-floor plan.
The dwellings, with mirror-image plans, are transformed from day (right) to night (left)
use by fold-away beds and sliding partitions.

109. Le Corbusier and Pierre Jeanneret: Maison Loucheur project: perspective.
The frame is of steel, the party wall of rubble stone.

Chapter 8   From Intermediate Technology to Regional Urbanization 1929–1946

The combination of time-honoured building methods with prefabricated light-weight technology came with Le Corbusier's Maison Loucheur proposal of 1929. Here rubble-stone walling was combined with exposed steel-frame construction and light-weight components in the first version of his *maison à sec*, that is a house assembled out of industrially produced prefabricated parts, including all the exterior panelling, the interior fittings, and a single sanitary unit, comprising a WC, a shower and a wash-hand basin.   108 Through the use of sliding partitions and fold-away beds, each 44-square metre (490 sq. ft) unit was when transformed from day to night use capable of accommodating two adults and four children. In the prototype, a pair of dwellings are supported in part   109 by free-standing steel stanchions (*pilotis*) and in part by a rubble-stone party wall. This last, to be made of native stone, was envisaged not only as mediating universal civilization through local culture but also as providing continual employment for local craftsmen and builders.

While the roof of the Maison Loucheur was implacably flat, the presence of vernacular references in Le Corbusier's architecture reasserts itself in the roof forms employed in a number of incidental works that he designed at the end of the 1920s and in the first half of the 1930s. The initial indications of this shift are in his projects for 'Ma Maison' of 1929 and the Maison Errazuris of 1930 – the former involving a return to vaulted forms such as he had conceived for the   18 Maison Monol, the latter introducing monopitch roofs. 'Ma Maison'   111 was a hypothetical house and studio for his own use, sketched out while en route to Buenos Aires on the S.S. *Massilia* in 1929. While the residential section of the house adhered to the format of the flat-roofed Purist prism, the studio was covered by two pairs of inclined conical shell vaults, similar in section and profile to those employed by the concrete engineer Eugène Freyssinet in his railway repair sheds at Bagneux that were under construction at around the same time. One should note in passing that Freyssinet was often a source of inspiration for Le Corbusier.

The reinterpreted agrarian syntax employed in the Maison Errazuris ostensibly came from the exigencies of having to build a

ERRAZZURIZ

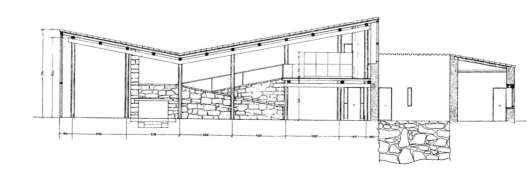

8982

110. Le Corbusier and Pierre Jeanneret: Maison Errazuris, Chile, 1930: interior.

111. Le Corbusier and Pierre Jeanneret: Maison Errazuris: section.

modest vacation house on an extremely remote site. Projected for Chile, it gave rise to what would soon become his characteristic neo-vernacular manner, an expression that was at one and the same time archaic and modern. The long and relatively narrow two-storey house, built of rough-cut, load-bearing stonework, was covered by two monopitch roofs of unequal length covered in Spanish tiles and draining towards a point one-third of the way along the length of the dwelling. This was Le Corbusier's first use of a pitched roof since his early work in La Chaux-de-Fonds. While the rubble-stone walls were externally finished in smooth plaster, the traditional roof-form was offset by large window openings and by an interior volume which, besides being double-height with a mezzanine sleeping-loft, was animated by a ramp connecting the two floors. The latter, together with the fireplace and inner walls, was to have been built out of exposed rubble stonework. The rather brutal material, along with the stripped tree trunks of the exposed structural frame, jointly conveyed a feeling of primitive rusticity. Le Corbusier wrote in 1934 in terms that falsely suggested the house had already been built:

This house was built on the edge of the Pacific Ocean. Since a technically skilled labour force was not available, we employed elements existing on the site that were easily handled: walls made of large blocks of stone, a framework made of tree-trunks, a covering of local tiles and as a result a pitched roof.

The rusticity of the materials is in no way a hindrance to the expression of a clear plan and a modern aesthetic.[1]

A version of the Maison Errazuris was actually realized a few years later in Japan, to the designs of the Czech-American émigré architect Antonin Raymond. He translated the rubble-stone walling into roughly dressed timber construction covered with thatch – close in spirit to the traditional Japanese timber farmhouse or *minka*. The two levels of the double-height living volume were again linked by an exposed ramp, here built out of logs. Publishing photographs of Raymond's Karuizawa House in his *Oeuvre complète 1929–1934* as though they were living proof of the tectonic validity of his Errazuris project, Le Corbusier was ironic about the plagiarism and praised the house for its intrinsic qualities, for the fact that it was an elegant variation of the same type-form and for revealing the inherent affinity of Japanese culture for modern architecture:

We were pleased to discover in this month's Architectural Record *of July 1934 a number of illustrations reproducing a very pretty house*

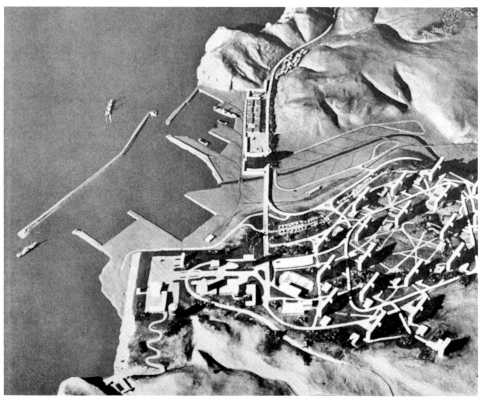

134

built by Mr. Raymond, near Tokyo, in Japan. The reader ought not to be deceived, it was not photographs of our house but rather a creation by Mr. Raymond! The least one can say is that great minds think alike! Be that as it may, we have had true satisfaction in seeing ideas that are dear to us realized with such taste. A digression is in order here: it is certain that the art of architecture in Japan is better prepared than our western counterpart to exploit successfully the modern architectural thesis. Japan possesses an admirable tradition of dwelling. It has at its disposal an exceptionally refined and spiritual craftsmanship. The old Japanese tea houses are adorable works of art.

Moreover, the Japanese have adopted the principles of modern architecture. They have applied them with undeniable flair. They are capable of endowing modern architecture with discernible refinements.[2]

Despite the successful realization in 1933 of the Immeuble Clarté in Geneva, and the equally refined Pavillon Suisse and the Porte Molitor apartment building in Paris, Le Corbusier's growing ambivalence towards the machine age nonetheless surfaced at this time and would persist in various ways throughout the rest of his career. His doubt in this regard was due to many causes, not least perhaps to the rejection of his international competition designs of the late 1920s and early 1930s. In addition to these setbacks, there was the particular disappointment he felt over his Maison Loucheur proposal. The failure of the State to implement his prefabricated prototype once again frustrated his vision of realizing a Taylorized low-income house comparable to the Model T Ford. Along with his desire to replace the typical overcrowded working-class ghetto by low-rise housing set amid green went his complementary aim of transcending the sentimental rusticity of the Anglo-Saxon garden suburb through a new form of regional urbanization.

Primitive building techniques and sophisticated components appeared as expressive elements in Le Corbusier's architecture from the Maison Loucheur onwards. We encounter comparable mixtures of off-site, prefabricated, and on-site, in-situ construction in the shop-built timber windows and rubble-stone walling of the vacation house that he built for Madame Hélène de Mandrot near Toulon in 1931. Three other equally 'archaic' works were to be realized in the next few years: the Maison de Week-end at La Celle-St-Cloud near Paris and the Maison aux Mathes near Bordeaux, both of 1935, and, at another scale altogether, the canvas-covered Pavillon des Temps Nouveaux, designed in 1936 for the Paris International Exhibition of 1937. While the troglodyte dwelling at

112. House for Madame de Mandrot, Le Pradet, near Toulon, 1931. Construction is of load-bearing rubble stone throughout, with wooden fenestration.

113. Le Corbusier and Pierre Jeanneret: plan for Nemours, Algeria, 1935: model. At the right are apartment blocks overlooking the harbour; at the left, the civic centre; above, the industrial zone.

114. Le Corbusier and Pierre
Jeanneret: Maison de Weekend,
La Celle-St-Cloud, 1935: isometric.

St-Cloud recalled Le Corbusier's Maison Monol of 1919 as well as
the vaulted Mediterranean megaron from which it was derived, the
Paris exhibition pavilion returned him to the nomadic tent, as this
had appeared in *Vers une architecture* in an archaeological reconstruction of the Hebrew Temple in the Wilderness.[3]

This mixing of industrial technology with pre-industrial building
technique was not the only paradigm shift during this period, as we
may judge from his abandonment of an anthropomorphic, centralized city model in favour of the linear city format that he adopted for
the Czech industrial town of Zlín in 1935. That year seems to have
been a watershed in urban design at other levels as well, for both in
Zlín and in Nemours in North Africa he abandoned the *à redents*
residential pattern in favour of free-standing slab blocks.

The single-storey, vaulted, turf-covered Maison de Week-end at
St-Cloud was to remain influential for the rest of his career, and it is
typical of Le Corbusier's new-found empiricism that this diminutive
hybrid dwelling should involve a subtle and poetic synthesis of time-
honoured agrarian building methods and advanced engineering
technique. This last was initially evident in the structural module of
the shell concrete vault on which the plan of the house was based.
This square module, standing free in the garden of the house as a
canopy, consisted of a thin shell supported at each of its corners by
equally thin reinforced concrete piers. When this module was used
within the body of the house to form the vaulted roof, the piers
were partially replaced by load-bearing rubble-stone walls. With
the Maison de Week-end, the expressive tenor of Le Corbusier's
architecture categorically shifted from the sculptural ethos of
Platonic form to the tectonic articulation of the construction itself.
He observed:

115. Le Corbusier and Pierre
Jeanneret: Maison de Week-end:
interior.

*The designing of such a house demanded extreme care since the
elements of construction were the only architectural means.*

*The architectural theme was established about a typical bay
whose influence extended as far as the little pavilion in the garden.*

*Here one was confronted with exposed rubble-stone walling,
painted white on the interior, plywood being used on the ceiling and
the walls, exposed roughly coursed brickwork for the chimney, white
ceramic tiles on the floor, Nevada glass block walls and a table of
cipollino marble.[4]*

While Le Corbusier sometimes justified the primitive means
adopted for such hybrid works on the grounds of the remoteness of
their sites, such a justification was hardly plausible in the case of the
Pavillon des Temps Nouveaux, which was all the more remarkable

114, 18

149

89

114,
115

116

for its combination of archaic and modern technology in the realization of an enormous tent held in place by wire cables running over free-standing latticework girders in steel. The aeronautical metaphor evoked by this dirigible-like structure was also evident in the pivoting entry door that, tapering at its extremities like an airplane wing, enabled the visitors to enter and leave the pavilion as though they were themselves as volatile in their movement as the turbulent air passing over an aerofoil. This aerodynamic association was reinforced by the placing of a model aircraft on the axis of the 'flow'. With its cruciform formation in plan, this model also alluded by association to an underlying spiritual, even religious, character, an implication carried further in the the space itself, where on entering one encountered an acoustic shell rising behind the speaker's rostrum like a baldacchino behind a pulpit. To the right of this rostrum, on the central axis of the space, the principles of the CIAM Athens Charter of 1934 were displayed on an undulating three-dimensional plaque – evocative of an open book – as though they were the Mosaic Tables of the Law. These spiritual associations were seemingly at variance with the quasi-Popular Front slogan emblazoned on the acoustic shell: 'UNE NOUVELLE ÈRE A COMMENCÉ... UNE ÈRE DE SOLIDARITÉ' (a new era has begun... an era of solidarity), although that slogan surely also possessed a spiritual ring.[5]

116. Le Corbusier and Pierre Jeanneret: Pavillon des Temps Nouveaux, Paris, 1937.

117. Le Corbusier and Pierre
Jeanneret: Pavillon des Temps
Nouveaux: elevation, plan
and section.

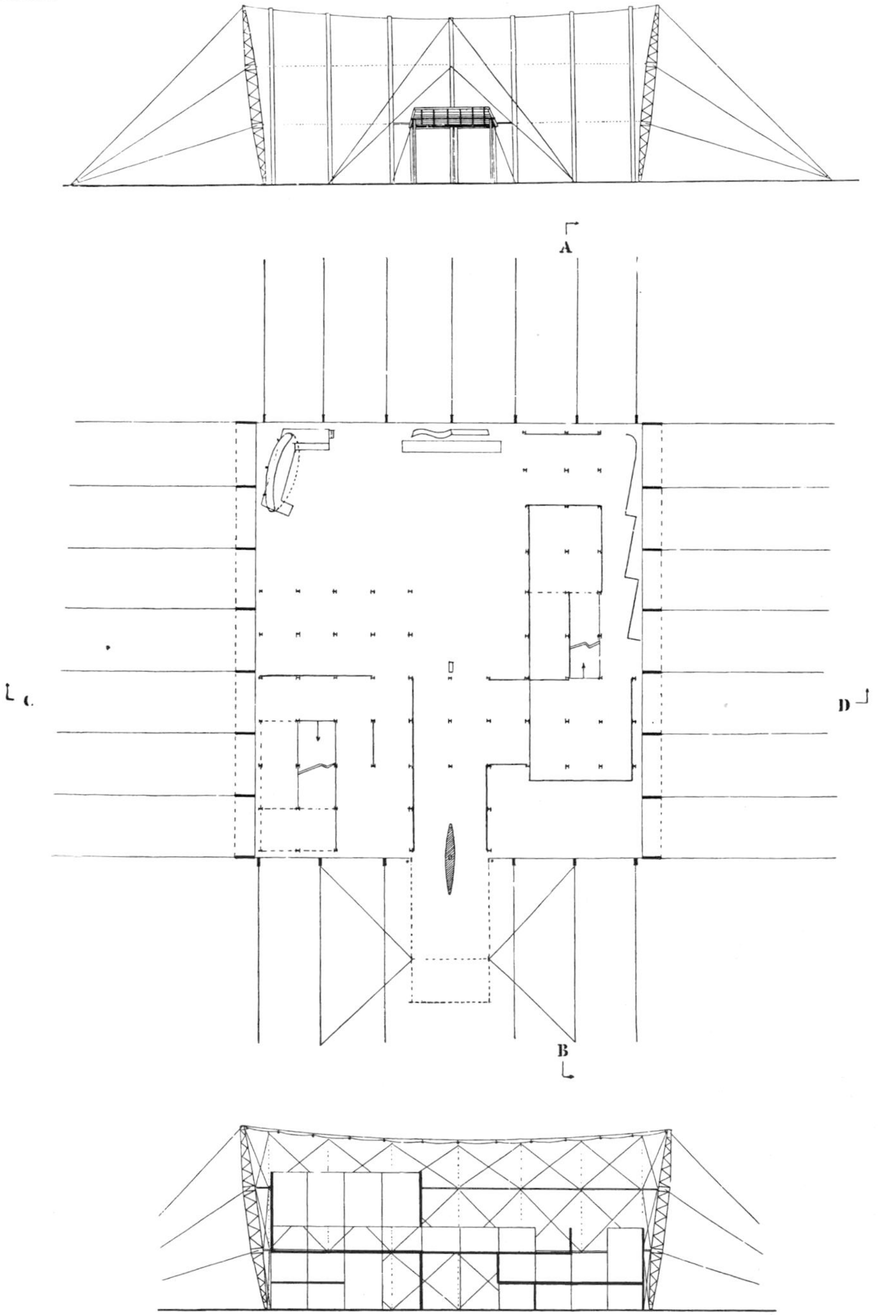

118. Le Corbusier and Pierre
Jeanneret: Pavillon des Temps
Nouveaux, Paris, 1937: interior.

119. Le Corbusier and Pierre Jeanneret: project for 'Îlot insalubre no. 6', around the rue du Faubourg St-Antoine, Paris, displayed in the Pavillon des Temps Nouveaux: site plan and block section. This slum clearance project uses the *à redent* typology of the Ville Radieuse as infill housing.

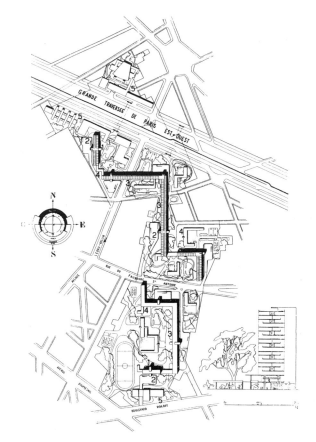

Following the ramped itinerary of the exhibition within, the visitor would have encountered, in succession, the Athens Charter, a brief history of Western urbanism, and Le Corbusier's 1937 plan for Paris together with his proposals for an exemplary piece of slum clearance, known as 'Îlot insalubre no. 6'.[6] The exhibition also con- 119
fronted the visitor with other equally didactic propositions, such as Le Corbusier's 1936 project for an open-air stadium capable of accommodating 300,000 people, and his plan for the reorganiza-
tion of the country's agriculture through his Radiant Farm proposal 107
of 1934. Both these projects had manifest political implications, the one providing an open-air arena suitable for mass meetings and demonstrations, the other implying a cooperative collectivization of agriculture, a project to which Pierre Jeanneret was especially dedicated. The stadium, with a vast elliptical velarium suspended over the tribune, had in common with the Pavillon des Temps Nouveaux the fact that it was predicated on the technique of cable suspension.

The colours used for the canvas roof and elevations of the Pavillon des Temps Nouveaux were as significant as its internal furnishings. The façade had three full-height panels coloured blue/white/blue and a red portico which, in combination, surely alluded to the French *tricolore*, plus a yellow roof which bestowed the light of a future golden age on the labyrinthine exhibition space beneath. Thus while the façade evoked national unity, the roof, flanked by green and red panels, recalled Le Corbusier's 'joies essentielles – soleil, espace et verdure' (essential joys – sun, space and greenery) that he began to reiterate around this time as a slogan. The red portico stood for the socialist welfare provisions of the Popular Front, and the inscription emblazoned on the pivoting entry door openly declared the didactic intent of the building:

Pilot museum of popular education (urbanism)
Visitor: this is the strict science of urbanism.
Urbanism may bring misery to the city and to the countryside; it may also bring the essential joys.
Urbanism as the total manifestation of the lyricism of an epoch.[7]

Despite the pre-industrial tectonic references, these 'primitive' works still made extensive use of advanced technology. Thus just as the week-end house at St-Cloud and the Maison aux Mathes were assemblies of rubble walling, concrete vaults, monopitch roofs, timber, plywood, asbestos cement, plate glass and glass lenses, the inverted tent of the Pavillon des Temps Nouveaux made spectacular use of steel-cable suspension in such a way as to allude to techniques that had already become familiar in the field of aeronautical engineering.

Unlike the large steel-framed multi-storey curtain-walled structures which Atelier 35S realized between 1930 and 1933, these smaller works pioneered an 'intermediate' technology in which men would be free to combine primitive and sophisticated techniques according to their needs and resources. Something of this timeless but simultaneously modern spirit was surely also implied by Le Corbusier's setting up a polychromed plaster cast of an archaic Greek *kore*, the *Calf-bearer*, in his studio as part of Louis Carré's 'Exposition d'Art dit "Primitif"' held there in 1935.[8] Five years later, 'primitive art' of a more non-Eurocentric, anthropological character came to the fore in Le Corbusier's exhibition 'La France d'Outre-Mer' of 1940, laid out in the Grand Palais in Paris as a rich cultural legacy drawn from France's overseas colonies.

Further recourse to primitive building modes repeatedly appeared in Le Corbusier's work throughout the late 1930s and early 1940s, first in an unrealized 'log cabin' projected for the Jaoul family in 1937 and then in the rubble-walled, pitch-roofed, low-rise housing designed for the Lannemezan company three years later. This approach became even more basic in the 'Maisons murondins' project of 1940, in which Le Corbusier adapted traditional *pisé* (rammed-earth) construction to the provision of temporary post-war housing. Something equally retardataire from the standpoint of building technology appeared in the barrel-vaulted mud-brick 120 house projected for a M. Peyrissac for a site at Cherchell, North Africa, in 1942. The latter was a structural prototype for the 'Roq' 143 and 'Rob' housing designed for Cap Martin in 1949. These two terrace housing projects, reminiscent of the Aegean vernacular, were derived from the St-Cloud Maison de Week-end of 1935 114 (as was also the case with the Peyrissac house and the low-rise, barrel-vaulted housing designed for Édouard Trouin's terrain at La Sainte-Baume in 1948). The dense, stepped terraces projected for the steeply sloping sites of both Roq and Rob were already presciently critical of the random deployment of free-standing individual vacation houses that have since destroyed large sections of the Côte d'Azur.

120. Sketch for the Maison Peyrissac, Cherchell, North Africa, 1940.

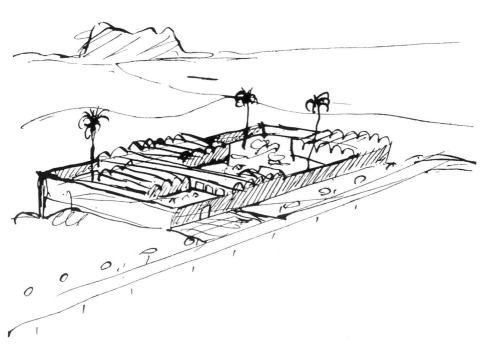

The fourth volume of the *Oeuvre complète*, covering 1938–46, came out under Le Corbusier's name alone. It is divided into two sections, the first of which features the work of his partnership with Pierre Jeanneret prior to the closure of the studio in rue de Sèvres after the German invasion in June 1940. Aside from the monument to Vaillant-Couturier and the 'Musée à croissance illimitée' (museum of unlimited growth) projected for Philippeville in North Africa, the last two years of the 1930s saw little work of consequence. The most interesting projects were the 'maisons monteés à sec' or MAS houses, to be assembled 'dry' out of prefabricated parts, and the closely related 'écoles volantes' that were portable school buildings designed to serve shifting post-war refugee populations. Both projects were worked out in association with the metal fabricator Jean Prouvé, although Le Corbusier failed to acknowledge this in the *Oeuvre complète*; an omission that is all the more surprising when one recalls that for Le Corbusier Prouvé was the ideal partner, a 'constructeur' specializing in light-weight metal construction.[9] As in the Maison Loucheur, the metal-roofed *écoles volantes* were predicated on a light steel frame with insulated clip-on laminated plywood

121. Le Corbusier and Jean Prouvé: prototypical prefabricated house (*maison montée à sec*, or MAS), 1940: elevation. The building has a steel frame clad in modular steel panels.

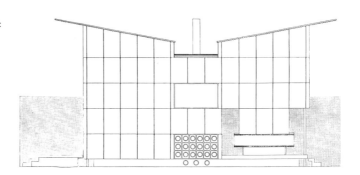

122. Le Corbusier and Jean Prouvé: prototypical prefabricated school (*école volante* or 'flying school'), 1939. The steel-framed structure is clad in light-weight modular panels.

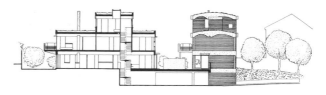

123. Maisons Jaoul, Neuilly, Paris, 1952–54: section and ground-floor plan. Twin houses for members of the same family, built on top of a subterranean garage.

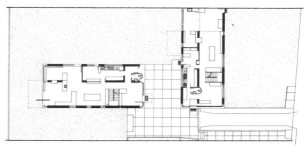

124. Maisons Jaoul: view from above, showing the brick walls, timber and plywood window panels, and turf-covered concrete vaults.

panels of an equally light section. What is particularly striking about these works is the ease with which Le Corbusier passed from the modular, industrially fabricated, metal panels of the MAS house to the heavy-weight, rubble-stone, load-bearing side walls of his Lannemezan house of virtually the same date.

Le Corbusier's sequestered existence in Paris during the German occupation made him particularly susceptible to the existential ethos of the epoch, and this rather sombre mood still finds reflection in the impacted, load-bearing brick walls of the Maisons Jaoul completed at Neuilly, Paris, in the mid-1950s. This vaulted double house (for André Jaoul and his son Michel Jaoul), with its narrow, somewhat claustrophobic timber and plywood fenestration, its rough shuttered concrete, Catalan tiles, and crude brickwork with unstruck mortar joints, was an affront to those architects who had been nurtured on the myth that modern architecture was necessarily machinist and planar and above all sustained by an elegant and articulate structural frame. As the British architect James Stirling put it, only to follow suit in his own work immediately afterwards,

there is no reference to any aspect of the machine at Jaoul either in construction or aesthetic... These houses... are being built by Algerian labourers equipped with hammers and nails and, with the exception of glass, synthetic materials are not being used.[10]

These intermittent forays into archaic building methods were accompanied by an equally radical shift in Le Corbusier's urban thinking. After his first encounter with the emerging megalopolises on the East Coast of the United States in 1936, he seems to have realized that modern urbanization was an organic process in which one could not meaningfully intervene except in a relatively open-ended manner. He saw that it had to be formulated in terms of a growth system, based on certain dynamic principles rather than on some kind of preconceived *tabula rasa*.

From the mid-1930s on, agriculture became an important part of Le Corbusier's regional thinking, going back to his first proposals for the reorganization of French farming methods. In the ensuing decade his Radiant Farm of 1934 evolved into the prototypical co-operative village of 1938 and, later still, became expanded into the 'unit of agricultural exploitation' as set forth in his book *Les Trois Établissements humains* (The Three Human Establishments) of 1945. This in turn was a further elaboration of the thesis that he had initially advanced in 1941 in *The Four Routes*. Where the four routes paralleled the four Aristotelian elements, comprising (1) highways (earth), (2) railways (fire), (3) waterways (water), and (4) airways (air), the 'Three Human Establishments' were identified as (1) the unit of agricultural exploitation, (2) the linear-industrial city, and (3) the radio-concentric city of exchange. In these two texts and in a third, covering very similar themes, that he issued in 1946 under the title *Manière de penser l'urbanisme* (published in English as *Concerning Town Planning*), Le Corbusier reiterated the basic units of production for this new regional paradigm: the Radiant Farm dedicated to *primary* industry, the Green Factory dedicated to *secondary* industry, and the traditional radio-concentric city of exchange, devoted to that sector known to economists as *tertiary* industry.

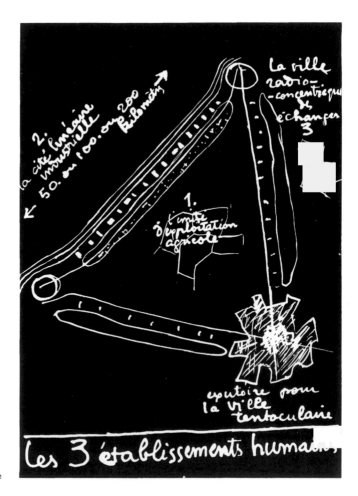

125. Diagram of the Three Human Establishments.
1 unit of agricultural exploitation
2 linear industrial city
3 radio-concentric city of exchange

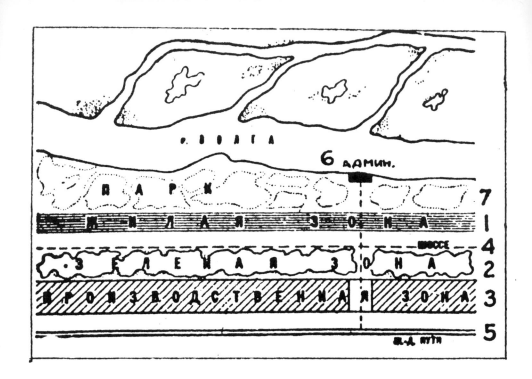

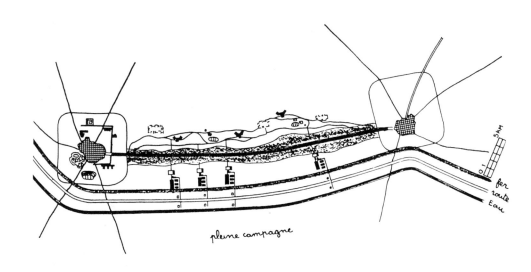

pleine campagne

126. N. A. Miliutin: master plan for the town of Traktorskoi at Stalingrad, embodying his paradigmatic linear city format.
1 residential zone
2 green buffer zone
3 industry
4 road system
5 railway system
6 community centre
7 parkland zone

127

126

As we have seen, Le Corbusier's linear industrial city model was derived from the work of the Soviet linear-city theorist Miliutin. It adhered fairly closely to the first four zones of Miliutin's 'industrial linear city' of 1930, comprising a transport zone, which Le Corbusier subdivided into three parallel freight routes for road, rail and canal traffic; an industrial zone with its Green Factories; a green zone with a high-speed (non-commercial) highway running down its spine; and a residential zone with supporting facilities, such as schools, playing fields, etc. Miliutin's parkland band is absent from the Corbusian model, since it is incorporated into the residential zone. At the same time, the agricultural sector, treated as a more or less continuous linear band in Miliutin's theoretical formulation, has now been transformed into clusters of polygonal agricultural settlements within the interstices of the triangulated grid established by the pre-existing radio-concentric cities. Le Corbusier proposed linking the cities not as in the past by a traditional road system but by Miliutin-style linear industrial strips.

While studying the topographical distribution of urban settlements in southern Germany in the 1930s, the German geographer Walter Cristaller discovered that traditional towns and villages happened to be located according to the coordinates of a triangular or hexagonal grid. While we do not know when or how Le Corbusier became familiar with Cristaller's work, it seems likely that this was the catalyst for his regional planning strategy of the 1940s, wherein existing market towns would be linked together by linear industrial strips and agricultural areas would be spontaneously organized in such a way as to conform to the pre-existing land-settlement pattern. Le Corbusier's neo-humanist, centralized ideal city had by now been totally relinquished, along with the seamless white architecture of the Purist era. With the end of the war in 1945, he had finally come to terms with the Pandora's box of regional urbanization, a process that would be greatly accelerated during the next decade by mass ownership of the automobile.

127. Prototypical linear industrial city, combining three of the four 'infrastructural' routes.

Chapter 9   Towards a New Habitat 1922–1960

Le Corbusier was preoccupied with the collective dwelling in one way or another throughout his career. His concern began with his auspicious visit to the Charterhouse of Ema in 1907, and resurfaced as an aspiration in the early 1920s when he first began to work on his 'Immeubles-Villas' prototype, of which the very title declared his Babylonian intention – namely, to provide multi-storey apartment buildings consisting effectively of stacked two-storey houses, complete with hanging gardens.

While the generic monastery proffered a paradigm for sustaining a balance between individual and collective life, it was obviously an unsuitable vessel for family occupation at a metropolitan scale. Apart from the ancient Babylonian model, the inspiration behind the Immeubles-Villas seems to have been Charles Fourier's concept of the *phalanstère*, posited at the beginning of the 19th century as an ideal agro-industrial, communal dwelling, which was fully elaborated in socio-spatial terms by Victor Considérant in his *Description du phalanstère et considérations sociales sur l'architectonique* (Description of the Phalanstery and the Social Aspects of its Architecture) of 1848. This utopian vision was probably brought to Le Corbusier's attention by the socialist architect Tony Garnier, whom he had met in 1919, a year after the publication of the latter's two-volume folio, *Une Cité industrielle*. While Garnier's ideal city did not feature a phalanstery, excerpts from Émile Zola's Fourierist novel *Travail* (Work, 1901) were inscribed on the entablature of its central assembly building. The fact that the form of the *phalanstère* had been derived from the aristocratic baroque palace rendered it no more suitable as a pattern of residential aggregation for a socialist city than a monastery.

As Peter Serenyi has pointed out,[1] the communal prototype that was more readily applicable to metropolitan conditions was Henry Jules Borie's 'Aérodomes' of 1865. That this may have been the ultimate model for Le Corbusier's *blocs à cellules* of the Ville Contemporaine (1922) is suggested first by the fact that Borie sought greatly to increase the overall density of Haussmannian Paris by introducing large multi-levelled residential blocks, and second by the fact that he visualized linking these blocks with aerial bridges.

Abandoning his *bloc à cellules* prototype after 1922, Le Corbusier did not return to the theme of the free-standing communal dwelling until after his visit to the Soviet Union in 1928. There, the Narkomfin communal apartment building realized by Ginzburg and Milinis in Moscow in 1929, together with the *dom kommuna* (communal dwelling) typology evolved by Ginzburg's Stroikom research group, seem to have prompted him to reconsider the sectional structure of his mass housing prototype. After seeing the various *dom kommuna* sections proposed by the OSA group, he began to move away from his standard two-storey dwelling unit (as embodied in the Pavillon de l'Esprit Nouveau of 1925) in order to arrive at an alternative dwelling type that could be

32, 33

128. Le Corbusier and Pierre Jeanneret: section of a typical cross-over duplex block of the Ville Radieuse or 'VR unit', 1934.

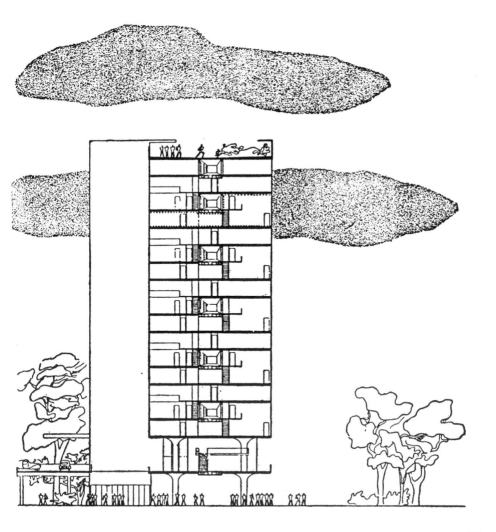

129. Le Corbusier and Pierre Jeanneret: plan of the typical 'transformable' single-storey VR apartment of the Ville Radieuse. Dotted lines with arrows indicate sliding partitions subdividing the children's bedrooms at night.

1 living room
2 master bedroom
3 bathrooms
4 kitchenette
5 dressing room
6 children's bedrooms

combined into apartment blocks with greater economy and variety. His first step in this direction was the 'Immeuble pour Artistes' project of 1928, where interlocking minimal dwellings are shown as being spatially transformable by sliding partitions, along the lines of the Maison Loucheur.

He subsequently broached the possibility of single-storey apartments of varying size and configuration in the 'VR units' designed for the set-back residential housing stock of the Ville Radieuse in 1934. Here once again he returned to the theme of industrially produced, light-weight, stackable units, contained within a continuous curtain wall. These apartments were conceived as transformable *machines à habitation*, without the luxurious private terraces which had been such an essential feature of the Immeubles-Villas. While keeping the skin-tight curtain wall, the *pan de verre*, he would come to abandon the single-storey VR apartment typology in favour of the cross-over duplex prototype, fed by internal corridors.

Le Corbusier's initial response to the challenge of the Soviet *dom kommuna* was his proposed development of 1932 for the Domaine de Badjara (Oued Ouchaia) in Algeria, comprising ribbons of semi-detached houses following the contours and four large communal blocks. These last consisted of a set-back prototype in which the basement was given over to parking and auxiliary services, while the two-storey ground floor accommodated an entrance hall, a communal restaurant, and visitors' parking. This communal undercroft was capped by four tiers of double-height units which, unlike the cross-over duplex units projected for the

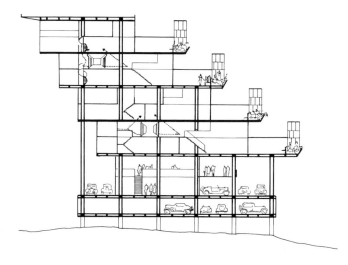

130. Le Corbusier and Pierre Jeanneret, Durand Unité block, Domaine de Badjara, Oued Ouchaia, Algeria, 1932: section.

Ville Radieuse slab in 1934, did not lock over and under an internal corridor. Equally inspired by Henri Sauvage's stepped apartments in the rue Vavin, Paris, of 1912, the Oued Ouchaia block assumed a stepped transverse section with overhanging bedrooms on its southern face and garden terraces facing north. Three fundamental principles seem to have determined this design from the outset: first, the decision to leave the existing vineyard site as intact as possible; second, the provision of partially elevated access roads for both the communal blocks and the houses; and lastly, the use of a stepped section not only to provide terraces but also, with the aid of *brise-soleil*, to distinguish between the individual unit and the communal dwelling as a whole.

131. Le Corbusier and Pierre Jeanneret, Durand Unité block, Oued Ouchaia: model.

132. Unité d'Habitation,
Marseilles, 1946–52.

The Unité d'Habitation at Marseilles, initially projected in 1945 132–141 as the result of a direct commission from the then Minister of Reconstruction, Raoul Dautry, is one of the most singular achievements of Le Corbusier's late career, as relevant today as a generic model as it was at the time of its erection. Aspiring to the civil engineering scale favoured by the engineer François de Pierrefeu, Le Corbusier treated the Unité in such a way as to transcend the normative dimensions of a typical medium-rise slab block. Rendered in massive, in-situ reinforced concrete construction, it was elevated on a bridge-like platform that with its battered cantilevered sides was supported by giant, tapering Egyptoid *pilotis*, also made of rough-boarded concrete. The whole recalled, but at a much more monumental scale, the monolithic reinforced concrete downstand beams and cantilevered deck carrying the steel

133. Le Corbusier with a model of
the roof of the Unité, Marseilles
(cf. III. 139).

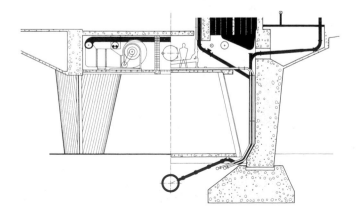

134. Unité d'Habitation, Marseilles:
section through *pilotis* and service
undercroft (the 'terrain artificiel').

superstructure of the Pavillon Suisse. Le Corbusier conceived of his 'unités d'habitation de grandeur conforme' (rendered in the *Oeuvre complète* as 'dwelling unities of congruent size') as 'cités-jardin verticales' (vertical garden cities), which was in categoric opposition to the horizontal, low-rise Anglo-Saxon garden city commonly adopted elsewhere for expansion on the urban periphery.

Sponsored by the French state, Le Corbusier embarked on the design of the Marseilles Unité as though it were his first undertaking of a truly pioneering potential – a work in which two basically different modes of fabrication could be brought together, that is to say the *béton brut* concrete frame, cast in situ from timber formwork, and a sequence of prefabricated components to be hauled into position and assembled dry within the frame. This hybrid approach to fabrication went so far as to envisage complete apartments being hoisted directly into position as prefabricated units, an idea depicted in a provocative photomontage where a godlike hand simply inserts factory-made dwellings into the frame, like stacking bottles in a wine rack. A sketch by Le Corbusier confirmed the metaphor, although this was not the manner in which the units could finally be fabricated and assembled.

After five years on site and five successive Ministers of Reconstruction, the Marseilles Unité was finally realized on the Boulevard Michelet. It was set at an angle to the boulevard so as to afford optimum sun exposure and to avoid the *mistral* wind from the north. The short description that accompanied its publication in the *Oeuvre complète* of 1946–52 can hardly be improved upon as a synthetic account of its organization:

135. Unité d'Habitation, Marseilles, 1946–52: the independent crossover duplex being 'slid' into the structural frame. (The hand is that of Le Corbusier's assistant, Roger Aujame.)

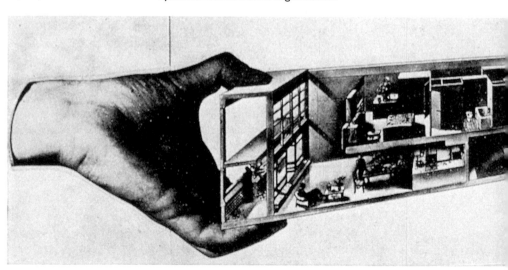

The building stands on pilotis. The ground below is unencumbered, and given over to pedestrians. There is parking for cars and there are paths for bicycles.

The terrain artificiel ['artificial ground', comprised of a massive folded-plate concrete structure carried on the pilotis] contains the air-conditioning plant, elevator machinery, and diesel generators.   134

The building contains 337 apartments of 23 different types, ranging from the smallest, for bachelors or childless couples, to large apartments for families with 3 to 8 children.

The apartments are arranged in pairs, interlocking, along corridors called 'internal streets' which run down the length of the building. The first characteristic of the typical apartment is that it is on two floors like a private house. The apartments are insulated from each other by lead boxes (sound insulation).   137

The living room runs through both storeys, and has a ceiling height of 4.80 metres [15 ft 9 in.]. A large window 3.66 metres wide and 4.80 metres high [12 ft x 15 ft 9 in.] reveals the magnificent surrounding landscape. The kitchen fittings are built in. They include: an electric stove with three plates and an oven, a double sink with automatic garbage disposal, a refrigerator, a large work-table, cupboards and shelving, and an extractor hood connected to the central ventilating system.   141

The Unité is served by 5 superimposed internal streets. Halfway up (levels 7 and 8) is the shopping street for provisions (communal services), which includes: shops for fish, charcuterie [pork products], meat, groceries, wine, dairy products, fruit and vegetables, as well as a bakery and a shop selling prepared dishes. Delivery to one's apartment can be arranged. A restaurant, tea room and snack bar provide meals. There are also a laundry, ironing room, drycleaner, drugstore and hairdresser, and a sub-post office, tobacconist, newsagent, book shop, and pharmacy. Along the same corridor lies the hotel accommodation.   136

On the top floor (level 17) are a nursery and a kindergarten, from where a ramp leads directly to a roof garden set aside for children. There is also a small paddling pool for children.   138

The roof terrace, which is both a hanging garden and a belvedere, provides a gymnasium, an open-air space for training and gymnastics, a solarium, a 300-metre [985 ft] running track, a buffet-bar, etc.[2]

136. Unité d'Habitation, Marseilles,
1946–52: cross section.
1 portico
2 entry
3 service duct
4 internal street
5 shops
6 nursery school
7 roof deck

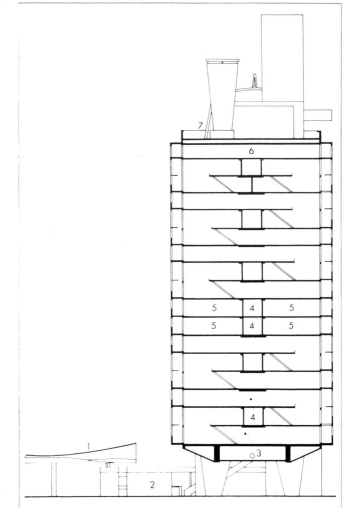

137. Unité d'Habitation, Marseilles:
perspectival section.
The up-going duplex A locks over
the down-going duplex B. The
central corridor or 'internal street'
affords access to both.

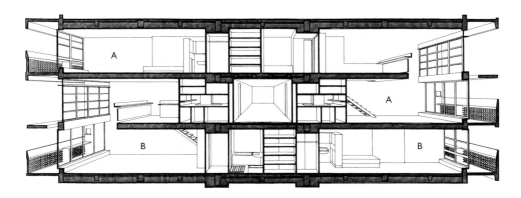

With its gymnasium, outdoor theatre space-cum-cinema screen, nursery school, paddling pool and running track, this roof was a full incarnation of the communal, rendered as a space of public appearance and set against the backdrop of distant mountains, in such a way as to evoke the agoras of the antique world.

138. Unité d'Habitation, Marseilles: children at the roof-top paddling pool.

139. Unité d'Habitation, Marseilles: roof deck superstructures (cf. Ill. 133). The flared concrete cowl ventilates the stacked bathrooms below.

With the exception of the south-facing units where all the
rooms had the same orientation, each transverse duplex unit had a
double exposure, with some rooms opening to the morning sun
and the landscape and others facing towards the evening sun and
the sea. Given the crossover duplex section, this meant that half the
double-height living spaces were graced with dawn light and half
with twilight, the reverse applying to the children's bedrooms on
the opposing face.

The asymmetrical interlocking crossover section, with half the
units passing over and half passing under the central internal access
corridor, produces positive and negative units in terms of the
convenience of the internal circulation. In this regard, the *up-going*
units tend to be preferable: one enters directly from the internal
corridor-street to kitchen/dining/living level, then takes the internal stair up to the master bedroom on the mezzanine over the living
space, before finally passing through to the services and the paired
children's bedrooms on the other side of the block. In the *down-
going* units, on the other hand, one enters the kitchen/dining space
which is on the mezzanine level and from there descends to the service core and the children's bedrooms beyond. One then has to
double back to reach the living space and master bedroom
arranged en suite. Internally sited bathroom units situated above
and below the *rue intérieure* are organized with great ingenuity, so
that in each duplex there are separate parents' and children's bathrooms. The narrow paired children's bedrooms are treated as
transformable volumes, which by virtue of a central sliding wall may
be divided for night-time use or opened up into an ample play space
during the day. The modulation of the *brise-soleil*/balcony layer on
either side of the block is equally ingenious, in that the horizontal
and vertical *brise-soleil* are so arranged as to exclude high-angle
summer sun and to admit low-angle winter light.

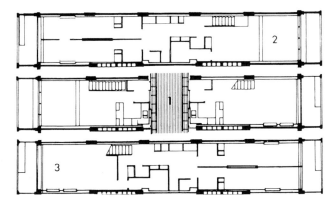

140. Unité d'Habitation, Marseilles,
1946–52: plan of typical crossover
duplex units.
1 internal street
2 up-going unit
3 down-going unit

Despite the ingenuity with which all of this was resolved, one nonetheless questions the ultimate *raison d'être* of the interlocking duplex section. It had originated in the Soviet Union in the late 1920s when the *dom kommuna* was projected as a vehicle for 'social condensation', Moisei Ginzburg's Stroikom research team going on to design a number of split-level, interlocking sections of various kinds, all of which were inspired by the naïve assumption that a new society could be literally brought into being through the application of dwelling units having a spatially interwoven character.

While the Marseilles Unité was designed for family life, Le Corbusier shared the Soviet avant-garde faith in the cultivation of the 'new man' who would come to transcend the limits of bourgeois society. He held on to this belief despite the tyranny of Stalinism in the Soviet Union and the violent upheaval of the Second World War. It is this conflicted legacy perhaps which gave renewed currency to the psycho-sociological, anarchic vision of Charles Fourier, which as Peter Serenyi has observed was first overtly referred to by Le Corbusier at the time of the Marseilles Unité, in his *Manière de penser l'urbanisme* (*Concerning Town Planning*) of 1946.[3]

Needless to say, the erection of such a complex megastructure as the Marseilles Unité required the services of many technicians; and it is they, the architects and engineers who worked together as a team under the name ATBAT (for Atelier des Bâtisseurs, 'builders' workshop'), who were responsible for the 2,785 drawings and other documents required to complete the building. Le Corbusier was totally indebted to this team and above all to his collaborators, the architect André Wogensky and the engineer and aircraft designer Vladimir Bodiansky. (The latter broke away soon afterwards to become the director of a splinter group known as ATBAT Afrique.) Equally essential to the ultimate realization of the work was the faithful and persistent patronage of the last Minister of Reconstruction, Eugène Claudius-Petit.

In the course of achieving this prototypical work, Le Corbusier was able to demonstrate, to himself and to others, the efficacy of three particular methods that were to emerge as an integral part of his post-war practice. The first of these was the use of *béton brut*, shuttered concrete, as a material that in strong sunlight would contrast in a striking way with other, more precisely finished elements, such as the pre-cast concrete *brise-soleil* and balconies that were attached to the building's exterior, along with the dry, light-weight panelling that was installed within. The second method was the macro and micro dimensioning of the entire work in accordance with Le Corbusier's 'Modulor' system of proportion, which he first published in 1950. Based on the time-honoured Golden Section proportion of 1:1.618, this system comprised two superimposed Fibonacci series that he called 'red' and 'blue' serial dimensions, derived from a hypothetical standard human stature of 1.83 metres (6 ft). Consistently applied, this dimensional system not only governed the main proportions of the structure but had the effect of proliferating Golden Section proportions throughout the building down to the smallest detail. The third method consisted of a systematic application of polychromy, demonstrated on this occasion by differentiating between adjacent duplexes by painting the vertical re-entrant planes of the balconies in different colours. This bestowed upon the otherwise grey mass of the building a vibrant, multi-coloured optical effect that constantly changed as one moved around the floating mass of this stranded 'ocean liner'.

142. Modulor Man shown in different postures in relation to different harmonic furniture dimensions, 1946.

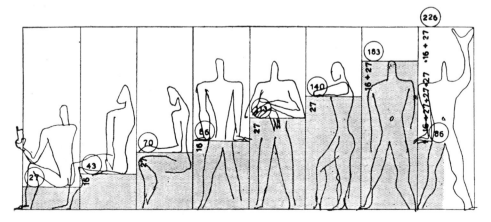

Four other Unités were actually built – at Rezé-lès-Nantes (1953), Berlin (1956), Briey-en-Forêt (1957), and, after Le Corbusier's death, at Firminy-Vert (1968). Le Corbusier also proposed similar Unités for a number of ambitious urban expansions that were to remain unrealized, including, at the behest of Dautry, a 1945 plan for St-Dié comprising eight such blocks and, a year later, an equally ambitious proposal for La Rochelle-Pallice consisting of ten Unités. In addition, three other multiple Unité schemes were projected: Strasbourg in 1951, where two blocks were grouped about a single cylinder; Marseilles-Sud also in 1951, comprising three blocks and two cylindrical towers; and finally Meaux in 1956, with five blocks in formation clustered about two cylindrical elements. In each instance, the perceptual centre of the composition was occupied by cylindrical towers attaining the same height as the blocks, Le Corbusier justifying this variation in building form on the grounds that the towers would contain smaller apartments for bachelors and childless couples.

Marseilles-Sud was in many respects the most significant of Le Corbusier's unbuilt housing sectors since it demonstrated a new realism, in that the overall scheme was extremely heterogeneous. Above all, it advocated the introduction of a quantum of two-storey housing, which would have helped to integrate the high-rise apartment blocks into the scale and texture of the existing urban fabric. At the same time, this rather *ad hoc* assembly was served by a hierarchical infrastructure comprising Le Corbusier's '7 Vs': V1 was a long-distance highway with limited access, V2 a feeder road, V3 a distributor, and V4 a traditional street serving a specific neighbourhood. This access system was further subdivided into a network of minor routes leading to houses (V5), 'interior streets' in blocks (V6), and dedicated paths serving schools, clubs and playing fields (V7) – all held within the organic parkscape flowing around and under the blocks.

The Unité built at Rezé-lès-Nantes in 1953 was a much more economical version of the Marseilles prototype, especially because it realized the elevated 'artificial ground' in a much less costly and monumental manner. Here the loss of the heroic scale of the *pilotis* in the Marseilles Unité was compensated for, at the level of the plinth, by canting every other cross-wall in and out from the building line, thereby modulating the rhythm of the support system so as to introduce a double-bay dimension at the level of the *pilotis*. Nantes varied from Marseilles in other significant ways, above all in the apartments themselves, which were smaller and subtly modified in respect of internal privacy. The acoustical insulation of the living space from the master bedroom was greatly improved by reducing the size of the double-height volume linking the mezzanine and the main floor. The approach to the block remained equally picturesque, however, in that the main entry entailed crossing a short concrete bridge suspended over the surface of an artificial moat. As in Marseilles, the roof was surmounted by an open-air theatre space and a nursery school, this last being randomly fenestrated with small rectangular windows that were filled with translucent and coloured glass. Nantes was also the occasion on which Le Corbusier openly acknowledged that his *béton brut* aesthetic aspired to the monumental grandeur of Egypt, in part suggested by the Egyptoid Modulor Man relief cast into the concrete close to the entry. Anticipating a future when the full significance of this work would be understood, he wrote:

Once the pouring of the concrete is completed, recessed mouldings appear in the face of the concrete, thus achieving a situation similar to that in which the Egyptians prepared sculptured frescos in their temples 5000 years ago. That is to say the architecture brings forth here that by which surface and volume are known (the recognition of the wall), that by which the materials, their place in the work, the meaning of the times, the rigorous schedule and the discipline of the job site are also recognized. For that recognition, one counts upon the generations yet to come.[4]

As we have noted, three other Unités were realized soon after Nantes. The first of these was completed in 1956 on the Olympic Hill in Charlottenburg, Berlin, while the second was built (in a greatly reduced version) at Briey-en-Forêt in 1957. Neither of these works satisfied the architect, the one because it was built with a pedantic precision that he deemed unsympathetic, the other because the dwelling units were too small. Moreover, in neither case were the apartments realized in accordance with the original space standards, as was also to be the case with the last Unité, built at Firminy-Vert in 1968.

Despite the manifest failure of the state to develop and improve on the initial prototype, the Marseilles Unité still stands as a breathtakingly heroic monument to a particular moment in time. Never was the utopian *modern project* so convincingly and thoroughly realized as in this work, and the fact that today it is more fully and completely lived in than ever before testifies to the validity of this vision, particularly when executed in a sympathetic climate at such an uncompromisingly monumental and collective scale. No-one has evoked this elegiac fulfilment more delicately than

William Curtis, when he wrote in 1986:

The usual roster of criticisms is that the apartments are too narrow, that the approach corridors are too dark, that the middle-level street cuts off this community from the world outside. To these, one must now add that the concrete of the roof terrace is weathering poorly in the salt air. But the present inhabitants of the building seem to have surmounted these problems, are in the building by choice, because they find it a pleasant place to live ... it is interesting to visit the unité between five and six in the evening in Autumn, when it is still hot enough to wear shorts and thin cotton dresses. People flood from work and school, leaving their cars under the trees; they dawdle by the banks of cypresses, or play tennis, or shop in the upper street. On the roof terrace, old men chat, catching the last afternoon sun while their grandchildren splash in the pool. The crags, in reality miles away, hover like models on the parapet ledge, their shadows turning from Cézanne blue to deep mauve. A ship pulls away from the port, dark against the shimmering sea ... The textured oblong broods like an antique viaduct above the trees, its bold mass and mighty legs evoking the great wall behind the Roman theater at Orange. In the tawdry imitations, skill, philosophy and poetry are absent. The unité takes a patiently worked out urban theorem and renders it in the terminology of a Mediterranean dream.[5]

143. Roq: low-rise, high-density, stepped terrace housing projected for a site below Roquebrune-Cap Martin, 1949.

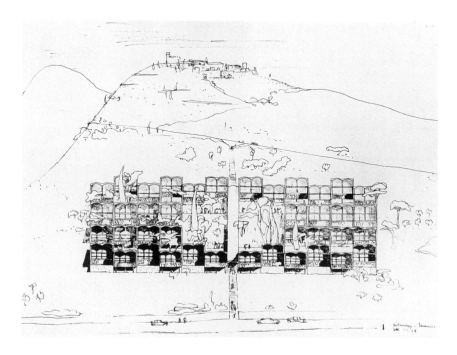

However, the Marseilles Unité is not the only compelling model of collective dwelling that Le Corbusier would leave behind him, as we may judge from the equally convincing Siedlung Halen outside 14 Bern, built in 1960 to the designs of Atelier 5.[6] While this was not literally designed by Le Corbusier, it is, as its architects were the first to concede, a virtual realization of his Roq and Rob housing 14. projected for Cap Martin in 1949. Despite the absence of the sea, as its terraces descend towards the valley of the Aare Halen is no less Mediterranean in spirit than the Marseilles Unité. Like the casbah in Algiers that was so unequivocally admired by Le Corbusier as vernacular urban form, Halen still remains an alternative housing model for megalopolitan application, as viable now as when it was built. We may think of it as an exemplary piece of carpet housing set within an all-enveloping sea of green; as a domain in which petit-bourgeois categories no longer apply. It is a world in which one can no longer discriminate with certainty between industrial norms and primitive building technique, between the archaic and the new, between the individual and the collective, between town and country, between artificial construction and natural form. It points towards a normative, ecologically valid pattern of middle-class land settlement that, while readily attainable, still remains 'sociologically' inaccessible.

144. Atelier 5: Siedlung Halen, Bern, Switzerland, 1960.

Chapter 10   The Sacred and the Profane:
Le Corbusier and Spiritual Form 1948–1965

In the immediate post-war years, Le Corbusier first approached the sacred in a somewhat mystical project for Édouard Trouin, sketched out in 1948 for a legendary site near Aix-en-Provence known as La Sainte-Baume. Here Trouin happened to own a large terrain of mountainous, unproductive ground in the midst of which was a sheer cliff face looking north to the Montagne Sainte-Victoire, with a long, slow incline on its opposite southern face dropping down towards the Mediterranean. Halfway up the sheer face lay a dark cave which was the legendary retreat of Mary Magdalene at the end of her life. According to local myth, she had been miraculously borne to the summit every morning on the wings of angels in order to offer her prayers to God. Le Corbusier's proposal for the site, at Trouin's suggestion, was to blast out three separate subterranean cisterns within the body of the mountain and to link these to the cave and to each other by ramped tunnels. The Dominicans who maintained jurisdiction over the site seem to have considered the project to be as much 'pagan' as it was extravagant, and rejected it out of hand.[1]

When Le Corbusier was first approached in 1950 to design Notre Dame-du-Haut at Ronchamp, by Canon Lucien Ledeur of the Besançon Commission d'Art Sacré, his first impulse was to decline; still smarting from his treatment at the hands of the Dominicans, he dismissed the Church as a dead institution. However, undeterred, Ledeur continued to pursue his architect with persuasive rhetoric:

We do not have much to offer you, but we do have this: a wonderful setting and the possibility to go all the way. I do not know whether you are committed to building churches, but if you should build one then the conditions offered by Ronchamp are ideal. This is not a lost cause: you will be given free rein to create what you will.[2]

It seems that Le Corbusier continued to have reservations until he visited the site in the company of Ledeur, when he was seduced on the spot: 'I had the impression that he had forged an immediate bond with the landscape', Ledeur remarked in retrospect.[3]

This was hardly surprising, given that to a much greater degree than at La Sainte-Baume the belvedere site opened out to a

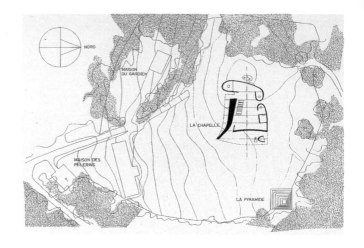

145. Notre Dame-du-Haut, Ronchamp, 1950–55: site plan. Around the chapel are the caretaker's house (upper left), accommodation for pilgrims (lower left), and the pyramidal monument (lower right).

panoramic landscape of remarkable beauty, looking north to the last foothills of the Vosges, east towards Belfort, west towards the Langres plateau and south towards the Jura. From the very outset, Le Corbusier imagined the shape of the chapel as a combination of convex and concave, somewhat crustacean forms (partially derived from polychromed wooden sculptures, *Ozon* and *Ubu*, that he had made with the Breton cabinetmaker Joseph Savina between 1940 and 1947[4]) which would respond to what he called the 'visual acoustics' of the landscape. He sought further to augment his somewhat cryptic evocation of 'visual acoustics' with a proposal to furnish the chapel with a repertoire of electronic music, especially composed by Olivier Messiaen for broadcasting throughout the terrain from loudspeakers mounted in an adjacent steel-framed carillon.

For Le Corbusier, the hilltop site rising above the village of Ronchamp was auspicious not only because of its cosmological, panoramic dimension – its 360-degree view of the world – but also because of its momentous history, the fact that it had successively been a pagan sun temple, a Roman fortress, a 4th-century Christian sanctuary, a place of miracles, and, last but not least, the site of a spontaneous pilgrimage by French and Germans alike, who first assembled here on 8 September 1873 to give thanks for the termination of the Franco-Prussian war.

Acknowledging this commemoration and a more ancient religious pilgrimage, both of which are still celebrated today, the site and the chapel were treated as two symbiotic elements. The site initially presents itself as the culmination of the pilgrimage route with a quasi-propylea made up of two single-storey monopitch buildings set skew to each other. These *béton brut* structures, covered with sod, comprise the pilgrims' refectory/dormitory and the caretaker's house. From this point the pilgrims climb a steep path that ascends towards the monumental southern face of the chapel, 146 the concave 'acoustical' form of which both welcomes them and gathers them on a grass *parvis* in front of an outdoor altar and elevated pulpit facing east. Here, depending on the time of year, some 12,000–30,000 people assemble as the congregation of an 'open-air cathedral' set on a natural acropolis that is bounded on its northeastern flank by a small pyramidal monument dedicated to those who lost their lives in the Second World War. The chapel itself consists in the main of a white, plastered mass, which is sculpturally structured about two contiguous *concave* fronts on the southern and eastern elevations and two *convex* backs on the northern and western faces. This plastic counterpoint is crowned by a *béton brut* shell roof which cantilevers its heavy form outwards on the southern and eastern elevations and ingeniously contrives to conceal itself behind whitewashed walls to the north and west.

146. Notre Dame-du-Haut, Ronchamp: general view from the south.

The dramatic play between grey concrete and white limewashed roughcast, inflected according to the cardinal points, is

147. Notre Dame-du-Haut, Ronchamp, 1950–55: interior looking west. Note the sliver of light between the roof and the southern wall, on the left.

reinforced by the manner in which light enters the interior, which may be seen as an orientational complement to the 'acoustical' displacements that shift from one face of the chapel to the next as one circumambulates the site. Apart from the multicoloured windows of the battered southern wall, and the star-like perforations and the narrow window both let into the eastern choir wall, the constantly changing light of the muted interior comes from three light cowls that rise out of the sculptural mass of the nave walls as three semi-cylindrical forms. Derived in part from the vernacular of Ischia and in part from Hadrian's Villa, each of these cowls covers a side chapel. The largest and highest cowl, situated at the southwest corner, faces north, while the other two, equal in size, are placed back-to-back on the northern elevation and face east and west. Where the largest cowl changes its luminosity solely from the cast of the sky, the two smaller ones gain their full light with the rising and the setting of the sun – the plastered and coloured inner shaft of the eastern cowl glowing deep red at dawn, and the similarly treated western cowl turning gold with the last rays of the sun. All three cowls are equipped with light baffles which Le Corbusier called *brise-lumière*.

The principle of the Trinity (Father, Son and Holy Ghost), as represented by the light cowls, governs many features both inside and out. Each part is linked reciprocally to the next throughout the stone-paved, roughcast interior, with axial seams running down the ¹⁴⁷ paving to connect the high altar at the eastern end to the subsidiary altars of the three side chapels facing east, west and north. The floor of the nave slopes gently down towards the main altar, while the raised floor of the sanctum slopes in the opposite direction. There is a similar reciprocal spatial play between the internal and external altars, with the figure of the Virgin, framed by a square window, suspended between them in such a way as to be readily visible from both sides of the eastern wall. The internal and external altars are made out of all but identical oblong blocks of stone, while the corresponding pulpits, cast integrally with their access stairs, are made of *béton brut*. A balcony in the north-east corner of the chapel, finished in roughcast, is continued, via a discreet door, to form a corresponding external balcony, the two combining in plan to form a *yin-yang* figure, a primary icon in Le Corbusier's personal iconography, standing for the diurnal passage of the sun.

All in all, inside and out, the chapel celebrates the ascent and descent of the sun together with the waxing and waning of the seasons, integrated into the life cycle and the rhythmic order of nature. This surely accounts for the decline of the volume and the roof towards the closed end of the western wall, within which are embedded two confessionals that are the cause of a swelling at this point in the external wall. This swelling finds an echo in a double-barrelled concrete gargoyle discharging storm water from the roof. The water falls into an ovoid concrete cistern that contains three symbolic forms, a hollow cylinder and a major and a minor pyramid, an assembly that seems to allude once again to the Holy Trinity.

The northern elevation, which flows uninterruptedly out of the western face, is split into two parts by the back-to-back light cowls. The east and west faces of these cowls are extended as vertical seams in the plaster below, dividing the wall surface into two separate sectors. The fenestrated sector, to the east, is flanked by a stringless concrete stair giving access to two superimposed levels of offices, situated above the sacristy and the adjacent chapel.

While the overall form of the Ronchamp chapel was obviously related to the whitewashed vernacular of the Mediterranean and above all to Le Corbusier's beloved cities of the M'zab – most particularly, as Danièle Pauly suggests, to the thick walls of the Sidi Brahim mosque in El Atteny – it is equally clear that, in typological terms, it was also a subtle transposition of the structure and the

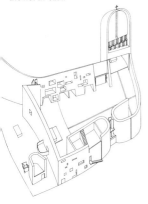

148. Notre Dame-du-Haut, Ronchamp: axonometric from the north-east.

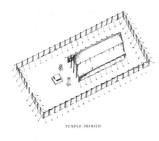

TEMPLE PRIMITIF

149. Reconstruction of the Hebrew Temple in the Wilderness, from *Vers une architecture*, 1923.

150. Prototypical exhibition pavilion for Liège and San Francisco, 1939. The double-square plan is covered by four-way lenticular steel trusses supporting paraboloid roofs, carried on tapered latticework pylons.

form of the Pavillon des Temps Nouveaux of 1937, which in its turn had been inspired by a reconstruction of the Hebrew Temple in the Wilderness that was used as a didactic illustration in *Vers une architecture* (see p.137). One can hardly fail to remark here on a typological/metaphorical shift in which the nomadic tent of the Temple, the *sacred*, becomes the secular inverted tent of the Pavilion, the *profane*, and this, when transposed into Ronchamp, again becomes the *sacred*. Thus, the inverted shell roof of the chapel has its origin in the double catenary curvature of the canvas covering the 1937 Pavilion, which also sloped from front to back in order to discharge storm water. Other structural and symbolic analogies are evident here, above all in the steel cable and canvas structure of the Pavilion which may be said to have resembled the structure of a dirigible turned inside-out. It is significant that the studio model used to refine the crustacean form of Ronchamp should recall not only that steel cable armature of the Pavilion but also aerodynamic form in general, by virtue of the common aeroplane modelling technique employed, that is to say a translucent tissue stretched over a wire skeleton.

Other persistent aerodynamic references are present in Le Corbusier's architecture of the late 1930s, for instance in the exhibition pavilions that he designed for Liège and San Francisco in 1939. These double and quadruple parasols, each square in plan, were projected as hollow, lenticular, space-framed structures supported at the midpoint of their bounding trusses. Thus each square parasol cantilevers at its four corners about a pylon situated at mid-span. He returned to this parasol theme in 1950, but in that instance the parasol roof was projected as being made from folded and welded steel plates, as in his Synthèse des Arts Majeurs pavilion projected for the Porte Maillot in Paris at the same time as his first sketches for Ronchamp. This double parasol theme in welded steel would be realized in the Heidi Weber pavilion, completed in Zurich on the lake front in 1967.

The hyperbolic space-frames of the Liège and San Francisco pavilions surely lie behind the complex curvature of the hollow double-layered concrete shell roof at Ronchamp, while trussed light-weight airframe construction re-emerges in the tubular lattice-work core of the pivoting entrance door – significantly, a reworking of the pivoting door in the Pavillon des Temps Nouveaux. Finally, a similar structural lattice is to be found in the thin reinforced concrete frame that supports the battered southern wall of the chapel, of which the interstices are filled with rubble stonework taken from the ruins of the pre-existing church, largely destroyed through bombardment during the German retreat at the end of the Second World War. This infill wall stops just below the eaves of the roof to reveal the concrete ribs that project to support the shell in such a way as to give it the appearance of floating above the roughcast plasterwork of the wall. These point supports admit a sliver of light on the interior running between the soffit of the roof and the walls on the southern and eastern faces. At intervals within the southern wall the infill is omitted and chamfered windows are introduced, their apertures filled with clear and painted glass which, while not strictly stained glass, was nonetheless an evocation of a time-honoured ecclesiastical tradition.

Finally, one should note that the double-shell roof at Ronchamp is as much the hull of a ship, with a hidden keel running down the centre, as it is a petrified tent or the distorted wing of a plane. This tectonic reference returns us to the ancient conjunction of church and ship embodied in the derivation of the word 'nave' from the Latin for ship, *navis*. This marine metaphor is confirmed by Danièle Pauly's reading of the chapel.

The high vertical line of the southeast corner calls out to the visitor, thus drawing him towards the east where he finds the outdoor chapel. This route is the same as that taken by faithful worshippers on pilgrimage days as they proceed from the main door in the south towards the open-air altar. This corner adopts the swell of a ship's prow, to which the hull of the roof appears to cling. Following the same concept of dynamics, the form of the east side of the chapel resembles a full sail or an aeroplane's wing... [5]

151. Notre Dame-du-Haut, Ronchamp, 1950–55: wire space model seen from the south.

This conjunction returns us to an oscillation between the nautical and the aeronautical – to a polarity that was always an intrinsic part of Le Corbusier's work and one which seems to assume a particular connotation here as it shifts between the aquatic origin of all life and the ultimate transformation of this aqueous state into the aerial, a metamorphosis paralleled in the diurnal cycle of evaporation and condensation, which he had experienced vividly from the air in 1929 in the rainforests of Latin America (p. 204).

Behind the two main religious works of Le Corbusier's career, the Ronchamp chapel and the monastery of La Tourette, lay the Dominican intellectual Father Alain Couturier, who after co-founding the review *Artsacré* in 1936 was to be personally involved in patronizing contemporary artists with religious commissions; it was due to him that Henri Matisse was asked to decorate and design vestments for the small chapel of St-Paul-de-Vence in 1948. Father Couturier was convinced that the decline of the Church in the 20th century, with its shrinking congregations, was due to the philistinism of the Church itself, to its habitual tendency to commission works of mediocre artistic quality. This led him to advance the name of Le Corbusier to Canon Ledeur as the architect for Notre-Dame-du-Haut at Ronchamp; and in 1953, even before the chapel was consecrated, he secured a further ecclesiastical commission for Le Corbusier: the Dominican monastery of Ste-Marie de La Tourette, to be built near Eveux-sur-Arbresle, close to the city of Lyons.

If Ronchamp led back via the Pavillon des Temps Nouveaux to the Hebrew Temple, La Tourette brought Le Corbusier back to the Charterhouse of Ema in Tuscany and to Mount Athos in Greece, via the Cistercian monastery of Le Thoronet in Provence which, notwithstanding that it served a different religious order, was recommended by Couturier as the generic model to be followed.

While Ema and Mount Athos were ideal monastic types inasmuch as they were both elevated on high ground overlooking a spectacular landscape, the subtle placement of the Charterhouse of Pavia, which Le Corbusier encountered in 1911 on his second visit to Italy, seems to have been equally seminal for his handling of the site at Eveux, where service and pedestrian access had to be provided from an original entry to the site from the north-east, thereby linking, at two distinct levels, the new monastery to the old rambling château that had previously served as an improvised residence for the Dominicans. Due to this double access, separated by a drop of some 10 metres (33 ft), the building came to present two different faces to the visitor, depending on whether it was

152. La Tourette, Eveux-sur-
Arbresle, 1957–60: aerial view from
the south-west.

153. La Tourette: plan of the
lower ground floor.
1 servery
2 refectory
3 chapter house
4 atrium
5 ambulatory
6 crypt altars
7 high altar
8 vestry
9–10 courts
25 church

154. La Tourette: plan of level 5.
1 cells for the sick
2 infirmary
3 guest cells
4 cells of teaching monks
5 cell of the monk in charge
   of the students
6 cells of student priests
8 cells of student brothers
9 cells of lay brothers
10–11 sanitary facilities
25 church

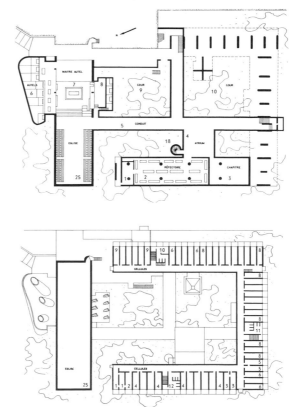

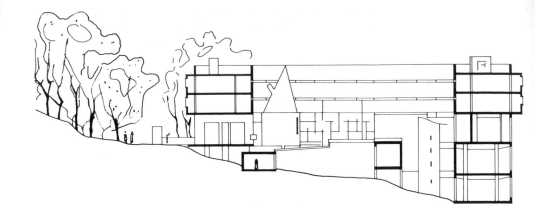

155. La Tourette, Eveux-sur-
Arbresle, 1957–60: east–west
section. Cells occupy the two
topmost levels; below them on
the side facing the valley (right),
the refectory is on the first floor,
with lecture rooms and common
room on the second floor. The
pyramidal-roofed oratory stands
in the 'cloister'.

approached from the high ground in the woods where the main
entrance was situated, or from the low ground in the valley where
the heroic monumental mass of the monastery rose above a rolling
greensward that, passing through an adjacent wooded landscape,
descended further into a distant valley as far as the eye could see.
No-one has perhaps better characterized the dichotomous interplay between the building and the site than Colin Rowe, when he
wrote in 1961:

> ...architecture and landscape, lucid and separate experiences, are like
> the rival protagonists of a debate who progressively contradict and
> clarify each other's meaning.
>
> Above all, the nature of their interaction is dialectical; and thus the
> building, with its church to the north, liturgically correct in orientation,
> separated from but adjoining the living quarters which face the sun, is
> presented as though it were a thesis for discussion; and thus the site
> inevitably rises to function as counterproposition. There is a statement
> of presumed universals and a contrary statement of particulars. There
> is the realist proclamation and the nominalist response, the idealistic
> gesture, the empiricist veto. But if this is a procedure with which Le
> Corbusier has long since made us familiar, and if such is his particular
> mode of logic, there is, of course, here in the program a curiously
> pragmatic justification of its exercise. For it was, after all, a Dominican
> monastery which was required. An architectural dialectitian, the
> greatest, was to service the requirements of the archsophisticates
> of dialectic... [6]

156. La Tourette: refectory, with
pans de verre ondulatoires.

La Tourette was a synthesis of the two heterotopic paradigms
that were to prevail throughout Le Corbusier's career; on the one
hand the monastic type-form, on the other the transatlantic liner,

which in this instance went beyond the characteristic bridge super-structure as we find that reinterpreted in the Villa Savoye. The domestic corpus of La Tourette, namely the two layers of monks' cells which cap the complex, is suspended high above the valley on attenuated concrete piers. Thus the main residential body of the building may be seen as analogous to the portholed hull of a liner, tethered, as it were, to the high ground of the ridge, while the public spaces of the 'vessel' – the classrooms, library, refectory, etc. – are housed underneath. Beneath this 'buoyant' mass the rolling land-scape sweeps in like a metaphorical sea, surging about the rather random reinforced concrete props and blades upon which the entire bulk is suspended.

Apart from this interplay between building and site, La Tourette was also an attempt to re-cast the monastic type in modern terms; in the first instance by replacing the traditional circulation pattern of the cloister with a more efficient system of distribution, linking midpoint stair cores on three sides of a virtual courtyard through 153 a cruciform conduit that eventually terminates in the church attached to the northern side of the complex. As Anton Henze would point out, this innovation embodied a surprising etymologi-cal/typological correspondence in the German language, whereby the traditional cloister, the *Kreuzgang*, was transformed into a cruciform volume, a *Kreuz*,[7] in part, at least, because it was difficult to impose a conventional cloister on such a steep slope. In effect, Le Corbusier transformed the traditional type into an elevated asymmetrical corridor, built of reinforced concrete, capped by sod, and enclosed with floor-to-ceiling glazing. This last was also the occasion for introducing a new type of fenestration that Le Corbusier called *pans de verre ondulatoires* (undulating glass panels), where the glazing is given a syncopated rhythm by being broken up by vertical concrete mullions into panels of varying width, interrupted at intervals by full-height pivoting ventilating louvers, called *aérateurs*. The same syncopated curtain-wall system was also applied to the refectory and the classrooms. Elsewhere, 156 where fronting onto the inner court, the incidental corridors and the semi-public spaces were faced in a checkerboard fenestration comprised of glass interspersed with panels of concrete.

The disturbing inaccessibility of the court (where the land falls away beneath the suspended cruciform corridor) is reinforced by a number of strident elements that disrupt the space still further: in 152 the first instance, the free-standing concrete cube of the oratory capped by a pyramid; in the second, a monopitch concrete roof ris-ing above the atrium signifying the communal core of the circulation system. This atrium may be read as a surrogate of the traditional cloister that, in conjunction with the cruciform ambulatory, serves to link the church, the sacristy, the refectory and the chapter house. Above the lower floors containing services and classrooms, which vary in number and height according to the fall of the land, the monastic cells crown the building on three sides. These may be seen as mini-megarons, the modular dimensions of which vary in width from 1.83 to 2.26 metres (6 ft to 7 ft 5 in.), according to whether the cell is designated for a novice or for a priest. Each cell has a door at one end and a balcony at the other, with sufficient space in between to provide for a bed, bookshelves, a closet and a desk.

157. La Tourette, Eveux-sur-Arbresle, 1957–60: interior of the church, looking west from behind the high altar.

158. La Tourette: crypt with stepped altars.

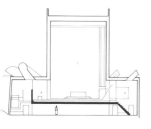

159. La Tourette: transverse section of the church.

As at Ronchamp, the church itself is a *tour de force*, in part 157–159 because of its stark simplicity that harks back to the volumetric purity of the early Christian church as Le Corbusier had experienced this in S. Maria in Cosmedin in Rome, and in part because of the introverted plasticity of the crypt or 'lower church' situated to the north of the main vessel and the equally spartan form of the sacristy located to the south. All of these auxiliary side spaces are top-lit by *canons à lumière*, three ovoid funnels above the lower church and seven south-facing prismatically sectioned shafts above the sacristy. Where the latter pick up the sun at its zenith, each of the light cannons above the crypt is precisely angled so as to receive a shaft of sunlight at the time of the equinoxes. Inside this space, the deep red and white internal surfaces of the concrete funnels are to be read against a cobalt blue ceiling, together with adjacent canted concrete walls painted yellow and black, exemplifying once again Le Corbusier's passion for polychromy. In contrast, the stone-paved concrete nave maintains a grey luminosity throughout except for the red and green clearstorey lights that flank it on either side. This polychromatic treatment affords a vibrant enrichment of the high altar since the reflected colours, often of a red hue, spill into the space at either side of the raised sanctum at different times of the day. The elevation and subtle proportion of the altar (together with the void beyond it) and the largely windowless volume of the nave – save for the aforementioned clearstoreys, a zenithal light, and a window to the right of the altar – combine with stark wooden furniture to give the space an early Christian, almost pagan, aura, comparable to that which he had attained at Ronchamp.

157
147

The one figure who was engaged with this project from the very beginning was the Greek musician/engineer/architect Iannis Xenakis, who was one of Le Corbusier's most trusted assistants from the time he joined the office in 1947 to his peremptory dismissal from the studio in August 1957 (p. 214). While Le Corbusier surely sanctioned every step he took, it is clear that Xenakis played a salient role in the work, from its initial conception through to the application of the Modulor system to every dimension, along with the extremely subtle rhythmic articulation of the *pans de verre ondulatoires*. As Xenakis informs us, the combinatorial number system used for the syncopation of these elements was derived from the Golden Section and was virtually the same as the system he would adopt for orchestrating his composition *Metastasis*. His own words written after the event are extremely revealing, not only with regard to the nature of their collaboration, but also with respect to Le Corbusier's growing preoccupation with the concept of the total work of art – his desire to enrich the visual arts with some form of musical expression, evident in his commissioning of *musique concrète* from such avant-garde composers as Olivier Messiaen and Edgar Varèse. As at Ronchamp, he entertained the wild idea of broadcasting electronic music over the rustic domain surrounding the monastery; a wilful complement, we must say, to the medieval tradition of the belfry calling the faithful to prayer. This latter-day preoccupation with the *Gesamtkunstwerk* was not without its irony, since both the architects and the client seem to have overlooked the need for an organ in the church, so that they were reduced to installing the instrument in an appendage at the back of the church at the last minute. However, concerning the use of the Modulor in both architectural and musical composition, Xenakis' words could hardly be more revealing:

156

*In June of 1954, I was studying the glass openings, 366 centimeters
[12 ft] high, for the level of the common rooms and classrooms.
I found out the vertigo of combinatories in architectural elements after
having experimented with them in music. In fact, in Metastasis for
orchestra, which I was finishing at the same time… [It] was the source*

of another much more radical work of architecture that I conceived
two years later. This was the Philips Pavilion at the 1958 Brussels
World's Fair which I designed and made out of the ruled surfaces much
like my fields of string glissandi which suddenly and for the first time
in the history of music opened the way to the continuity of sound
transformations in instrumental music.[8]

Xenakis's interest in glissandi form and ellipsoid geometry gives an unusual poignancy to the curious fate that brought him and Le Corbusier together, for he was able to consummate not only Le Corbusier's lifelong preoccupation with harmonic proportion but also his penchant for non-orthogonal geometry, which ran back to his admiration for the work of Eugène Freyssinet in the early 1920s and to his appreciation in 1932 of the plastic potential of the hyperbolic paraboloid vault as that appears in the roof of Antoni Gaudí's parochial school of 1909 attached to the Sagrada Familia church in Barcelona.

In retrospect, the Philips Pavilion, commissioned by Philips, the Dutch radio and electronics corporation, for the Brussels World Exhibition of 1958, may be seen as the penultimate essay in Le Corbusier's excursus into the sacred, despite the fact that it could hardly have been more removed from orthodox religion.

160. Philips Pavilion,
Brussels World Exhibition, 1958.

Nevertheless, its hyperbolic form, combined with Le Corbusier's *poème électronique*, projected a kind of cosmic synthesis such as had previously been the exclusive province of the Church. Moreover, a recurrent tectonic transformation (invariably dedicated to a similar kind of didactic synthesis) runs continuously through Le Corbusier's work from the Pavillon des Temps Nouveaux of 1937 to the Philips Pavilion. This typological evolution, with multiple metaphoric overtones, invariably entailed some form of double curvature, due either to catenary suspension, as in the 1937 tent, or to hyperbolic, space-frame structures in his exhibition pavilions of 1939. Moreover, as we have seen, there is the trace of a similar geometry in the ribbed double curvature of the concrete shell roof spanning over Ronchamp.

The Philips Pavilion was a culmination of Le Corbusier's preoccupation both with electronic music and with the ideal of the total work of art, since while he commissioned Varèse to write a multi-track electronic score that would accompany the 480-second kinetic light display, he himself selected the images for this spectacle and controlled the pattern of coloured filters to be superimposed over the projections. This schedule, together with the script (the *minutage*), determined the coordinated sequence of images and sounds to be projected against the complex curvature of the hyperbolic shell vaults which constituted the body of the Philips Pavilion.

As with the Pavillon des Temps Nouveaux, this was an audacious project, designed and realized at the eleventh hour by a team of architects, musicians and structural engineers, together with Philips's own technicians, in a common display of talent, daring and solidarity.[9] No one had ever built a piece like this before, and some measure of its pioneering character may be gauged from the fact that the shells were constructed out of pre-cast concrete diamond segments, each one of varying curvature, cast against a full-scale sand mould and bound together structurally by pre-stressing cables, inside and out. These last stabilized the shape and force of each vault as the multifaceted space of the inner volume passed from one ridge chord to the next.

Le Corbusier's retort-like sketch for the Philips Pavilion dating from September 1956 seems to have served as the point of departure for the third and final church of his career, St-Pierre at Firminy-Vert, initiated in 1960 by Eugène Claudius-Petit, who by then was mayor of Firminy. Le Corbusier only accepted this commission because of his long friendship with Claudius-Petit, combined with the fact that the church was intended to serve as a complement to the youth club and the stadium which he had previously designed for the same client on an adjacent site. Significantly enough, he would refuse another church commission outright in the following year.

Derived in part from a 1929 sketch for a church at Le Tremblay, in part from the cooling-tower form as he used this in the Assembly 165 in Chandigarh, the primary volume and mass of the Firminy church were predicated on the progressive transformation of a square plan into a hollow conic shell – a geometric shift that is clearly indicated by a string model made in the studio in November 1961.[10] The building divides into two parts, into the *profane* two-storey podium accommodating the sacristy, the presbytery and the parish hall, and the *sacred* volume of the church itself that also consists of two levels – the horizontal floor of the sanctuary, and the warped plane of the seating suspended within the nave. Two prominent forms give an organic character to the design: the dramatic plasticity of the tiered seating, and the cone of the 'cooling tower' which illuminates the sacred space from above. While the presbytery and parish hall are entered at ground level from the west, the church is reached from the south via a ramp and an exterior portico. Unfinished at the time of his death, the Firminy church was fully developed as a design between 1962 and 1964 and subsequently brought to the contract drawing stage by José Oubrerie over the years 1970–79. Although partially constructed, it is still incomplete.

There remains the enigma of Le Corbusier's own beliefs, for he denied, on numerous occasions, that he subscribed to any form of religious faith. In common with Tony Garnier and with the technocratic élite with which he was so closely associated in the late 1920s, Le Corbusier excluded all forms of institutionalized religion from his vision of society. Nevertheless while denying any kind of affiliation he wrote: 'Into my work I bring so much effusion and intense inner life that it becomes something almost religious.'[11]

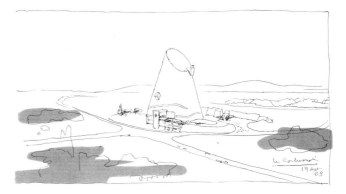

161. St-Pierre, Firminy-Vert, 1961–65: panoramic sketch, 1963.

Chapter 11   Passage to India 1950–1965

The strain of the archaic that runs through Le Corbusier's architecture after the early 1930s seems to attain its greatest fulfilment in India, where, at the age of 63, he found himself at long last working under state patronage and in the name of a society that was still largely pre-industrial. Sought out in his atelier in rue de Sèvres by the Indian government representatives, the engineer P. L. Varma and the administrator P. N. Thapar, he was officially charged with the planning of Chandigarh, the new capital of the Punjab, in November 162- 1950. This commission was a consequence of the Hindu-Muslim 16■ partition of India after the country gained its independence in 1947, with Lahore, the old capital of the Punjab, becoming incorporated into Pakistan, thereby creating an immediate need for a new capital.

The design had initially been commissioned by the first prime minister of India, Jawaharlal Nehru, from the American planner Albert Mayer. Mayer's outline plan was derived in large part from the model villages and towns that he had prepared for India soon after Independence; but he was prescient enough to realize that he did not have the requisite talent and/or training to design the Capitol, and to that end he employed the Polish-American architect Matthew Nowicki. Nowicki had barely begun to work on the project before he was killed in an air crash in 1950. It is ironic, given his antipathy towards the American way of life, that Le Corbusier should derive his own scheme for Chandigarh from a sketch plan by Nowicki. By adopting it as a point of departure he was able to transcend Albert Mayer's irregular garden-city layout, although he retained the neighbourhood concept on which the Mayer plan had been based. Like Nowicki, Le Corbusier located his government Capitol to the north of the main body, while the gridded plan of the city itself would unfold about a central axis to the south.

In spite of the colonial legacy of an efficient rail and harbour network throughout the subcontinent and the established prosperity of the textile industry in Ahmedabad, India was still in the main an agrarian society. Le Corbusier seems to have felt privileged to be working for such a society, since its time-honoured cyclical way of life still remained somewhat isolated from the vicissitudes of Western progress. It was a moment 'Avant le big money', as Le Corbusier noted in his Sketchbook E18 of 1951.[1] On the other hand, like his magisterial client, Nehru, he was hardly sympathetic to the anti-industrialism of Mahatma Gandhi's 'Quit India' movement, which had been ultimately responsible for the elimination of colonial rule. As idealistic as Nehru, Le Corbusier imagined that it would still be possible to combine advanced technology with a thousand-year-old peasant culture. In December 1950 we find him writing to his British collaborators, Jane Drew and E. Maxwell Fry:

At this moment in the evolution of modern civilization India represents a quality of spirit, particularly attractive. Our task is to discover the architecture to be immersed in the sieve of this powerful and profound civilization and the endowment of favourable modern tools to find it a place in present time.[2]

However much Le Corbusier might rail against what he called the 'Oxonian' conspiracy, which presumably meant the tendency of English-educated Indian architects to favour Mayer's garden-city layout, his own ideas as to an appropriate urbanism for a Third World situation were not entirely convincing. In generic terms, he seems to have found himself caught between the regional urbanization arguments of *Les Trois Établissements humains* of 1945 and the zoning principle of the CIAM Athens Charter of 1934, in which he

162. Chandigarh, India, 1950–65: master plan and model of the Capitol. From left to right, the structures are the Secretariat (Ill.167), Assembly (Ill.165), Governor's Palace (unrealized), High Court (Ill.164), and Open Hand (Ill.168).

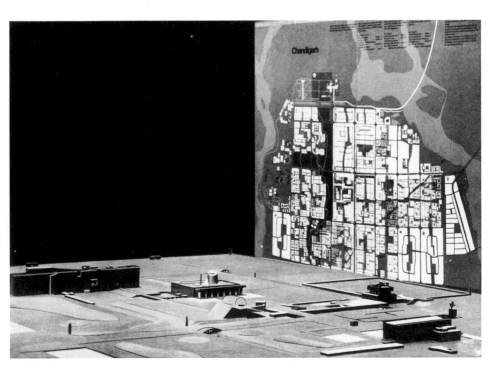

had insisted on dividing the modern city into separate zones for work, dwelling, and recreation, while relying upon transportation as the sole agent capable of uniting these zones into a workable and perceivable whole. In Chandigarh the transport infrastructure was an orthogonal grid, complemented by Le Corbusier's somewhat mystical hierarchy of the seven routes or *voies*, which he called the '7 Vs' (see p.163). Despite this hierarchical conception, which differentiated between the V1 regional roads coming into the city from the hinterland and the V2 roads that constituted the major intersecting axial boulevards of the city (an evocation perhaps of the Roman *cardo* and *decumanus*), Le Corbusier and his colleagues found it difficult to arrive at an appropriate grid for the residential matrix, as is evident from the 1,200 x 800-metre (3,940 x 2,625 ft) residential sectors that comprised the neighbourhood units,[3] surrounded on all four sides by the V3 road network. Movement about this monumental street grid on foot or by bullock cart was not made any easier by the provision of bus stops at 200-metre (656 ft) intervals, a rhythm taken straight from the Parisian transportation system. Moreover, the intersecting sectorial axes – a north–south greenway band (V7), and an east–west bazaar street (V2) – had the effect of dividing up the residential zone still further, with the paradoxical result that the physical fabric of the city became not only overscaled but also somewhat difficult to negotiate and perceive. Notwithstanding the non-orthogonal V5 distributor roads looping through each residential sector, the roads in general tended to be too wide and too far apart: while the designers of Chandigarh expressed their admiration for the mixed-use vitality of the relatively narrow traditional Indian street, they nonetheless superimposed a street grid that would have been justifiable only in a country in which mass ownership of the automobile was the norm. It was as though the ideological split between Nehru and Gandhi found a direct reflection in the infrastructure of Chandigarh, testifying to a confrontation between two entirely different world-views.

It was not that Le Corbusier was incapable of imagining a form of habitat more appropriate to the real needs of the poor. On the contrary, as his and Jeanneret's 'peon' housing project for Chandigarh of 1952 suggests, he was fully able to meet such requirements. Conceived as a horizontal version of his Roq and Rob stepped terrace housing proposals of 1949, and designed to fit the subdivision of the residential sectors into units of 110 square metres (1,200 sq. ft) per family, this was predicated on a single subdivided basic volume, set under a concrete vault spanning

14:

2.26 metres (7 ft 5 in.) and resting on brick cross-walls. With a covered living area raised upon a shallow podium, this minimum dwelling for four persons was capable of expansion on to exterior verandahs at either end of the megaron, facing private yards at front and back. However, the fact that he sensed the impossibility of achieving a successful fusion between the First and Third Worlds, particularly at a residential scale, may well explain why he confined himself to the design of the Capitol, comprising the Assembly, the High Court, the Secretariat, and the Governor's Palace (this last unrealized). A somewhat desperate remark to Maxwell Fry that he was only interested in art speaks to this, although this was somewhat at variance with his appreciation of the Indian way of life as a truly human modus that was already threatened by modernization. As he wrote in Sketchbook E18:

At Chandigarh people will walk without automobiles and New York's Fifth Avenue and 42nd Street will be grotesque. Calm, dignity, contempt for envy: Perhaps India is capable of maintaining herself at this point and establishing herself at the head of civilization.

—They begin work at 10 o'clock in the morning. Why not? They walk by people and trees and flowers. They leave at 4 o'clock. Why not? All of a sudden, a car horn! The police jeep. There is the enemy. It's inadmissible in the midst of this peace acquired through an instinctive wisdom.

On the next page he continues to jot down a set of loosely connected thoughts about a society where the primary mode of getting around is on foot:

Simla March 15. Fin d'un Monde. People use their legs: pedestrians. Walking ½ hour or more, men and women, straight. Joy of walking, not tired, Chandigarh a walking city and no cars. The pedestrian is alone in the V4's and V7's.

Thapar and Varma are as calm as time immemorial. Offices in the USA?!!! Pierre [Jeanneret] thinks that the Indian people will be caught up in that passion.[4]

Despite the somewhat sceptical and ambivalent attitude that Le Corbusier displayed towards the inevitable modernization of India, it is known that he nonetheless admired the heroic scale of Sir Edwin Lutyens's Viceroy's Palace in New Delhi (1923–31), and indeed he would approach the design of both the Capitol and the city in equally monumental terms. Thus the 400- and 800-metre (1,312 and 2,625 ft) planning modules of the city seem to have been derived from the distribution of monuments with respect to the central axis of Paris, so that the distance between the Capitol and the commercial centre equalled the span between the Louvre and the Place de la Concorde.[5] At the same time, he designed the accommodation of the commercial centre as though it were a neo-Sittesque version of an Indian *chowk* or bazaar. Yet although he made an effort to evoke the space of the traditional bazaar, he failed to reproduce its well-shaded interstitial fabric in modern terms. Moreover, despite his fascination with the elegant posture of Indian women, dressed in *saris*, gracefully bearing heavy loads upon their heads, and his countless sketches of Indian cattle, his architectonic sympathies remained more with the Mughal empire than with the Indian village vernacular. Hence the passing allusion in designs for the Capitol to the astronomical observatories at Delhi and Jaipur and his transformation of the arcuated Diwan-i-Am of the Red Fort in Delhi into the parabolic arches of the Chandigarh High Court.

In more general terms the Capitol may be seen as a reworking of his Cité Mondiale of 1929, inasmuch as its primary institutions – the Assembly, the High Court and the Secretariat – echo the equally monumental disposition of the lecture hall, library and museum in Paul Otlet's hypothetical world campus. This was not the only feature in common, since both complexes were ordered about a set of regulating lines which in each instance established the proportional relationships between the monumental structures in such a way as to achieve a certain spatial resonance between them. We may regard this plastic interplay over large distances as a demonstration of Le Corbusier's 'ineffable space', his *espace indicible*.[6]

163. Chandigarh, India, 1950–65: plan of the Capitol.
1 Assembly
2 Secretariat
3 Governor's Palace
4 High Court
5 Tower of Shadows
6 Martyrs' Monument
7 Open Hand

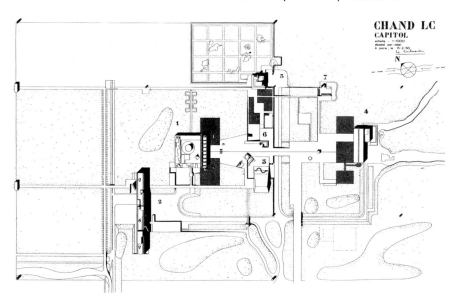

CHAND LC
CAPITOL
echelle · 1.1000
dessiné par- tolati
à paris , le 8-2-56.
N

At another level the Capitol seems to be comparable to a multi-levelled Mayan acropolis, where monuments are disposed according to auspicious cosmological alignments against a vast natural backdrop. Apart from fundamental morphological differences arising out of the different programmes, the three palatial buildings of the Capitol were distinguished from each other by the deployment of climatically based tectonic devices that Le Corbusier perfected in India – the parasol, the double roof, the frustum and the hyperbolic vault – together with the ubiquitous *brise-soleil*. Thus the High Court (1951–55) was composed of two 164
fundamental tropes: a long vaulted parasol divided into eleven bays that provided a shade roof for the entire structure, and a syncopated, rhythmic *brise-soleil* that differentiated between the eight standard courts and the main tribunal. The entry to the building was treated as a four-storey breeze hall, divided by three full-height piers which support vaults above and are painted green, yellow, and red. The switch back and forth of the exposed concrete ramp situated behind this space enabled Le Corbusier to create a particularly dramatic sculptural play between the inclination of the ramps and a series of irregular voids cut out of the supporting central wall.

The striking profile of the Assembly (1953–61) comprised a 165
concrete frustum or 'cooling-tower' shape, rising over the circular plan of the principal chamber to pierce through the ceiling of the surrounding hypostyle hall and topping out, 40 metres (130 ft) above ground level, in an observation deck linked by a metal walkway to a free-standing concrete lift-shaft of the same height. The

164. High Court, Chandigarh, 1951–55.

165. Assembly, Chandigarh,
1953–61.

166. Assembly: ground-floor plan.
1 main entrance
2 assembly hall
3 assembly chamber
4 vestibule
5 offices

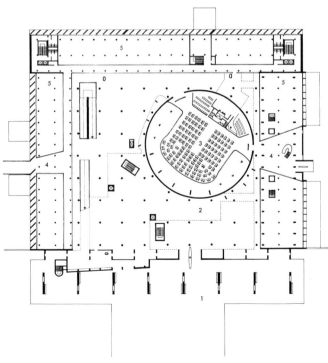

vertical mass of this shaft served to mediate, in a sculptural sense, between the truncated 'cone' over the main chamber and a con- 165 crete pyramid poised over the square council chamber. The entrance itself took the form of a monumental portico facing south-east, its supporting blade walls pierced by irregular holes in order to facilitate cross-ventilation. In effect this structure was an enormous gutter-cum-parasol, seemingly derived, in its sectional form, from Le Corbusier's habitual sketches of the horns of a bull. Le Corbusier displayed comparable plastic virtuosity in the convex interior of the parliamentary chamber itself, lined with organically shaped sound-absorbing acoustic 'clouds'. One should also note that the frustum shape created a Venturi effect that served to facilitate the natural ventilation of the space.

The straight vertical *brise-soleil* shielding the perimeter offices of the Assembly are answered at a distance by the predominantly horizontal *brise-soleil* of the Secretariat (1951–58), a continual 167 rhythm interrupted on its south-eastern face by a fugal interplay of deep, double-height balconies, recalling an abstract trope that had first appeared in the high-rise office building that Le Corbusier had projected for Algiers in 1938. This orthogonal 'oculus' plus two enclosed free-standing ramps, situated at either end of the Secretariat slab and lit by small openings, are the main relieving elements in an otherwise relentless façade some 254 metres (833 ft) in length. Le Corbusier's description of his treatment of this façade, from a climatic standpoint, reveals a great deal about the effort he

167. Secretariat, Chandigarh, 1951–58.

made to create an appropriate modern architecture for the Indian subcontinent. Thus he writes:

The exterior is of rough concrete, that is to say, the vertical brise-soleil, the parapets and the horizontal brise-soleil, the acroterium which stands out against the sky – leaving visible the rooftop accommodations which are to be used for a club and for receptions. The two large ramps in front of and behind the building serve all floors and are likewise in rough concrete. They offer a very beguiling solution of the circulation (morning and evening) for the 3000 employees. Vertical circulation is ensured by batteries of elevators matched by a staircase running in both directions encased in a vertical spine rising from ground level to the summit of the roof. Rough concrete similarly caps the two end walls bringing out the effect of the standard sheet-metal formwork. The block of ministerial offices has been the object of very careful research in regards to the sculptural relief given to rough concrete by the effect of diverse types of brise-soleil. The rough concrete again interposes in the fenestration of the two main façades: more than 2000 units of a unique design – one stanchion type 27 x 7 cm in section and 366 cm high – constitute the 'undulatory glazing'. This concerns an application here of the Modulor which permits the stretching of a veil of glass extending the entire length and height of the building, interrupted by elements called 'ventilators' which comprise a shutter of sheet-metal pivoting vertically from floor to ceiling across an opening of 43 cm and capable of being opened to any desired width, from 1 millimeter up to 23 centimeters; covered, in addition, by a curtain of copper mosquito-netting. Thus, an enormous saving of money and maintenance was realized with this fenestration, when compared with wood or metal.[7]

The use of the Modulor in plan to hold these diverse and distant forms together was emphasized in section by the treatment of the topography as a vast relief, from the creation of artificial hills to the judicious retention of clumps of mature trees at strategic points, from the deployment of extensive reflecting pools, modelled after Mughal precedent, to the use of the English traditional ha-ha or sunken fence as a device by which to establish the boundaries of the Capitol precinct. All these modifications of the surface were further reinforced by the provision of a recessed roadway, one floor below ground level, reserved for automobiles and bicycles. This lower level would have been given further spatial significance, as part of a gigantic low relief, incised into the ground, had it been accompanied by the sunken paradise garden projected for the Governor's Palace. The same level provides a continuous datum for

168. The Open Hand, Chandigarh.

Le Corbusier's other symbolic elements, for the 'Fosse de la Considération' or Monument to the Martyrs of Indian Partition (ostensibly designed for spontaneous assembly), the 'Tour des Ombres' (Tower of Shadows), and lastly 'La Main Ouverte' (The Open Hand), finally realized in 1985 as a light stressed-skin structure able to pivot in the wind like a weather vane.[8]   168

As Caroline Constant reminds us, the Capitol at Chandigarh was laid out at an aeronautical scale, legible as much in terms of time as in terms of space, thereby transcending, as she puts it, 'the limitations of humanist perspective to achieve a new legibility that he associated with the Cosmic'.[9] She goes on to argue that

He sought to transcend this difference in scale by infusing modern spatiality with mythopoeic content. The vast pedestrian esplanade linking the Assembly and High Court was inspired in spirit and detail by airport runways, while the reflecting pools to reduce the visual distance derive from Mughal precedents. The shifted ground plane, with its artificial mounds, reflecting pools and sunken courts, represents a sacred landscape created ex nihilo. Large earth mounds positioned to enhance the perceptual sequence allude to the distant mountains and contribute to the primal imagery. These landscape elements and the monuments intended to populate the esplanade suggest myriad nuances of meaning, as if to amplify their spatial significance.[10]

Seen in this light, it is clear that a crucial element missing from the Capitol is the Governor's Palace, which Nehru decided to omit on the grounds of its undemocratic character. Its absence indubitably compromises the rhythmic and quasi-Asiatic character of the whole. This much was surely confirmed by a full-size mock-up in canvas of the main elevation on the occasion of the 50th anniversary of the founding of Chandigarh.

India afforded Le Corbusier the opportunity of executing some ten substantial works, large and small, in the space of some fourteen years, in Chandigarh and in Ahmedabad. This last, the wealthy textile capital of Gujarat State, graced his career with two late masterworks: the modest Sarabhai House (1955), built in the midst   169
of the family compound, and the equally significant Millowners'   171,
Association Building, completed in 1954, under virtually the same   172
patronage.

The Sarabhai House is in many respects an Asiatic recasting of the St-Cloud Maison de Week-End of 1935, only now the rubble   114
stone has been replaced by load-bearing brick cross-walls, while the concrete roof structure is even more evident in the deep downstand perimeter beams, accented with gargoyles, that both crown

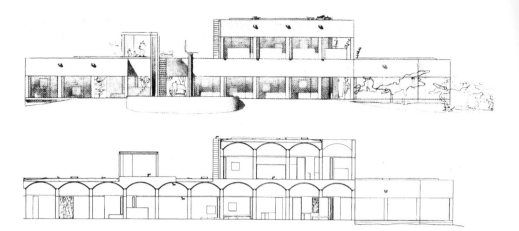

169. Sarabhai House, Ahmedabad, India, 1955: south elevation and section.

the building and cap the ends of its Catalan vaults. The grass-covered roof, more extensive than in Paris, has now become a world apart, a kind of secret 'parterre', connected by a concrete toboggan-run to the plunge pool that enlivens the garden proper. No one has assessed the subtle stature of this work more perceptively than Sunand Prasad. He writes:

The house is principally an interior or more precisely a system for creating a set of connected habitable spaces that flow simply to the outside. The actual plan is not very important and has indeed slowly and naturally changed in the thirty years of occupation by the original inhabitants…As Awand Sarabhai grew up, the house was re-arranged – room use was changed, open verandas were covered to make a library, etc. – all without significantly altering its character.[11]

Ahmedabad presented Le Corbusier with an occasion for further exploring the parasol theme as this had already been touched on in the third of his Four Compositions in his *Précisions* of 1929. This parasol paradigm had in fact been realized in the Villa Baizeau built at Carthage, Tunisia, in 1928. Interrelated features of the Villa Baizeau reappear in his designs for the Chimanbhai and Hutheesing houses, two free-standing *palazzettos* projected for Ahmedabad in the early 1950s. As it happened, the design for Hutheesing would eventually become the basis for the Shodhan House, its plans being effectively sold to another owner for realization on a different site. The characteristics that these share are: (1) the development of the *brise-soleil* in depth so that the space between the louvers becomes partially encapsulated within the cubic volume of the house itself; (2) the activation of the enclosed space through the introduction of a *promenade architecturale* in the form of a central ramp passing up

194

through the entire volume (cf. the Villa Savoye); and (3) the treat- 67–69
ment of the upper storeys as a belvedere from which to overlook
the landscape. Two other buildings, erected in the Americas – the
Villa Curutchet (1949) and the Carpenter Center for the Visual 182
Arts (1964) – belong to the same typological series, but since lie
outside the Indian subcontinent they will be treated separately.

The interlocking section of the Villa Baizeau with its flat slab
parasol was expressly contrived for the purposes of cross-
ventilation and sun control. It is easy to see how this would
naturally suggest itself as a viable type for India, given that Le
Corbusier was confronted with a climate in which relentless sun
and torrential rain both demand shelter. As others have indicated,
the most striking Indian precedent for this form of covered open-
sided terrace construction was to be found in Akbar's ill-fated
capital of Fatehpur Sikri, erected towards the end of the 16th
century. Thus the parasol of Carthage emerged from the repertoire
of Le Corbusier's Purist period to fuse with the Mughal tradition.
At the same time, the general deportment of these *palazzetto*
designs returned Le Corbusier to his neo-Palladian 'house/palace'
preoccupations of the late 1920s.

The priority given to shade and cross-ventilation in the
Carthage section makes itself particularly evident in the
Millowners' Association Building at Ahmedabad, above all in the 171,
structuring of its institutional presence about a breeze hall, which, 172
beginning at the level of the *piano nobile*, was given over to executive
use. The long access ramp to this 'noble' level served, in conjunction
with the relegation of the clerical staff and the restaurant to
the ground floor, as a means for establishing a palatial sense of

170. Shodhan House, Ahmedabad, India, 1956.

decorum. As to the way in which this hierarchy was reinforced by the detailing, Sunand Prasad has written:

The horizontal distance which the visitor has to travel is used to gain almost effortlessly a storey in height so that the grand approach arrives directly at the triple-height hall on the first floor. To guard the side of the ramp to the left, against the secluded lawn, is a low concrete wall with an inward-sloping shelf on top while to the right, against the car parking area and reaching to the ground floor, is a massive handrail supported on thin rods. As well as stopping people from falling off and providing something to hang on to, the 'balustrade' on the left feels safe to perch on the edge of and overhang the lawn; its wide, sloping top, which throws off rain, allows it to be relatively low, thus offering a sense of openness on the ramp. The ingeniously curved profile of the great rail on the other side makes for a 'buttock-rest' as well as an easy grip for the hand. Its paired steel supports, thin as the reinforcement hidden in the concrete, one upright, one braced against side thrust, stand on concrete stubs that grow out of the ramp. The whole composition – the solid base making special mounts for the insubstantial vertical supports, which in turn support the substantial, closely observed horizontal rail – is a poem about the heavy and the light, transparency and protection, in a new language of the materials of modern industry bound together by profoundly understood functional rigor. Together the elements of the ramp make a rich discourse on these qualities, on publicness and privacy, and on the experience of the body moving up through space; a discourse that is sustained within the building in the route that from the end of the ramp proceeds on and up to the roof-garden.[12]

171. Millowners' Association Building, Ahmedabad, India, 1954: main approach.

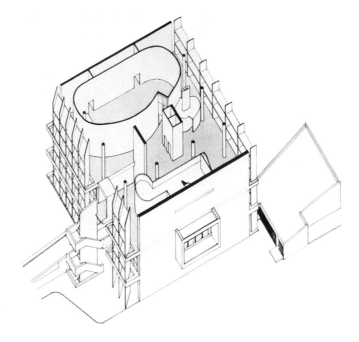

172. Millowners' Association Building: axonometric showing the breeze hall containing the elliptically planned assembly space and surrounding foyer plus mezzanines (drawn by John Pettit West III).

As in the Maison Cook, the Millowners' Building elevates the traditional *piano nobile* of the *palazzetto* type to the second floor, despite the fact that the monumental exterior ramp delivers the general public to the single-storey reception/secretariat accommodation located on the first floor. An honorific, double-height breeze hall space completes the representational programme of the building on the floor above. Apart from the elevator shaft linking all levels, this open space is furnished with an auditorium, a bar, a mezzanine-cum-minstrels' gallery and a diminutive curvilinear-sided pod containing male and female lavatories. The free-standing auditorium, oval in plan, pierces the flat roof of this space to crown the top of the building with a separate, elevated parasol. The profiling and surface treatment of the ovoid auditorium stress the contrast between the calm volume of the prism and the dynamism of the shell form poised within. The parabolic inner track of this shell, cutting like a blade against the outer cubic form, is emphasized by the diagonal plywood lining of the interior, patterned in such a way as to oppose its orthogonal container.

This dialectical opposition, which always plays such an essential part in Le Corbusier's imagination, expresses itself at Ahmedabad in the double articulation of the entire composition. Thus the elliptical lecture hall is opposed not only to the outer cube but also to

172

the dog-leg stair, which in its turn assumes an active figural character in relation to the passive orthogonality of the basic volume. And what is true for these primary elements applies with equal force to the smaller components. The vertical *brise-soleil* of the front façade contrast with the horizontal sun-screening of the rear elevation, facing the river. By a similar token, the elliptical forms of the bar and lavatories are set in opposition to the sculptural counterform of a diminutive dog-leg stair leading to the mezzanine and the roof. Finally, in the interlocking *yin-yang* enclosures of the male and the female toilets we are presented with organic forms that may be said to be as dialogical as they are metaphorically erotic.

Le Corbusier's involvement with India lasted until April 1964, when he came to Chandigarh for the last time in order to attend the inauguration of the main door to the Assembly, enamelled in part with his famous icon of the twenty-four-hour cycle.[13] In all Le Corbusier visited India some twenty-three times in fourteen years, slightly less than the two times a year stipulated under the terms of his initial contract. By 1962 most of the major works of the Capitol were already completed, and while he had responded with his characteristic brilliance to the symbolic challenge of designing a capital for the Punjab, he fell short of mastering the subtleties of an extremely varied and taxing climate, for although he understood the need to protect buildings from the sun, he failed to comprehend the best way of dealing with hot breezes or for that matter of protecting interiors from the impact of the monsoon, both of which demanded some measure for closing a building down against ambient heat or heavy, windswept rain. Moreover, he failed to note that the thermal capacity of uninsulated concrete is such as to make it extremely hot in summer and unbearably cold in winter.

All the same, while he misread key aspects of the Indian vernacular and was inspired instead by the monumentality of the Mughal empire, he nonetheless captured something of the spirit of India, for as William Curtis has noted, 'the sophisticated foreign primitivist intuited links between his own contrived pantheism and the deeply rooted cosmic myths of India's ancient religions'.[14] This led to the superimposition of an iconography, particularly in the Capitol, that was as much his own cosmology as it was a reflection of the Indian mythic tradition. Hence the cross-cultural resonance of the 'signs' cast into the *béton brut* of the Capitol or alternatively enamelled onto the door of the Assembly or woven into the giant tapestries of the High Court by Kashmiri weavers. These cryptic images, part traditional, part hermetic, comprised such items as the seal of Mohenjo Daro, the bull of Shiva, the scales of justice, the tree of life, the crescent moon, the wheels of the sun, a snake, a tree, an ear of corn, a Modulor Man, and even primitive drawings made by the construction workers themselves. All were signs of another civilization as it were; a culture of his imagination lying beyond the fateful processes of time.

Half a century after its foundation, with a population of 750,000, already fifty per cent larger than its projected size, Chandigarh must be regarded on balance as a success at more than one level. Its economic prosperity has since prompted the foundation of two extramural settlements – the SAS Nagar and Panchkula townships – not to mention sundry squatters' camps dotted about the periphery of the initial 52-sector grid. Moreover, despite the size of the sectors, their introspective character and the separation of the commercial centre from the Capitol, at least 20 of the 29 sectors of the first phase were virtually fully developed as self-contained neighbourhood units at the time of Le Corbusier's death in 1965. The wide roads, which seemed absurd at the beginning, are now much appreciated in a city containing nearly a half a million automobiles. And if there is a shortfall today in terms of infrastructure, it is the desperate need for some sort of high-speed public transit system, be it bus or light rail.

As far as the residential fabric is concerned, it has to be conceded that the Corbusian design team failed to anticipate how Indian society would develop under the impact of modernization and how, where prosperous, it would also begin to demand air-conditioning, not to mention the other accoutrements of the consumer society, all of which have led to a departure from the traditional way of life for which the dwelling units had been origi-nally designed. At the same time, despite the abandonment of the Mayer plan, Chandigarh has become a garden city after all, for it is covered with profuse vegetation throughout, to the extent that much of its fabric is concealed from the average visitor when driving through. On the other hand, the Capitol itself remains one of the great unfinished landscapes of the modern world, and one only hopes that the various state authorities will soon find the resources necessary to finish and maintain the surface of this spectacular earthwork rather than let it deteriorate further in its present partially ruined condition.

Chapter 12 *Le Poème de l'Angle Droit*

While alchemical themes had been latent in Le Corbusier's thought from the very beginning, figurative imagery appeared in his architecture with the League of Nations project of 1927, as we may judge from the sculptural group shown poised over the secretary general's pavilion on its lake front elevation. Comprised of a lion, a horse, a man and an eagle, this figurative cluster seems so arbitrarily composed as to suggest that it was nothing more than a graphic convention for the representation of honorific statuary.[1] With Le Corbusier, however, one cannot simply assume that the gesture was entirely innocent, and it is arguable that each figure of the group had a particular symbolic if not mythic significance.

It would seem that the horse and the man were transpositions of the Deutsche Werkbund symbol that Peter Behrens had installed on top of the German Embassy realized to his designs in St Petersburg in 1912. This icon, featured again in Behrens's Festhalle built for the Deutsche Werkbund exhibition of 1914, was in fact a version of the classical *Dioscuri*, who had first appeared in modern architecture as representations of Prussian statehood on top of K. F. Schinkel's Altes Museum of 1830 in Berlin. While in the

173. Le Corbusier and Pierre Jeanneret: League of Nations project for Geneva, 1927: detail of the sculptural group above the secretary general's pavilion.

Schinkel version (based on the antique *Horse-Tamers*) the heavenly twins Castor and Pollux are barely able to hold their spirited charges in check, in Behrens's group (based on the *Dioscuri* at the Capitol) these rampant beasts become pacified at the hands of *Übermenschen* who, like the horses, are frontalized and stare impassively ahead. Partially returning to the theme – a reference surely to his brief apprenticeship with Behrens – Le Corbusier isolates one of the *Dioscuri* and brings both horse and man back to life.

In the League of Nations sculptural cluster this figure of a man standing at ease is juxtaposed with the image of a bird poised for flight. It is possible that this is self-referential, in that Le Corbusier had represented himself as a eagle in an ironic caricature sent to his parents in 1909.[2] According to mythic tradition, the eagle symbolizes the spirit. It is the initial character of the Egyptian hieroglyphic system, representative of the sun and luminosity.[3] Le Corbusier's Nietzschean identification of himself with an eagle also links him to Behrens, since Behrens had been equally obsessed with this image during the period of his 'Zarathustrastil', a manner which attained its apotheosis in a house he built for himself in Darmstadt in 1901. We know that in 1908 Le Corbusier read and underlined Nietzsche's *Thus Spake Zarathustra*, where an eagle is prominently featured along with a snake as Zarathustra's 'animals'. The eagle's constant circling under the sun at high noon epitomized for Nietzsche the law of the eternal return.[4] Thus Le Corbusier seems to have associated himself with Zarathustra's eagle as an image of immortal power on the threshold of his artistic maturity. This narcissistic identification is quite removed from the slightly sinister, ironic, post-1945 characterization of himself as a crow, wherein he returned to that early play on words in which Ozenfant had encouraged him to adopt the pseudonym Le Corbusier, the meaning of which may be loosely construed as 'the crow-like one'.[5] Unlike the eagle, this black avian image would prove assimilable in his later life to the alchemical concept of the *nigredo*. In the Swiss psychologist Carl Gustav Jung's influential *Psychology and Alchemy*, first published in 1944, 'the *nigredo* or blackness is the initial state' corresponding to primordial chaos, or, at a more personal level, to spiritual depression or more generally to a condition of death and putrefaction that must of necessity precede rebirth.[6] The traditional alchemical symbol of the *nigredo* is the raven.

The attributes of the left part of the League of Nations group are more difficult to decode, partly because the horse is an ambivalent symbol. In this instance, however, it is surely the opposite of the calm, neoclassical figure of a man, inasmuch as an untamed horse may be seen as representing the turbulent or more Dionysiac side of human character. Thus the male figure may be read as a symbol of control, suggestive of the role played by Le Corbusier's cousin Pierre Jeanneret. However, if we turn to the other outriding figure, a lion, we find another image that might be associated with Jeanneret, since in size, position and posture the lion balances the Corbusian eagle. The traditional elemental attributes of the lion are sulphur and the sun, which would give Jeanneret an appropriately Apollonian cast, although in alchemical lore the lion is also associated with Mercury.

Irrespective of the significance that may be attributed to these images, what is certainly suggested by this sculptural group is Le Corbusier's obsession with the double,[7] not only in relation to his own split personality – caught until 1928 between Charles Édouard Jeanneret, the Purist painter, and Le Corbusier, the architect[8] – but also in terms of the highly symbiotic relationships that he was in the habit of establishing with his closest associates. Hence the use of the compound pen-name 'Le Corbusier-Saugnier' for the author of *Vers une architecture* when it was first published in essay form, 'Saugnier' being a pseudonym of Amédée Ozenfant. Hence also the other crucial interdependency, namely Le Corbusier's partnership with Pierre Jeanneret, which was made to seem all the more intimate by the fact that both men carried the same last name.

Like Ludwig Mies van der Rohe, who added his mother's maiden name, Rohe, to his simple patronym in order to imply a noble origin,[9] Le Corbusier was moved to acquire through an assumed pseudonym the suggestion of an aristocratic heritage. Above all, he seems to have been proud of the fact that the family name, Jeanneret-Gris, could be traced back to a minor 17th-century aristocratic line in the Languedoc.[10] In the latter part of his life he speculated about the propitiousness of this affiliation, since it linked him to the Manichean tradition of the Cathars, the so-called Albigensian heretics. Thus he declared to Jean Petit:

The frontiers of the land of my birth are part of the topographical and geographical areas on the edge of the great French migrations of the past. My origins lie in the South of France; the name Jeanneret is spelt 'Janeret' in the pays d'Oc, and, quite simply, we are Albigensians...[11]

In the light of this connection, the case can be made that Le Corbusier's dialogical habit of mind, that is his tendency to think in terms of interdependent opposites, had its ultimate origin in Albigensian dualism, since the Cathars (from the Greek, meaning 'purified') gave equal weight to the forces of good and evil. The late

Swiss architect Bernard Hoesli once remarked that during his apprenticeship in the rue de Sèvres studio Le Corbusier would often allude to minor irritations as testifying to the presence of the devil, remarking, 'vous voyez, l'ennemi est partout' (you see, the enemy is everywhere).[12]

The Cathars were unable to accept that the Christian God could have created a world so full of pain and suffering. In consequence, they totally rejected the cross and the sacraments, and went on to associate the principle of goodness with the spirit, and that of its opposite with the body. This dualist view led them to pursue an extremely puritanical way of life, favouring vegetarianism, meditation, and sexual abstinence, save for the purpose of procreation. Suicide was seen not as a mortal sin but as the triumph of spirit over matter. Given this tradition, it is at least possible to see Le Corbusier's fatal seizure while swimming off Cap Martin in 1965 as a form of inadvertent suicide, since this would have been consistent not only with his assumed Albigensian identity but also with his dualistic, alchemical preoccupations, coming close to the final sublimation of the body in the female ocean while swimming towards the male sun.[13]

Subject to a great deal of scholarly attention in the 1940s, above all by Jung, alchemy may be regarded as an extension of this dualistic world-view into the 20th century. The most important dichotomous figure in the alchemical cosmos is Mercury. In one aspect this figure is a dark demiurge, the creator of all earthly matter; in another it is the ultimate dematerialization of the spiritual principle. Jung would favour the dualistic characterization of Mercury as the 'Uroboros', that is as the quintessential union of opposites represented through the image of a mythical reptile swallowing its own tail. A further personification of Mercurial duality is to be found in the caduceus, comprising a wand with two winged snakes intertwined about its shaft – an image that would coincidentally resemble the abstract scale of interlocking proportions (the 'red' and 'blue' series) that accompanies Le Corbusier's characteristic figure of the Modulor Man, dating from 1946. Unlike the Christian godhead who descended from above and then returned to heaven, the pagan Mercury mythically ascends from earth to sky and then descends as part of the same continuous cycle. In this regard, the Mercurial as a principle may be said to have much in common with the precipitation cycle of the earth's atmosphere as we find this at a cosmic scale in Le Corbusier's moving account in *La Ville Radieuse* (1935), when recalling his experience of witnessing cloud formations while flying above the pampas in Latin America:

174

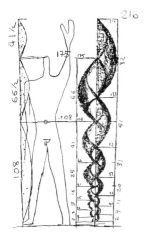

174. Modulor Man, as sketched on the ship *Vernon S. Hood,* 6 January 1946.

4:00 A.M.: The sun appears over the rim of the plain; the dew lies on the grass, in the hollow of every leaf. Since the sun sank the evening before, the cool of the night has turned what was vapour in the air to droplets lying on the ground.

8:00 A.M.: The scattered waters, now ascending, are driven far up from the earth by the luminous arrows of the sun, which, as they strike the ground, are transformed into caloric power: a force is produced that presses down upon the plains and lifts the vaporous layers up on its shoulders into the sky

10:00 A.M.: ...they are now small clouds floating over the plain. From where it flies above them, an airplane can discern their tactics: they are a team, they are a formation, a task force: they are appearing everywhere. They are the water's army.

Noon: The sun is in its glory. Its arrows strike vertically down into the earth; and they light furnaces upon it...Violence threatens, rivalries become apparent, the certainty of conflict emerges, and a battle is imminent. The air is filled with an electric charge.

The army of the water masses for an attack: colossal vertical clouds billow high into the sky and obscure its face.

5:00 P.M.: The first lightning flash streaks down, followed by tremendous thunder. All is terror and lashing rain, while darkness covers the unleashing of the storm...

6:00 P.M.: The earth is refreshed, the sky is clear. The sun, larger and clearer now, dips towards the plain again. Its movement becomes apparent, the speed of its descent almost alarming...

This prodigious spectacle has been produced by the interplay of two elements, one male, one female: sun and water.[14]

While alchemical dualism would not fully take hold of Le Corbusier's imagination until after 1945, his spiritual and artistic personality suffered a profound change in the late 1920s. The metamorphosis is most noticeable in his painting, which becomes increasingly post-Purist, as in his *Le Déjeuner au phare* of 1928 or his *Composition avec une poire* of the following year. In these works he begins to mix Purist motifs such as glasses, bottles, corkscrews, matchboxes and dominoes with elements of a more ambiguous and organic character such as a well-worn leather glove, together with a range of flotsam that he had long since been in the habit of collecting – pebbles, shells, flints, cordage, roots, driftwood, fossils and bones, all of which had been ravaged by the sea and bleached by the sun. His identification of these items as 'objets à reaction poétique'[15] may have been derived from André Breton's earlier use of a similar term. Le Corbusier became preoccupied with such evocative forms in the company of Fernand Léger, whose meticulous yet lyrical drawings of leaves, tree trunks, sides of meat, old gloves, overalls, and above all flints manifested a similar interest in his exhibition *Objets* of 1934.[16] Aside from their common reference to organic forms eroded by nature and time, the two men were also simultaneously engaged in a glorification of the working class. In this regard gloves, and later hands, were to have an allegorical status for Léger. They were seen as testifying to the heroic engagement of the manual worker in the arduous daily task of production – hence Léger's synthetic poem of 1951, 'Les Mains à la mémoire de Maiakovski'.[17]

175. Sketch of the tropical climate cycle, from *La Ville Radieuse*, 1935.

For Le Corbusier, influenced throughout his life by his initial exposure to the Arts and Crafts ideology of Charles L'Éplattenier, the image of the hand eventually acquired an even more universal significance, transcending, as it were, the socialist-cum-artisanal implications that seem to have been invariably associated with the image in Léger's painting. Le Corbusier was susceptible to John Ruskin's assimilation of a hand to a tree and vice versa,[18] which he later transformed into an image of an open hand raised up towards the sky. In 1937, in his book *Quand les cathedrals étaient blanches*, he refers to the tree as being the friend of a man whose branches bud forth each spring to form 'a new open hand'.[19] In the same year, he projected a large sculptural image of an outstretched hand, conceived as an appeal to revolutionary action, in his monument to Vaillant-Couturier. He returned to this image in 1947 in a sketch of a partially open hand, lying recumbent, close to the ground. In that instance it was no longer a call to arms but rather a call to faith, a connotation that is made explicit by the inscription beneath the drawing, that reads 'as if it were the façade of a cathedral'.[20] This analogical image of a digitally encapsulated volume seems to have been inspired by Auguste Rodin's famous sculpture of 1908 featuring two elongated half-open hands, partly spiralling upwards to create a space between them, bearing the title *La Cathédrale*. Some four years later, he would produce his first sketches for a colossal Open Hand as a monument to be erected in the Capitol of Chandigarh in India. This was conceived from the outset as a cosmic image; as an *axis mundi* linking heaven and earth. As he told Constantino Nivola during a visit to New York:

The open hand is a plastic gesture imbued with a profoundly human content; a symbol that is all too appropriate to a liberated and independent earth. A gesture that calls for the fraternal and solid collaboration of all men and all nations of the earth. It is also a sculptural and plastic gesture that is capable of incorporating the sky and engaging it with the earth.[21]

The shift towards the organic in Le Corbusier's painting in the mid- to late 1920s was accompanied by the introduction of the female figure, as we find this in his quasi-mythical *Deux figures, soleil et lune* (1928). This abandonment of Purist abstraction in favour of the figurative had been initiated even earlier and more directly in Le Corbusier's Léger-like silverpoint studies entitled *Fisherwomen* (1926).[22] In the 1930s, his painting acquired an increasingly erotic and esoteric character, as in *La Main et le silex* (1930) or *Deux Femmes au repos* (1937), the latter being apparently inspired by

Eugène Delacroix's *Les Femmes d'Alger* of 1833.[23] The human figure will also appear in his works at a mural scale, such as the untitled tapestry that he designed for Marie Cuttoli of Aubusson in 1936 – a medium which he embraced again with considerable acclaim after 1958.[24] 55

Similar forms appeared, also on a mural scale, in his *Sgraffite à Cap Martin* (1938), three interlocking linear figures inscribed into the plaster of an undercroft wall below Eileen Gray's E1027 house at Roquebrune-Cap Martin. This neo-Purist house had been realized to the designs of Gray in collaboration with the architect Jean Badovici in 1929. Throughout the 1930s, after it had been given by Gray to Badovici, Le Corbusier was in the habit of vacationing there – without Gray's knowledge and, it now seems, with only grudging acceptance on the part of Badovici. Le Corbusier painted seven other polychrome murals inside the house between 1938 and 1940. These wall pieces, together with the large photomurals that he created for the Pavillon des Temps Nouveaux in 1937, represent the apotheosis of his post-Purist image-making prior to the outbreak of the Second World War. In this context *Sgraffite à Cap Martin* stands out as a canonical work, not only because of its application 176

176. *Sgraffite à Cap Martin*, on a wall below Eileen Gray's house, E1027, at Roquebrune-Cap Martin, 1938.

of the technique of *mariage de contours* to a figurative subject, but also because of its representation of two women (referential once again to Delacroix) between whom there emerges the image of a primordial child. In my view, this is also possibly a reference to the alchemical *rebis*, particularly since this idea of an offspring stemming from a hermaphroditic couple may also be associated with the alchemical work or *opus*. Hence also the significance of the trace of a swastika, or a sun wheel, in the mural, recalling perhaps all too consciously the alchemical wheel or *rotas*, evoking the cyclical succession of the seasons plus the rising and falling of the *opus circulatorium*.

Significantly enough, given his preoccupation with the double, bisexuality is a theme to which Le Corbusier referred throughout his life, as we may judge from the numerous drawings and paintings depicting lesbian encounters. These are sometimes represented as occurring across racial lines, as in a striking watercolour of 1917 featuring a black and a white woman.[25] Could this also have been, at the same time, an early, literal allusion to the transformative power of the alchemical *nigredo*?[26]

Antithetical reconciliations in which polar opposites are fused together to give rise to a third term are a constant theme in his plastic work throughout the 1940s and early 1950s. Among such quasi-mythic conjunctions, we may cite the Medusa/Apollo image that is the end plate in *La Maison des hommes* (1942), or the mythical encounter of Pasiphaë with the white solar bull, their union giving rise to Cretan Minotaur, an image that appears as the first plate of another lithographic suite, entitled *Unité*, published in 1953. An equally synthetic myth/image, of a female horned figure with a single wing cupped in a monumental hand, appears in his 1948 mural for the foyer of the Pavillon Suisse in the Cité Universitaire, Paris,

177. Cover of the booklet *Poésie sur Alger*, 1950.

above the inscription '…garder mon aile dans ta main'.[27] This representation reappears on the cover of a booklet entitled *Poésie sur Alger* (1950), where it is shown rising over the sea, above the corniche of Algiers, a levitation seemingly induced by the presence of the giant hand. Scholars are divided as to whether this image is part goat, and therefore a representation of Capricorn, or a female unicorn.[28] It has been suggested that the figure is assimilable in Le Corbusier's personal iconography to his wife Yvonne, whom he characterized as 'A woman of strong heart and will, integrity and propriety, Guardian angel of the hearth, of my hearth…In my "poem of the right angle" she occupies a central place…'[29]

Le Poème de l'Angle Droit (The Poem of the Right Angle), exe-cuted as a seven-part sequence over a seven-year period from 1947 to 1953, is structured after the format of the Eastern Orthodox iconostasis, the traditional screen of icons separating the altar from the nave that serves as a veil between the congregation and the celebrants of the Eucharist.[30] It was eventually published in 1953 as a portfolio of eighteen coloured lithographic plates interspersed with black-and-white sketches, accompanying a series of poetic fragments that conjointly assumed the form of a hermetic gloss to the plates. The key to the entirety was a schematic iconostasis 178 structured as seven rows of iconic squares, the successive sym-metrical tiers being associated with the first seven letters of the alphabet. Each tier comprised a different number of images: starting from the top, there are 5, 3, 5, 1, 3, 1 and 1 – in all a total of 19. And each was devoted to a different attribute and colour, as follows, again from the top: A *milieu*, environment (green); B *esprit*, spirit or mind (blue); C *chair*, flesh (violet); D *fusion* (red); E *caractère* (clear); F *offre*, offering (yellow), and G *outil* or instrumentality (purple).

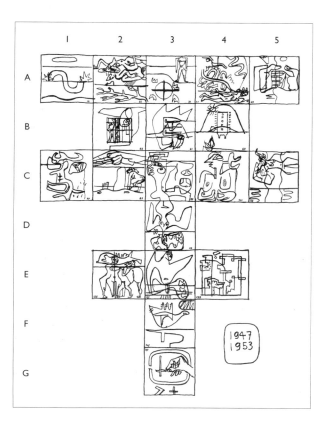

178. Iconostasis key to *Le Poème de l'Angle Droit*, 1953.

Incantatory and couched in rather cryptic language, the 'poem' unfolds its hermetic significance by opening with a five-square sequence representing the environment. It begins with the implacable law of the twenty-four-hour sun cycle as this varies from summer to winter (A1). The next image in this tier of Le Corbusier's iconostasis is the *aqua mercurialis* (A2),[31] represented as the ascent and descent of water in the earth's atmosphere due to the diurnal interaction between the ocean and the sun as this was first described as a cosmic revelation in Le Corbusier's *La Ville Radieuse* (p. 204). There follows in the central square (A3) the Mercurial image of Le Corbusier's Modulor Man standing erect (as a right angle) before the alchemical *rota* or wheel representing the four seasons. This synthetic icon is followed by a square representing the law of the meander (A4), demonstrating the principle by which the truth lies between two banks, as Le Corbusier had remarked while flying over Brazil. This may be seen as an aqueous dialectic at a cosmic scale wherein a river finds its final bed across time by oscillating as a meander between two banks. This initial sequence representing the environment closes with the division of the sensate world into polar opposites signified by the interlaced fingers of two hands meeting (A5), thereby dividing the image into interdependent parts – left/right, sun/moon, male/female, day/night, and even architect/engineer.

179. *Le Poème de l'Angle Droit*, plate A3: Modulor Man before the wheel (*rota*) of the four seasons.

The next row, comprising three squares set symmetrically on the axis of the iconostasis, is dedicated to the life of the mind and the three canonical underlying precepts of Le Corbusier's architecture, respectively the Modulor number system (B2), the Five Points of a New Architecture (B3), and the crossover section of the Unité block together with its ideal orientation (B4). The variable play of the summer and the winter solstices across this section is depicted as being mediated by *brise-soleil*, which serve to protect the building from over-exposure to the sun. This interplay between light and shade is posed in B3 above an image of a diminutive black owl, a representation of the alchemical *nigredo* but also traditionally symbolic of wisdom and death. From the irregular black field surrounding the white-line image of the owl there emerges a tiny black image of Mercury as the Modulor Man. In the text which accompanies B4 the invention of the *brise-soleil* is seen as assuring the triumph of modern sun-responsive architecture over classicism. As Le Corbusier puts it, 'Et Vignole – enfin – est foutu! Merci! Victoire!' (And Vignola is finally screwed! Alleluia! Victory!).

180

The third tier down, dedicated to the body, consists of five images, all of which are erotic in character with the exception of the first (C1), which features the creation of a bull's head out of *objets à réaction poétique*, a pebble, a piece of wood and a side of beef. This panel, accompanied by a rather cryptic reference to Beelzebub as

180. *Le Poème de l'Angle Droit*, plate B3: Five Points of a New Architecture.

another incarnation of the alchemical demiurge, recalls Le Corbusier's exile in the Pyrenees during the occupation of France. That low moment in his life was ominously coloured by the necessity of having his dog (named Pinceau, 'paint brush') put to sleep. In the four squares that follow (C2–C5) this death appears to be redeemed through the female principle. The last panel (C5) features the horned human figure flying horizontally over the sea. In the single panel of the next tier, representing 'fusion' (D3), this image is rotated into a vertical position with its horn penetrating into the lower part of the square, which features the traditional alchemical male/female engaged in the creation of a hermaphroditic *rebis*.[32] Of this image Daphne Becket has written:

The D3 lithograph stands for the large ambitions expressed in the Poème, that of a creation of art that would transfigure society itself. Understood in this way, the copulating couple refers to the creative act, or fusion/conjunctio in alchemical terms... Most of Le Corbusier's icons express either of two states or conditions. They manifest either stability, balance and harmony or a form of violence. Fusion is clearly of the latter variety, although it ultimately produces peace and tranquillity. The psychology is interesting here, because one form of this violence is derived from a fatalistic interpretation of the battle of good and evil, the other is a cathartic process necessary to creation... In the text for D3, Le Corbusier uses the metaphor of the alchemist, in relation to his role as artist/architect, to carry his great aspirations... [33]

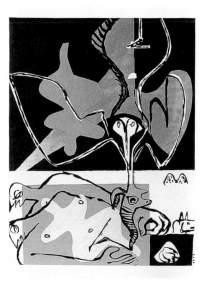

181. *Le Poème de l'Angle Droit*, Plate D3: Fusion. The inverted image of Capricorn descends to conjoin the hermaphroditic couple and the *rebis*.

According to Becket, the fifth tier, *caractère* (E), comprising three squares, is a major section in the lower half of the iconostasis. In the three squares Le Corbusier refers to himself, his design team and his wife, the last being the stabilizing complement of his own turbulent, creative temperament – his icono-*stasis*. This tier is followed by two single central panels one above the other: F, *offre,* and G, *outil.* Where F simply depicts the Open Hand 'from which to give and by which to receive', G shows another hand inscribing an ovular form, and within this image of the cosmic egg a cruciform intersection. This, needless to say, is the ultimate representation of the right angle, as an intersection of two opposed conditions, the horizontal and the vertical – the embodiment in fact of the alchemical *coincidentia oppositorum*. Here the right angle of the poem, as drawn by Le Corbusier's hand, is depicted as a prerequisite for the creation of a rational new condition, existing in harmony with the surrounding natural world.

Le Corbusier's alchemical poem exposes to arcane ends his compulsively gnostic habit of mind. It reveals more clearly than anything else why he always insisted that the secret of his architecture lay in his painting. It also accounts for the constant recurrence of number mysticism in his work: 'les cinq points d'une architecture nouvelle', 'les trois établissements humains', 'les quatre routes', 'les sept voies', etc. It further accounts for his invention of the Modulor as a harmonic alternative to the universal metric system of measurement. Derived from the Fibonacci series, the Modulor 'synthesized' two hitherto irreconcilable proportional systems – the side of a square first to its diagonal, and then to its Golden Section (1:1.618).[34]

While his post-Purist painting was never accepted as being of any artistic consequence by the Parisian curatorial élite – which accounts for Christian Zervos' damning review of Le Corbusier's 1953 retrospective exhibition staged in the Musée National d'Art Moderne[35] – it nonetheless pervaded his later work as a fertile *machine à métaphore*, enriching his architecture with a myriad of otherwise unimaginable formal-cum-metaphorical devices. Despite his overt rationalism and the generally liberative, even positivist character of the modern project as it passed through his hands, Le Corbusier was by no means alone amid the 20th-century avant-garde of the inter-war years in turning towards hermetic lore as an ultimate source of poetic inspiration, the other prime example in this regard being Marcel Duchamp, who, like Le Corbusier, admitted to dabbling in hermetic art without really 'knowing' it.[36]

Chapter 13   Fin d'un Monde: The Last Works 1939–1965

Whether it was derived from the European wartime ethos or not, there is something decisively existential about Le Corbusier's work and thought from the 1940s on. We may catch this mood in the cryptic, often self-deprecating aphorisms of his later years, his touching but sobering confession that every morning he feels as if he is waking up in the skin of a donkey, or the equally stoic existential aphorism that may be found in the text of *Le Poème de l'Angle Droit*, to the effect that one should do one's work in the bag of one's skin and give thanks to one's creator.

After the global disasters of the Spanish Civil War and the Second World War, when the previously assumed progressive benefits of the modern movement in all its aspects no longer seemed so self-evident, there emerged in Le Corbusier's *modus operandi* a decidedly stoic and somewhat improvised character. The confident, abstract, machine-age exuberance of his initial maturity now came to be overlaid with an expeditious archaism wherein the still manifest modern line was simultaneously suffused with the tactility of a reinterpreted vernacular. Nowhere was this existential spirit more evident than in the single-cell log cabin that he built at Roquebrune-Cap Martin in 1952 as a birthday present for his wife Yvonne Gallis, his so-called guardian angel identified as the mythical *Icône* in *Le Poème de l'Angle Droit*.

Five years later Le Corbusier was obliged to reorganize his atelier in response to the demands then being made by his more senior assistants, among them Tobito Acevido, André Maisonnier and Iannis Xenakis, all of whom had been with him since 1948. Feeling that they were insufficiently rewarded for all the responsibilities they assumed, these three were claiming higher salaries and, above all, seeking the right to sign drawings in their own names. Le Corbusier categorically rejected these demands, arguing that except for the association with his cousin he had always resisted any form of partnership. Thus towards the end of the August 1957 *vacances* he drafted a collective letter of dismissal. None of them received this, since he could not bring himself to send it; instead, he had the locks of his studio changed overnight, with the keys being issued only to faithful veterans such as Roger Andreini. A younger team was assembled, made up at the first level of responsibility

190

by Guillermo Jullian de la Fuente[1] from Chile and José Oubrerie[2] from Nantes, and at the second level by Alain Tavés, Pierre Paucheux and Robert Rebutato. The unsent notice of dismissal is of interest since it displays Le Corbusier's complex feelings about the limits of apprenticeship and more especially his recognition of the process by which one generation succeeds another. Entered with the incidental annotation 'Train Bleu, arrivée Paris, 8½ h., 28 aôut', the draft of the letter reads:

Modern Architecture has triumphed in France, it has been adopted. You may today find there a testing ground for everything that you yourselves have acquired with your own hands and also for [that which] your work with me has afforded you.

I thus give you your liberty beginning September 1st. It is of course understood that I shall fulfil all legal obligations in your regard and those which stem naturally from friendship insofar as circumstances shall permit me.

You have completed one phase of your life [at] 35 rue de Sèvres. I am quite persuaded that in full maturity you will make a brilliant career like all those who have preceded you here and who have made their own life.[3]

One of the first moves of the reconstituted atelier would be to recast the free-standing *palazzetto* model as it had been reformulated in Le Corbusier's post-war career first in Dr Curutchet's town house built in La Plata, Argentina, in 1949 and then in the Millowners' Association Building realized in Ahmedabad in 1954. The Curutchet house and doctor's office is the first domestic work in which the outer prismatic form of the envelope is established by a *brise-soleil* screen while the inner volume is activated by a ramp that passes through the main body of the space, which here takes the form of an atrium. It may also be seen as a frontalized transposition of the Villa Baizeau at Carthage of 1928. Once again it is possible to trace a 'genealogy' running through Le Corbusier's work, for whereas the Curutchet house conceals the activating ramp that will play a more visible and dynamic role five years later, it already displays a crowning canopy over its roof terrace, which, first deployed in the Villa Baizeau, would come to play such a salient role in the post-war work, not only in India, as we have seen, but also in the Carpenter Center for the Visual Arts at Harvard University, first projected in 1961 and realized some three years later in collaboration with Jullian de la Fuente and the Catalan émigré architect José Luis Sert. However, what had been the diminutive interlocking binary forms of the toilets in the Millowners' Association Building

171

182,
183

are now inflated as a plan configuration capable of incorporating the inner cube of the building on both sides. The Carpenter Arts Center may also be seen as adapting the breeze hall of the Millowners' Building, only now this feature becomes little more than a ramped aperture for the passage of pedestrians up and down from Quincy and Prescott Streets on the opposite sides of the building. This second-floor passageway, set at an angle to the surrounding street grid, gives access to the lung-like studio wing and orthogonal exhibition space as these are projected towards the Fogg Museum and the Harvard Faculty Club on either side.[4]

The resulting orthogonal/organic dialogue, constrained in Ahmedabad, was rendered more obtrusive at Harvard, asserting its dichotomous nature at every turn. The orthogonal format of the inner cube was thus offset by the push and the pull of the wings 'dilated', as it were, by the thrust of the pedestrian ramp passing between them. As with the breeze hall at Ahmedabad, the ramped passageway is the heart of the building from which all the other functions are variously distributed, with administrative and

182. Carpenter Center for the Visual Arts, Harvard University, Cambridge, Mass., 1961–64.

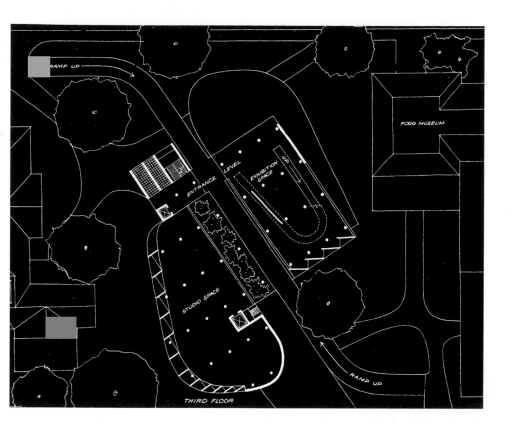

183. Carpenter Center for the Visual Arts: project site plan.

academic uses being relegated to the ground floor and the basement accommodating a lecture hall. A crowning top floor terminates the composition, both formally and symbolically, first through restating the form of the cube and second by incorporating a penthouse/atelier and a roof garden for the artist in residence. Departing from the orthogonality of the classical prism, but still committed to the Purist spirit, the Carpenter Arts Center seems to have been a link between the turbulence of Ronchamp (1955) and the more mediated plasticity of Le Corbusier's penultimate projects of the early 1960s: the church at Firminy, a computer centre for Olivetti, and a congress hall for Strasbourg.

Le Corbusier's rejuvenated atelier would soon start to work on another equally dualistic proposition, namely a reinterpretation of the lenticular double parasol roof first devised for the exhibition pavilions projected for Liège and San Francisco in 1939 (p.150) and reworked as a folded plate roof form for a pavilion at the Porte Maillot, Paris, in 1950. The paradigm would be returned to in 1962 as a double-square *yin-yang* folded concrete plate umbrella roof over a

146

161

187

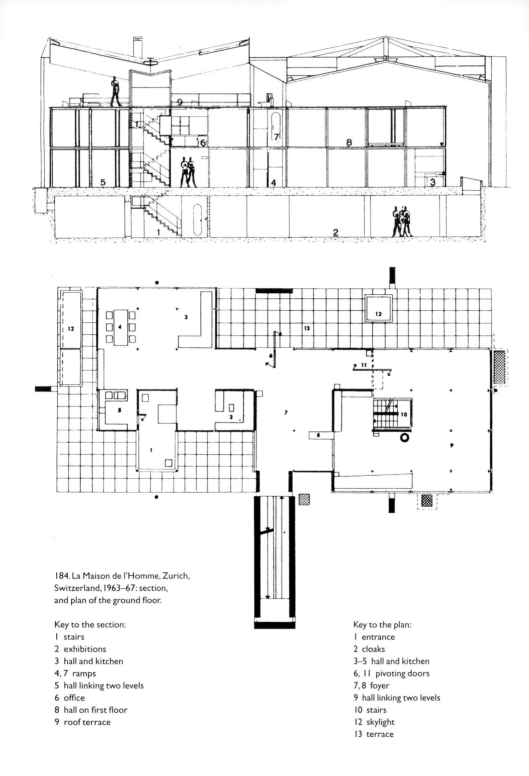

184. La Maison de l'Homme, Zurich,
Switzerland, 1963–67: section,
and plan of the ground floor.

Key to the section:
1 stairs
2 exhibitions
3 hall and kitchen
4, 7 ramps
5 hall linking two levels
6 office
8 hall on first floor
9 roof terrace

Key to the plan:
1 entrance
2 cloaks
3–5 hall and kitchen
6, 11 pivoting doors
7, 8 foyer
9 hall linking two levels
10 stairs
12 skylight
13 terrace

Stockholm art gallery projected for the Swedish collector Theodor Ahrenberg. Stubbornly pursued as a unique typological/tectonic concept for twenty-five years, the double-parasol pavilion would finally be realized in 1967 after Le Corbusier's death as Heidi Weber's 'Maison de l'Homme' on the lake front in Zurich. In this instance the *yin-yang* folded plates, sloping alternately up and down towards the perimeter, were made of sheet metal and supported by hollow steel columns on one axis and by steel tubes on the other. The parasols were stiffened by horizontal girders and separated from each other by a narrow interstitial bay. The pavilion beneath the double roof was a modular panel system in steel, first envisaged in 1949 and based on a cubic unit measuring 2.26 metres (7 ft 5 in.) on its sides. Influenced by Jean Prouvé's lightweight constructional systems, Le Corbusier attempted to employ the same cruciform section throughout as a kind of universal four-way joint; a proposition that proved difficult to achieve, given that the same structural section had to serve equally well in both a vertical and a horizontal direction.

184, 185

185. La Maison de l'Homme, Zurich.

Another highly plastic work, started just prior to his death, was a proposal for the French Embassy in Brasilia, a project which depended, as far as the chancellery was concerned, on a proposition that he had previously made but never realized for cylindrical residential towers in the projects for Strasbourg and Marseilles-Sud dating from 1951. The problem at Brasilia was how to arrange for the orthogonal subdivision of a cylindrical volume that was faced on the periphery with *brise-soleil*. Extended as partition walls in depth (thereby creating rooms), the *brise-soleil* also served as a common exterior treatment, thereby unifying the eight-storey cylindrical chancellery with the orthogonal four-storey ambassadorial residence. The combination of a cylinder and a parallelepiped provided an occasion for reworking a site-planning strategy that he had first deployed at the Villa Stein de Monzie. In the embassy project the two volumes were linked by a fluid, dynamically contoured landscape treatment, reminiscent of the work of Roberto Burle Marx. Wide ramped aprons descended from the raised ground floor of the ambassador's residence to provide a monumental approach to the entrance on one side and a private sun terrace on the other.

One of the most remarkable works to come from the atelier during the last five years of Le Corbusier's life was the Olivetti Electronic Centre, projected for Rho-Milan during the years 1962–64. Like the Carpenter Arts Center realized around the same time, this project had a dynamically plastic character, which was partly inspired by the exit and access ramps necessary to connect it to the Milan–Turin *autostrada*. Conceived as an urban mega-form, and in that regard reminiscent of the Plan Obus for Algiers of 1932, the Olivetti Centre assumed the shape of a low, pinwheeling orthogonal matrix from which various forms seemed to be thrown off in different directions. Once again the complex was fed by ramped pedestrian walkways emerging out of the terraced parking area. The continuously sloping pedestrian access system fed into different auxiliary uses on the raised ground floor (restaurant, electronic museum, etc.) while culminating in three amoeba-like cloakroom units on the laboratory roof. Each of these was divided into two segments, where men and women showered and changed into sterilized clothing. These changing facilities served as 'valves' by which to maintain the sterilized status of the clean areas below. The laboratory roof was projected as having an ingenious section that comprised V-shaped, long-span concrete beams filled with earth in order to sustain a roof garden, plus monitor lights set between the beams illuminating the laboratories below. The entire complex was crowned by two free-standing ten-storey slabs containing research offices, one of which was straight and the other partially curved.

92

186. French Embassy, Brasilia, Brazil, 1964: model. The ambassador's residence is in the foreground, facing the swimming pool; the chancellery is to the rear.

187. Olivetti Electronic Centre, Rho-Milan, Italy, 1962–64: roof-top plan of laboratories with cloakroom access and service manifold above.
1 entrance ramp
2 corridor
3 cloakrooms and showers
4 stairs down to laboratories

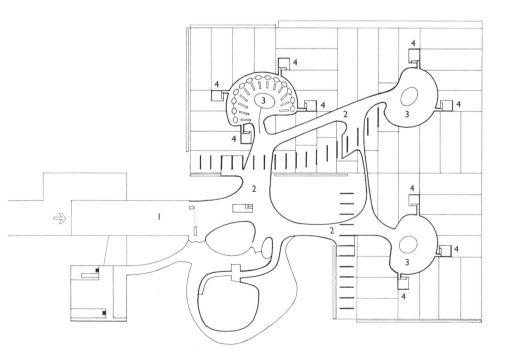

Le Corbusier's 1964 competition entry for a Congress Hall in Strasbourg led him to develop the spatial potential of continuously inclined surfaces further. The project comprised a bulky prism, intercepted by a wide ramp throughout its volume. Inspired by the work of Oscar Niemeyer, it was perhaps the most Brazilian building of his career, as evident from the freely planned floors that provided not only for a number of meeting rooms of varying size but also for a free-flowing foyer containing among other facilities a tourist office, a bank, a post office, a library, and a discotheque. The uppermost level would have accommodated two auditoria, of 300 and 1,000 seats respectively, while the ramped access itself ended in an inclined roof. This last, rendered as a *res publica*, was focused about an amphitheatre and an acoustical pylon, which, as at Ronchamp and La Tourette, was conceived as broadcasting electronic music.

During the very last year of his life Le Corbusier worked in close association with Guillermo Jullian de la Fuente and José Oubrerie, most particularly on a project for a hospital in Venice dating from 1964. Here he elected to interpret the hospital as a 'city in miniature', basing its modular order on the grain of the city and giving it a low profile in order to respond to the height of the surrounding fabric. Thus its 1.2-metre (4 ft) wide internal corridors conformed to the width of the average Venetian street, while even the nursing stations for each ward cluster recalled the diminutive *campi* that punctuate the Venetian fabric at regular intervals. Of this infrastructure Le Corbusier wrote:

188. Hospital, Venice, Italy, 1964: model.

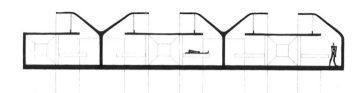

Each patient has a 'unité lit' at his disposal. This module of 3 by 3 metres [10 x 10 ft] is a unit in which the sick person is provided the best possible conditions in which to stay. The unit is provided with movable panels which permit, once closed, total isolation for bedside care. When these panels are open, according to the position in which the patient is placed, he benefits from a new perspective, for example the view of other units and of the medical hall arranged for that effect, with its interplay of natural lighting, etc.

It is anticipated for each 'unité lit' that there will be a glassed opening 3 metres by 1 metre [10 ft x 3 ft 4 in.], placed above a ceiling 2.26 metres [7 ft 5 in.] high. The glassed opening would not be visible to the patient, but would project natural light on a curved wall 3.66 metres [12 ft] high, located in front of it, which gives pleasant reflected light for the patient in bed.

A coloured panel placed on the outside of the unit gives colour to the reflected light, of an intensity which varies with the different times of day. These panels will be of different colours, creating variety for the different units. At the same time, the arrangement permits an exact control over the intensity of the light. All these factors are correlated to the psychological importance of colour on the spirits of the patients.[5]

It seems prophetic, given the imminence of Le Corbusier's death, that the figures of the patients stencilled on the drawings should have resembled Egyptoid homunculi lying on mortuary slabs. Le Corbusier's alter ego, the Modulor Man, was depicted in these renderings as a mortally wounded hero, suspended between life and death on the edge of the Lagoon and subject all the while to the therapeutic effect of colour and indirect light.

Organized on four levels, the 1,200-bed hospital was structured about an intricate system of circulation in which the first elevated level provided for entry, plus the administration and basic services; the second housed the operating suites and the nurses' accommodation; and the third was a ramped mezzanine system, giving access to patients' cells set at the topmost level. These cells were organized into fourteen wards, with a single central access corridor for each ward. As Le Corbusier's report indicated, one of the most dynamic aspects of the design was the provision of sliding walls that

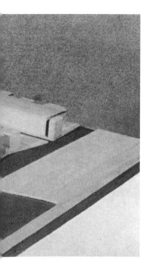

189

enabled each cell to be either isolated from or united with the neighbouring cells.

Regrettably, like most of his late projects, the Venice hospital remained unrealized. It is symptomatic of Le Corbusier's capacity for self-renewal that it seems to have been inspired by a design of one of his former assistants, the American architect Shadrach Woods. Like Woods's 1963 four-storey gridded proposal for the Free University of Berlin, the layered, carpet-like structure of the Venice hospital was to have been pierced by six courtyards in order to provide adequate light and air to the lower floors. Envisaged as being built partially on the land and partially in the water, it was inflected by two exceptional elements: by a bridge linking across a canal to a separate pediatric wing, and by a pier, accommodating a chapel and a mortuary, jutting out into the Lagoon.

The intensity and virtuosity of the architectonic microcosms that were proposed during the last two years of Le Corbusier's life remain as remarkable today as when they first appeared. Except for Louis Kahn, there is perhaps no other architect of the 20th century whose creative capacity increased rather than diminished during the final period of his activity. By engaging the imagination of the rising generation, Le Corbusier afforded them the opportunity to create under his leadership. Thus both Jullian de la Fuente and Oubrerie were able to play fertile roles in many of his last works, so that while Jullian made the running in the Carpenter Arts Center and the Brasilia embassy and Oubrerie carried the church at Firminy, both assumed a certain level of joint responsibility for the Venice hospital.

Le Corbusier's interest in hyperbolic paraboloids, dating from his first direct contact with the work of Antoni Gaudí in 1932, remained with him throughout his career and culminated not only, as we have seen, in such works as the Philips Pavilion but also in his penchant for catenary suspension systems, as we find these in the roof of the youth and cultural centre at Firminy (1960–65) and in the art school designed for Chandigarh in 1963 but not completed until 1969, four years after his death. Where the art school, with its short-span, in-situ concrete floors, used the catenary cables as permanent reinforcement, the hyperbolic roof at Firminy was built up out of pre-cast concrete panels laid on top of the catenary cables.

While it is not, chronologically speaking, a final work, Le Corbusier's single-cell vacation cabin at Roquebrune-Cap Martin (1952) is certainly some sort of last will and testament, since no work of his post-war career represents such a simple condensation of his thought. This diminutive monopitched *cabanon* – of framed construction, lined in plywood and designed to be clad in metal sheet, which was replaced at a late stage by a revetment of half-round logs – seems to have come into being almost as an afterthought in relation to two other structures that happened to be situated on virtually the same narrow precipitous site, isolated by the Nice–Ventimiglia railway on one side and by the Mediterranean on the other. Here in 1949, while staying in Eileen Gray's house, E1027, with a study team that had come to work with him on the master plan for Bogotá,[6] Le Corbusier met Thomas Rebutato, the future proprietor of a small tavern ('L'Étoile de Mer') to be built on the same site. The result of this encounter was not only the building in 1952 of Le Corbusier's vacation cabin, next to Rebutato's tavern, but also the realization in 1957 of Rebutato's *unité de camping*. This took the form of a modest, monopitched terrace of five timber-framed single-cell vacation dwellings, elevated on a concrete substructure. Each one of these rental units was to all intents and purposes a variation on the *cabanon*, with each cell accommodating two beds, a desk, a wash-hand basin and a closet within a 3.66 x 2.26-metre (12 ft x 7 ft 5 in.) plan.

The *cabanon* itself was ingeniously arranged within a square measuring 3.66 x 3.66 metres (12 x 12 ft), with a corridor 70 centimetres (c. 28 in.) wide on one side. It was organized geometrically

190. Cabanon, Roquebrune-Cap Martin, 1952.

in plan on the basis of four interlocking 226 x 86-centimetre (7 ft 5 in. x 2 ft 10 in.) rectangles spiralling about a central square measuring 86 centimetres (2 ft 10 in.) on its sides. While the arrangement of the furniture did not always accord with this underlying geometry, the implicit zones allocated to day and night use and the pinwheel placement of the windows corresponded to a helicoidal organization of the space. This particularly applied to the location and size of the windows, which were harmoniously dimensioned and judiciously placed so as to afford different views of the exterior. Thus a 33 x 70 centimetre (13 x 28 in.) window, set low over a bed, afforded an inland view from a corner of the north-east façade, while two 70 x 70 centimetre (28 x 28 in.) windows set above table-top height had views to the south-east and south-west respectively, with the latter affording a panoramic view over the distant bay below. Each window closed in a slightly different way, with the opening to the north-east being a single panel, side-hung, the one to the south-east having two side-hung leaves, and the one to the south-west being closed and/or augmented by a sliding/folding double-panelled shutter, lined on its inner face by a mirror, positioned so as to reflect the view when open.

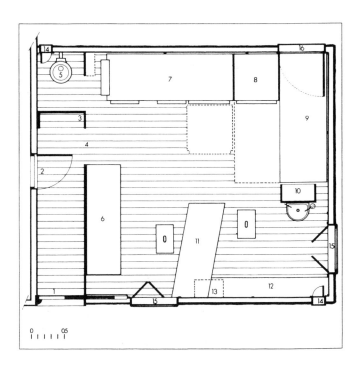

191. Cabanon, Roquebrune-Cap Martin, 1952: plan.
  1 entrance
  2 door to the restaurant 'L'Étoile de Mer'
  3 coats
  4 entrance to cabin
  5 WC
  6 cupboard
  7 bed
  8 low table
  9 bed
  10 'sanitary column' with washbasin
  11 table
  12 low shelf
  13 shelf
  14 vertical louvers
  15 window 70 x 70 cm
  16 window 33 x 70 cm

The *cabanon* was a brilliant exercise in the modulation of microspace, where each gesture of daily life found its corresponding piece of equipment or furniture, pitched at just the right height, width and scale to suit its optimum use within an extremely restricted space. Thus the beds were originally set at right angles to each other, with storage drawers beneath. The toilet was situated in the northern corner, screened from the entry hall by a light wall for hanging coats, while the so-called *colonne sanitaire*, with a stainless steel washbasin attached, was in the southern corner. Of all this Bruno Chiambreto has written:

In the first sketch for the cabanon, *a plan, not a single traditional element of architecture is represented: only pieces of furniture are indicated. At this stage of the project, they are the sole means of characterizing the space or the spaces of the* cabanon, *and only the placing of the furniture allows one to perceive the limits and the partitioning of the habitable volume. As a direct translation of the programme, the furniture here constitutes the first form by which the object comes into being.*[7]

It was perhaps symptomatic of his lifelong preoccupation with dwelling that the building of 'le petit cabanon' at Roquebrune should coincide with the creation of the Unité d'Habitation at Marseille in 1952. On the one hand one witnesses the quintessential primitive hut revisited in mid-20th-century terms, on the other the sole full-scale realization of Le Corbusier's Fourierist utopia, with a full range of social services, built as a self-contained but readily repeatable unit for future urbanization; in the first instance the most modest *Existenzminimum* imaginable for someone of Le Corbusier's stature; in the second, an invention that if it had been generally adopted and progressively refined from one prototype to the next, at varying scales, could have done much to ameliorate the tentacular megalopolitan urbanization that has engulfed the world at a cataclysmic scale over the last half-century. The gulf between the all but apostolic poverty of Le Corbusier's own vacational requirements and the profligate waste and pollution of industrial civilization clearly underlay much of the bitterness and rancour that inform the last text of his life, the anecdotal, somewhat rambling *Mise au point* (Into Focus) written at different times and recombined into various draft versions over the years 1960–65.

As Ivan Žaknić has pointed out in his illuminating study of the text and the circumstances attending its compilation, *Mise au point* is not a polished work, and since it was edited and published by Jean Petit in 1966[8] we have reason to doubt that the order of the fragments from which it is composed would have satisfied Le Corbusier had he lived to edit the final version. Moreover, as Žaknić remarks, 'Petit's *Le Corbusier lui-même* (1970) contains embedded pieces of *Mise au point*, and given his constant editorial presence during Le Corbusier's final years, it might be difficult to confirm a primary author for *Mise au point*.'[9]

Nevertheless, *Mise au point* is the closest that Le Corbusier ever came to writing an autobiography, and here we find, mixed with apocalyptic insight and stoic resignation, his understandable indictment of the irrational environmental policies pursued by modern society, be it pre- or post-industrial. After castigating the overblown character of the CNIT exhibition hall completed at La Défense, Paris, in 1958 to the designs of Bernard Zehrfuss and Jean Prouvé, Le Corbusier went on to condemn the maximization of modern technique, particularly where such technology displayed little regard for basic human needs or for the fundamental limits of an anthropomorphic scale. From the CNIT with its gargantuan scale he rapidly turned to the 'fiasco' that attended the realization in New York of the UN building, which, had it been detailed by himself or by Oscar Niemeyer, would have had the curtain wall of its secretariat slab protected by *brise-soleil*. From this complaint we find him shifting into a general lament for the lost promise of the machine-age civilization:

Everything became so confused after the wars of '14 and '39 that we lost our minds! Laissez-faire, lack of conscience, and carelessness overflowed. Sprawling cities were born, developed, and reached their apogee; a scandal, a disaster. Here New York, twelve million inhabitants; here London, ten million; and here is Moscow which is already at five million... This year, 1961, Paris is gloriously arriving at eight million inhabitants! It's done, they let it happen. Someone should have rung the alarm in time... But no one did![10]

As we have already observed, Le Corbusier's panacea for such chaos had been his book *The Three Human Establishments* of 1945, above all the strategy of deploying linear industrial cities to link up and augment existing radio-concentric cities of exchange, while preserving within the interstices of the resulting triangular infra-structure pockets of pre-industrial agricultural settlement. Evidently the Unité d'Habitation, standing free amid greenery, was an essential corollary of this concept, since it was one of the few housing paradigms available that would have been capable of dealing with the population explosion without destroying the pre-industrial landscape.

Alternately ironic, critical, self-pitying, pessimistic and bombastic, *Mise au point* nonetheless made it clear that for Le Corbusier nothing was capable of transcending the limits of individual existence but the work of the mind. As he put it July 1965, in anticipation of his own demise:

Nothing is transmissible but thought. Over the years a man gradually acquires through his struggles, his work, his inner combat, a certain capital, his own individual and personal conquest. But all the passionate quests of the individual, all that capital, that experience so dearly paid for, will disappear. The lair of life: death. Nature shuts off all activity by death. Thought alone, the fruit of labour, is transmissible. Days pass, in the stream of days, in the course of a life... At the age of 32, I was with the Esprit Nouveau, out of fervent conviction, loyalty, temerity, but also courage, accepting all risks. At 32 I wrote Towards a New Architecture, *a clear affirmation of a vision of reality (risks included), when the roots were being put down... Youth is toughness, intransigence, purity. Yet the spring stretches, has stretched. That is man's fate, his destiny. From childhood to the age of thirty what an intense uproar, what schemes, what accomplishments! He never knew, the little fellow. He went his way, the same way one sees ranks of boys (with their crew cuts) in Paris, going to the swimming pool with their class in the morning, or to the seashore on vacation, an intensity in their gestures, their remarks, their looks, their walk, the friendly gestures towards their friends. How much will remain of this vast potential, of so much purity?*[11]

Much of the same spirit obtains in a recorded interview that Le Corbusier gave to Hughes Desalle in May 1965, wherein he seems to embody the spirit of Rabelais and Cervantes, the two writers to whom he was inordinately attached, the one for his rebellious humour and audacity, the other for his image of Don Quixote as the ill-fated idealist at odds with history, whose grand aspirations were forever destined to fail and whose indomitable spirit would only be sustained through the ministrations of his all too pragmatic Sancho Panza; a figure that Le Corbusier readily associated with Pierre Jeanneret. Before Desalle's patient questioning Le Corbusier is by turn informative, testy, forgetful, vain, self-mocking, congenial, critical, and even at times still characteristically optimistic, particularly with regard to what was then the apparent willingness of the city of Venice to realize his hospital. And it was the fate of this last project that remained undecided when he walked down into the sea off Roquebrune for the last time on the morning of 27 August 1965 to fulfil his own dictum that in the end 'everything returns to the sea'.[12]

Notes

For details of works cited in abbreviated form, see the Bibliography (pp. 234–35).
O.C. = Oeuvre complète

Chapter 1 (pp. 8–19)
1 See Brooks, Formative Years, pp. 371–72 and 408–9. Jeanneret would, however, have seen Garnier's utilitarian buildings on a visit to Lyons in 1912.
2 Turner, Education of Le Corbusier, pp. 5, 6 and fig. 1.
3 Petit, Le Corbusier: Lui-même, p. 28.
4 See Brooks, Le Corbusier's Formative Years, p. 157.
5 Petit, Le Corbusier: Lui-même, p. 38.
6 Gresleri, Viaggio in Oriente, p. 45.
7 Le Corbusier, Towards a New Architecture, p. 206.
8 ibid., p. 101.
9 See Gresleri's entry on Ritter in Le Corbusier: une encyclopédie, pp. 349–50.
10 Turner, Education of Le Corbusier, p. 93.
11 ibid., p. 87.
12 Moos, Elements of a Synthesis, pp. 17–29.
13 See in particular the banded horizontal first-floor fenestration of Wright's Winslow (1893) and McAfee (1894) houses.
14 Contrary to subsequent interpretations, it now seems that this panel was to have been decorated. See Brooks, Formative Years, pp. 459–61.
15 It is interesting to note that the term 'tracés régulateurs' is taken from Auguste Choisy's Histoire de l'architecture, a copy of which Le Corbusier bought in 1913. See Brooks, Formative Years, pp. 444–49.
16 The house was to be fully documented with construction photographs in L'Esprit Nouveau, 6, 1921, except for the principal façades that were published somewhat anonymously two years later, in the section dealing with 'Les tracés régulateurs' in Vers une architecture.

Chapter 2 (pp. 21–45)
1 This was the title of Vers une architecture (1923) when it was translated into English by Frederick Etchells in 1927.
2 Brooks, Formative Years, p. 473.

3 See Taylor, Le Corbusier at Pessac, I, p. 15. Taylor argues that the system of demountable formwork for the Domino structure derived from a 1912 pamphlet of the American Portland Cement Association.
4 O.C. 1910–1929, p. 85.
5 Le Corbusier, Towards a New Architecture, pp. 242, 243.
6 Petit, Le Corbusier: Lui-même, p. 52.
7 L'Esprit Nouveau, 1, 15 Oct. 1920, p. 3.
8 R. H. L. Herbert, Modern Artists on Art, Englewood Cliffs, N.J., 1904, pp. 61, 62.
9 For the general rappel à l'ordre after the 1914–18 war see Kenneth Silver, 'Esprit de Corps: The Great War and French Art 1914–25', PhD thesis, Yale University, 1981.
10 See Le Corbusier, Après le cubisme, p. 57.
11 Le Corbusier, City of Tomorrow, p. 22.
12 Le Corbusier, Towards a New Architecture, p. 153.
13 ibid., p. 269.
14 Walter Gropius wrote two essays in the Deutsche Werkbund yearbooks on this theme: 'Die Entwicklung Modernes Industriebaukunst' (1913) and 'Die Stilbildende Wert Industrielles Bauformen' (1914). The second was accompanied by other articles on industrial design illustrated with photographs of locomotives, aircraft, automobiles and ships.
15 Le Corbusier, Towards a New Architecture, p. 92.
16 I am alluding to Marcel Duchamp's coinage of the term 'readymade' which first appeared with his Bottle Dryer of 1914.
17 Le Corbusier, 'Pour ne pas dire Citroën', in Vers une architecture, p. 200.
18 See O.C. 1910–1929, p. 31.
19 Around 1906, under the influence of the theatrical reformer Adolphe Appia, the Suisse-Romande composer Émile Jaques-Dalcroze transformed his concept of eurythmical training into a therapeutic art form. Albert Jeanneret seems to have become involved with the Jaques-Dalcroze method at its inception in Geneva in 1906, whereupon he gave up music in favour of teaching dance.
20 Benton, Villas of Le Corbusier, p. 70.
21 Le Corbusier, Almanach d'architecture moderne, p. 158.
22 See C. Courtiau on Pierre Jeanneret in Le Corbusier: une encyclopédie, pp. 213–16.

23 See the special commemorative issue of Aujourd'hui, Art et Architecture, 51, Nov. 1965, p. 10.
24 Benton, Villas of Le Corbusier, p. 37.
25 See Serenyi, 'Le Corbusier, Fourier and the Monastery of Ema', pp. 277–86.

Chapter 3 (pp. 46–57)
1 The City of Tomorrow is the title of the English version of Le Corbusier's Urbanisme of 1925, translated by Frederick Etchells and first published by John Rodker, London, 1929.
2 See Le Corbusier, Voyages d'Allemagne.
3 Brooks, Formative Years, pp. 368–70.
4 Le Corbusier, Towards a New Architecture, p. 59.
5 See Bruno Taut's Architektur-Schauspiel für symphonische Musik and his Die Auflösung der Städte, Hagen, 1920. Both books were in Le Corbusier's library.
6 O.C. 1910–1929, pp. 118–19.
7 R. Banham, Theory and Design in the First Machine Age, London, 1960, p. 253.
8 A. Sutcliffe, Towards the Planned City, Oxford, 1981, p. 171. See also P. M. Wolf, Eugène Hénard and the Beginning of Urbanism in Paris 1900–1914, The Hague, 1968.
9 Le Corbusier, Radiant City, p. 168.
10 Passanti, 'The Skyscrapers of the Ville Contemporaine', pp. 53–65.
11 Le Corbusier, Radiant City, pp. 133–34.
12 ibid., p. 132.
13 Cohen, Le Corbusier and the Mystique of the USSR, pp. 140–42. Pidoux's book, published in 1928 under the title La Science des plans de villes, was written in collaboration with Adolphe-Augustin Rey and Charles Barde.

Chapter 4 (pp. 59–69)
1 Le Corbusier, Decorative Art of Today, p. 75.
2 ibid., p. 76.
3 Loos, 'Die Abschaffung der Möbel', 1924, in Trotzdem, Sämtliche Schriften, I, p. 390.
4 Le Corbusier, Decorative Art of Today, p. 76.
5 ibid., pp. 77, 79.
6 Loos, 'Ornament and Crime', in The Architecture of Adolf Loos, London, 1987, p. 103.
7 Le Corbusier, Zodiac, 7, 1960, p. 57.
8 Arthur Ruegg, 'Équipement', in Le Corbusier: une encyclopédie, pp. 134–35.
9 Perriand, Un Art de vivre, Paris, 1985, p. 27.

Chapter 5 (pp. 70–87)

1 Le Corbusier, *Vers une architecture*, p. 96.
2 Loos's system of *Raumplan* or 'space-planning' depended, unlike Le Corbusier's *plan libre*, on sectional displacement. The term *Raumplan* was first coined by Heinrich Kulka, Loos's biographer.
3 Le Corbusier, *Précisions*, p. 134.
4 See Le Corbusier, 'Où est l'Architecture?', *L'Architecture vivante*, Autumn–Winter 1927, p. 25.
5 *O.C. 1910–1929*, p. 89.
6 *O.C. 1929–1934*, p. 24.
7 *O.C. 1910–1929*, p. 128. Le Corbusier characterizes the sliding window as 'l'élément mécanique-type de la maison'.
8 B. Reichlin, 'The Pros and Cons of the Horizontal Window: The Perret–Le Corbusier Controversy', *Daidalos*, 13, Sept. 1984, pp. 71–82.
9 Rowe, 'Mathematics', pp. 101–4; also Rowe, *Mathematics*, pp. 1–17. Judging from an exchange of correspondence between P. Morton Shand and Le Corbusier, it would seem that Le Corbusier acknowledged the viability of this critical comparison. (Rowe refers to the Villa Stein as the Villa Garches, which was the received usage in English criticism in the late 1940s and early 1950s.)
10 C. Rowe and R. Slutzky, 'Transparency: Literal and Phenomenal', *Perspecta 8*, 1963, pp. 45–54.
11 *O.C. 1929–1934*, p. 130.
12 Le Corbusier, *Une Maison, un palais*, p. 97.
13 R. Middleton, 'The Abbé de Cordemoy and the Graeco-Gothic Ideal: A Prelude to Romantic Classicism', *Journal of the Warburg and Courtauld Institutes*, V, 25, nos. 3–4, July–Dec. 1962.
14 Rowe and Slutzky, 'Transparency: Literal and Phenomenal', *Perspecta 8*, 1963, p. 53.
15 R. Quincerot, 'Palais des Nations', in *Le Corbusier: une encyclopédie*, pp. 285–86.
16 G. Ciucci, 'Premier congrès: Les acquisitions de l'architecture moderne', in *Le Corbusier: une encyclopédie*, pp. 88–90. See also J. Gubler, *L'Age de Homme*, Lausanne, 1975, pp. 145–61.
17 C. Courtiau, 'Paul Otlet', in *Le Corbusier: une encyclopédie*, pp. 278–79.
18 Teige, 'Mundaneum', *Oppositions*, 4,

Oct. 1974, p. 91 (transl. by L. and E. Holovsky of the original article published in *Stavba*, VII, 1929, p. 145).

Chapter 6 (pp. 88–115)

1 See Sigmund Freud, *Civilization and its Discontents*.
2 See J. Andel, 'The 1920s: The Improbable Wedding of Constructivism and Poetism', in *The Art of the Avant Garde in Czechoslovakia 1928–1938*, Valencia, 1993, pp. 21–60.
3 Cohen, *Le Corbusier and the Mystique of the USSR*, p. 44.
4 'La famine en Russie', *L'Esprit Nouveau*, 16, May 1922.
5 El Lissitzky first wrote to Le Corbusier in March 1924, but their cordial relations were short-lived. Prior to this the trilingual Constructivist magazine, *Vesch, Gegenstand, Objet*, edited by Ilya Ehrenburg and El Lissitzky, had published in its third issue in 1922 a number of pieces taken from *L'Esprit Nouveau*.
6 Cohen, *Le Corbusier et la mystique de l'URSS*, p. 29. For English translations of Malevich's essays see Troels Anderson, ed., *K. S. Malevich: Essays on Art*, II, Copenhagen, 1971.
7 Cohen (cit. at n. 3), p. 42.
8 ibid., p. 79.
9 Le Corbusier, *Précisions*, pp. 46, 48.
10 Cohen (cit. at n. 3), p. 146.
11 *L'Architecture vivante*, Autumn–Winter 1932, p. 26.
12 *O.C. 1929–1934*, p. 129.
13 C. Lodder, *Russian Constructivism*, New Haven/London, 1983, pp. 50–53.
14 Taylor, 'Piuttosto visionario…', p. 61.
15 Cohen (cit. at n. 3), pp. 88–92.
16 See Sumi, *Immeuble Clarté*.
17 For the sketches, see Sketchbook B4; for Josephine Baker, Petit, *Le Corbusier: Lui-même*, p. 68. Petit maintains that Le Corbusier first met Josephine Baker in Latin America on a coaster, the S.S. *Giulio Cesare*. See also *Le Corbusier: une encyclopédie*, pp. 59, 95.
18 See Moos, 'Urbanism and Transcultural Exchanges', p. 227.
19 Cf. Yona Friedman's 'Paris Spatial' proposal of 1958 and N. J. Habraken's concept of 'Supports', 1972.
20 Moos, 'Le Corbusier as Painter', p. 89. Moos cites Rafi, 'Le Corbusier et les Femmes d'Alger', p. 58.
21 McLeod, 'Le Corbusier and Algiers', p. 63.

22 M. Tafuri, 'Machine et mémoire: The City in the Work of Le Corbusier', in Brooks, *Le Corbusier*, pp. 209–11.
23 Le Corbusier, *Aircraft*, p. 12.
24 See H. Arendt, *The Human Condition*, Chicago, 1958, p. 262: 'we have found a way to act on earth and within terrestrial nature as though we dispose of it from the outside, from the Archimedean point'. Archimedes asserted that, given a big enough lever, balanced on a point outside the earth, we could move the planet.
25 Le Corbusier, *Aircraft*, p. 123.
26 Le Corbusier, *L'Art Décoratif d'aujourd'hui*, pp. 54–57.
27 *O.C. 1934–1938*, pp. 66–67.
28 See Moos, 'Urbanism and Transcultural Exchanges', in *Le Corbusier*, ed. Brooks, p. 231.
29 Giordani in *Le Corbusier: une encyclopédie*, p. 402.
30 Petit, *Le Corbusier Parle*, p. 48.

Chapter 7 (pp. 116–129)

1 McLeod, *Urbanism and Utopia*, p. 68.
2 Le Corbusier, *Towards a New Architecture*, pp. 288–89.
3 The two met through the architect Jean Walter and his wife. After splitting from George Valois, Lamour founded the neo-Saint-Simonian review *Grande Route*.
4 Alexander von Senger, anti-Semitic Swiss architect and author of the politically conservative tracts *Krisis in der Architektur* (Crisis in Architecture, Zurich, 1928) and *Le Cheval de Troie du bolchévisme* (The Trojan Horse of Bolshevism, Bienne, 1931). The other main critic from the extreme right was Camille Mauclair, who wrote in 1933 his anti-Corbusian tract, *L'Architecture va-t-elle mourir? La crise du panbétonisme intégral* (Is Architecture going to die? The crisis of exposed concrete).
5 Sorelian editor of *Mouvement Socialiste* and author of *Le Socialisme ouvrier* (1911), Lagardelle believed in regional autarchy as opposed to centralized parliamentary democracy.
6 Pierrefeu was a graduate of the École Polytechnique, a hydraulics engineer, and a pioneer aviator. After 1922 as director of a prominent civil engineering concern he built a number of hydroelectric dams in Algeria and Morocco. See the entry by Rémi Baudoui in *Le Corbusier: une encyclopédie*, p. 308.

7 Dr Winter was an ear, nose and throat surgeon. See the entry by Rémi Baudoui in *Le Corbusier: une encyclopédie*, p. 478.

8 Le Corbusier, 'La Guerre? Mieux vaut construire', *Plans*, 6 Jan. 1931, pp. 65–67.

9 Valois called for the abdication of parliament and a national-socialist dictatorship. See R. Fischman, *Urban Utopias in the Twentieth Century*, New York, 1977, pp. 223–24.

10 Pierrefeu, *Le Corbusier et Pierre Jeanneret*, 1930.

11 *Préludes, thèmes préparatoires à l'action*, 16 issues, 15 Jan. 1933–July/August 1936.

12 As a committed communist, Moussinac seems to have been opposed to Le Corbusier throughout the 1920s and 1930s. See J.-L. Cohen, 'Droite–gauche: invite à l'action', in *Le Corbusier: une encyclopédie*, pp. 309–13.

13 See Catherine Courtiau on Pierre Jeanneret in *Le Corbusier: une encyclopédie*, pp. 213–15.

14 The Third Republic, founded in 1870, became particularly factional in the inter-war period, there being 44 governments and 20 different prime ministers between 1918 and France's defeat in 1940.

15 *La Maison des hommes*, pp. 30, 32.

16 ibid., p. 194. Pierrefeu refers to the need to establish an equilibrium between the nano-planning of the state, the mores of the region, and the interests of the corporation of trades unions. He writes: 'the law giver [by which he means the architect] stands at the heart of the national doctrine of the "built domain" [*domaine bâti*], like a referee, you might say, between geography and the activities of man.'

17 One assumes that this was a self-conscious allusion to the Soviet concept of the 'general line'.

18 *La Maison des Hommes*, p. 204. Pierrefeu alludes directly in this final paragraph to Le Corbusier's split image of the sun (Apollo) and Medusa that occurs on the facing page in the French version of the text.

19 See entries by Patrice Noviant in *Le Corbusier: une encyclopédie* on ASCORAL (pp. 50–51) and *Les Trois Établissements humains* (pp. 414–17).

20 André Boll and his brother Marcel (a doctor) had been totally won over to Le Corbusier's world view in the early 1930s. See the entry by Rémi Baudoui in *Le Corbusier: une encyclopédie*, p. 77.

Chapter 8 (pp. 131–149)

1 *O.C. 1929–1934*, p. 48.

2 ibid., p. 52.

3 Based on Reinhold von Lichtenberg's reconstruction in *Haus, Dorf, Stadt, eine Entwicklungs-Geschichte des antiken Stadtbilder*, Leipzig, 1909. See Saddy, 'Temple Primitif', p. 40.

4 *O.C. 1934–1938*, p. 125.

5 There were other equally provocative statements throughout, such as 'Le paradoxe c'est la permanence de la notion romaine de propriété' (What is paradoxical is the survival of the Roman notion of property) and 'Tuer l'argent est la condition primordiale d'une mise en ordre du monde actuel' (Killing money is the precondition for reordering the present world).

6 *Ilôt insalubre* is a term still used to classify an unsanitary group of buildings bounded by streets or alleys. As late as 1925 only one-third of the dwellings in Paris were connected to the public sewers.

7 Le Corbusier, *Des canons, des munitions?*, p. 26.

8 *O.C. 1934–1938*, pp. 156–57.

9 Le Corbusier, *Modulor 2* (transl.), pp. 111, 112.

10 See Stirling, 'From Garches to Jaoul'.

Chapter 9 (pp. 150–166)

1 Serenyi 1975, p. 110.

2 *O.C. 1946–1952*, p. 194, retranslated.

3 Serenyi 1967/75.

4 *O.C. 1952–1957*, p. 180.

5 Curtis, *Le Corbusier: Ideas and Forms*, p. 174.

6 Siedlung Halen was the first major work by a group of neo-Corbusian architects who had been trained in the office of Hans Brechbuhler, one of Le Corbusier's assistants in the inter-war era.

Chapter 10 (pp. 167–183)

1 *O.C. 1952–1957*, pp. 24–36.

2 Interview between DANIÈLE Pauly and Canon Ledeur, March 1974. Cited in Pauly, *Ronchamp*, p. 59.

3 ibid., p. 60.

4 *Ozon* referred to the village in the Pyrenees where Le Corbusier remained in isolation with his wife Yvonne from 1940 to 1943. *Ubu* testifies to Le Corbusier's identification with the figure of Père Ubu, taken from Alfred Jarry's sardonic play *Ubu Roi* of 1909.

5 Pauly, *Ronchamp*, pp. 34, 36.

6 Rowe, 'La Tourette', pp. 188, 194.

7 Henze, *La Tourette*, p. 69.

8 Xenakis, 'La Tourette', p. 147.

9 See Treib, *Space Calculated in Seconds*. In addition to Xenakis and Varèse, Treib remarks on the essential roles played by Philips's art director, Louis Kalff, and by Hoyte Duyster, the structural engineer and builder, not to mention the film-maker Philippe Agostini. Jean Petit was charged with gathering the images for Le Corbusier and Agostini with preparing them for projection.

10 Eardley and Oubrerie, *Le Corbusier's Firminy Church*, figs. 44, 33.

11 As he explained to Jean Petit, 'I am not a churchgoer myself but one thing I do know is that every man has a religious consciousness of belonging to a greater mankind, to a greater or lesser degree, but in the end he is part of it. Into my work I bring so much effusion and intense inner life that it becomes something almost religious'; Petit, *Le Corbusier*, p. 183.

Chapter 11 (pp. 184–199)

1 See *Le Corbusier Sketchbooks*, II, p. 330.

2 Prasad, 'Le Corbusier in India', p. 279.

3 The idea of the neighbourhood unit, comprising housing, shops, parks and schools, had first been advanced by Clarence Perry in his Forest Hills Gardens, built on Long Island, N.Y., in 1913. See Evenson, *Chandigarh*, p. 114, n. 55.

4 See *Le Corbusier Sketchbooks*, II, drawings 362, 363, English translation pp. 30, 31.

5 Evenson points out that 800 metres separate the Louvre from the Place de la Concorde, the Place de la Concorde from the Place Clémenceau and, on the cross-axis, the Madeleine from the Chambre des Députés: *Chandigarh*, p. 99.

6 Le Corbusier, 'L'Espace indicible', pp. 9–17.

7 *O.C. 1952–1957*, p. 78.

8 For Le Corbusier and the image of the open hand, see below, p. 206.

9 Constant, 'Virgilian Dream', p. 86.

10 ibid.

11 Prasad, 'Le Corbusier in India', p. 302.

12 ibid., p. 300.

13 'La journée solaire de 24 heures est la mesure de toutes les entreprises urbanistiques.' For the first appearance of this icon, see *O.C. 1934–1938*, p. 25. For a full analysis of the iconography of the door, see M. Krustrup, *Porte Email*, Copenhagen, 1991 (published in three languages under the subtitles *Emaljeporten*, *La Porte émaillée*, *The Enamel Door*).
14 Curtis, *Le Corbusier: Ideas and Forms*, p. 191.

Chapter 12 (pp. 200–213)
1 See Oechslin, *Wettbewerbsprojekt*, p. 49; also Frampton, 'Le Corbusier's Designs', pp. 57, 58.
2 Petit, *Le Corbusier: Lui-même*, p. 35.
3 See J. E. Circlot, *A Dictionary of Symbols*, London, 1962, pp. 87–89.
4 M. Heidegger, 'Who is Nietzsche's Zarathustra?', in *The New Nietzsche*, ed. D. B. Allison, New York, 1977, pp. 64–79 (originally published in German in 1961). Of this double image of the eagle with the snake around its neck, Heidegger writes: 'In this mysterious embrace we already have a presentiment of how circle and ring are implicitly entwined in the circling of the eagle and the winding of the snake. So this ring, called *annulus aeternitatis*, sparkles: the seal ring and year of eternity.'
5 Amédée Ozenfant, *Mémoires 1886–1962*, Paris, 1965, p. 113.
6 C. G. Jung, *Psychology and Alchemy*, London, 1953. See Moore, 'Alchemical and mythical themes'. In his essay, Moore remarks that Jung's work, which first appeared in 1944, was accompanied by a renewed interest in the myth of the mother goddess and the primordial child. There are many French texts that may have influenced Le Corbusier in this regard, including René Guenon's *La Grande Triade* (1946) and Paul Senard's *Le Zodiaque* (1948).
7 For Le Corbusier and the double see J. P. Robert, 'Pseudonymes', in *Le Corbusier: une encyclopédie*, pp. 316–17.
8 Le Corbusier signed his paintings 'Jeanneret' until 1928, 'Le Corbusier' thereafter.
9 See F. Schulze, *Mies van der Rohe, A Critical Biography*, Chicago, 1985.
10 Petit, *Le Corbusier: Lui-même*, p. 22.
11 ibid., p. 23.
12 From a conversation with the author.

13 It was Jerzy Soltan who first told me at a seminar at Princeton University in the mid-1960s of Le Corbusier's desire to die while swimming for the sun.
14 Le Corbusier, *Radiant City*, pp. 77–78.
15 Le Corbusier, *New World of Space*, p. 33.
16 See *Fernand Léger, La poésie de l'objet, 1928–1934*, Centre Georges Pompidou, Paris, 1981.
17 See *Paris 1937–1957*, Centre Georges Pompidou, Paris, 1981, p. 207.
18 P. Sekler, 'Ruskin, the Tree and the Open Hand', in Walden, *Open Hand*, pp. 61–89. For Ruskin's influence on Le Corbusier, see also Gresleri, *Viaggio in Toscana*, p. 132.
19 Sekler (cit. at n. 18), p. 74.
20 ibid., p. 77.
21 ibid., p. 75.
22 Moos, 'Le Corbusier as Painter', pp. 88–107; also Rafi, 'Le Corbusier et les Femmes d'Alger', pp. 58–61.
23 Rafi, op. cit.; and see Papadaki, *Le Corbusier*, pp. 128–32.
24 See *Les Tapisseries de Le Corbusier*. From 1949 to 1956, Pierre Baudouin worked closely with Le Corbusier to produce more than 40 tapestries.
25 Moos, 'Le Corbusier as Painter', p. 93.
26 In the alchemical procedure, the *nigredo* is characterized as a phase of putrefaction in which opposites are dissolved. See S. Klossowski de Rola, *The Secret Art of Alchemy*, London, 1973, p. 10.
27 A line from Stéphane Mallarmé's 'Autre éventail de Mademoiselle Mallarmé': Moos, *Elements of a Synthesis*, p. 291.
28 Becket, 'Poème de l'Angle Droit', pp. 39, 50.
29 The goat is the interpretation advanced by Richard Moore ('Alchemical and Mythical Themes'); the unicorn is the thesis preferred by Daphne Becket ('Poème de l'Angle Droit'), who believes that the feminine French noun for unicorn, *licorne*, has an implication of female gender.
30 See Moore, 'Alchemical and Mythical Themes', p. 135.
31 ibid., pp. 135–36.
32 J. F. Moffitt, 'Marcel Duchamp: the Alchemist of the Avant Garde', in *The Spiritual in Art: Abstract Painting 1890–1985*, ed. M. Tuchman, New York, 1986, p. 259.

33 See Becket, 'Poème de l'Angle Droit', pp. 44, 45.
34 Le Corbusier, *The Modulor*, pp. 15–68. See also *Modulor 2* (transl.), pp. 44–59.
35 Zervos, 'Expositions'.
36 Moffitt (cit. at n. 32), p. 269. In 1959, Duchamp remarked: 'If I have practiced alchemy, it was in the only way it can be done now, that is to say without knowing it.' Duchamp contended that in a secular society such as ours, the true knowledge of alchemy had been irrevocably lost.

Chapter 13 (pp. 214–229)
1 Jullian de la Fuente first entered Le Corbusier's atelier in July 1958.
2 Oubrerie, who had begun his artistic career as a painter, first came in contact with Le Corbusier in 1958 while working on the construction site of the Pavillon du Brésil in the Cité Universitaire, and started as an assistant in the studio in the following year.
3 *Le Corbusier Sketchbooks*, IV, p. 420 (Sketchbook 58).
4 Colquhoun, 'Formal and Functional Interactions'.
5 *O.C.: Last Works*, pp. 134–35.
6 This group comprised amongst others José Luis Sert, Paul Lester Meiner, and Le Corbusier's old mentor William Ritter.
7 Chiambreto, *Cap Martin*, p. 38.
8 Petit, *Le Corbusier, Mise au point*.
9 Žaknić, *Final Testament of Père Corbu*, p. 2.
10 ibid., p. 93.
11 ibid., p. 87.
12 *O.C.: Last Works*, p. 173. This phrase comes from the first paragraph of 'Rien n'est transmissible que la pensée', which seems to have been another draft of *Mise au point*. Swimming against his doctor's advice, he died of a heart attack in the sea. This brought him close to his ideal of dying while swimming for the sun expressed in a casual conversation with André Maisonnier. See Žaknić, *Final Testament of Père Corbu*, pp. 60–81, p. 164, n. 127.

Bibliography

By Le Corbusier

• indicates an English translation of a work originally published in French

Aircraft, London, 1935
Almanach d'architecture moderne, Paris, 1926
Après le cubisme (with A. Ozenfant), Paris, 1918
L'Art Décoratif d'aujourd'hui, Paris, 1925 [Engl.: see The Decorative Art of Today]
• The City of Tomorrow [Urbanisme, transl. F. Etchells], London, 1929
• Concerning Town Planning [Manière de penser l'urbanisme], London, 1948
• The Decorative Art of Today [L'Art décoratif d'aujourd'hui, transl. J. Dunnett], Cambridge, Mass., 1987
Des Canons, des munitions! Merci! Des Logis... S.V.P., Boulogne-sur-Seine, 1938
'L'Espace indicible', L'Architecture d'aujourd'hui, special number, 1946
L'Esprit Nouveau, nos. 1–28, 1920–25
• The Four Routes [Les Quatre Routes], London, 1947
• The Home of Man [La Maison des hommes, transl. C. Entwistle and G. Holt], London, 1948
• Journey to the East [Voyage d'Orient, transl. I. Žaknić in collaboration with N. Pertuiset], Cambridge, Mass., 1987
La Maison des hommes (with F. de Pierrefeu), Paris, 1942 [Engl.: see The Home of Man]
Une Maison, un palais: À la recherche d'une unité architecturale, Paris, 1928
Manière de penser l'urbanisme, Paris, 1946 [Engl.: see Concerning Town Planning]
Mise au point [Engl.: see Žaknić, The Final Testament of Père Corbu]
Le Modulor, Paris, 1948
• The Modulor [transl. P. de Francia and A. Bostock], London, 1961/ Cambridge, Mass., 1968
Modulor 2, Paris, 1955
• Modulor 2 [transl. P. de Francia and A. Bostock], London, 1958/ Cambridge, Mass., 1968
New World of Space, New York, 1948
Le Poème de l'Angle Droit, Paris, 1989
Précisions sur un état présent de l'architecture, Paris, 1930
• Precisions on the Present State of Architecture and City Planning [transl.

E. S. Aujame], Cambridge, Mass., 1991
Quand les cathédrales étaient blanches, Paris, 1937 [Engl.: see When the Cathedrals were White]
Les Quatre Routes, Paris, 1941 [Engl.: see The Four Routes]
• The Radiant City [La Ville Radieuse, transl. P. Knight et al.], London, 1964
'Tapisseries Muralnomad', Zodiac, 7, 1960, pp. 57–65
• The Three Human Establishments [Les Trois Établissements humains], Chandigarh, 1976
• Towards a New Architecture [Vers une Architecture, transl. F. Etchells], London, 1927
Les Trois Établissements humains, Paris, 1945 [Engl.: see The Three Human Establishments]
Urbanisme, Paris, 1925 [Engl.: see The City of Tomorrow]
Vers une architecture, Paris, 1923 [Engl.: see Towards a New Architecture]
La Ville Radieuse, Paris, 1935 [Engl.: see The Radiant City]
Voyage d'Orient. Carnets 1–6 (facsimile), New York, 1988 [Engl.: see Journey to the East]
Les Voyages d'Allemagne. Carnets 1–4 (facsimile), New York, 1995
• When the Cathedrals were White [Quand les cathédrales étaient blanches, transl. F. E. Hyslop], London/Cornwall, N.Y., 1947

The Le Corbusier Archive
32 vols of drawings in the Fondation Le Corbusier, Paris, ed. H. Allen Brooks, New York, 1982

Le Corbusier: Oeuvre complète
Published in Zurich in 8 vols, all of which have been translated into English and other languages. The first 4 feature the work of Le Corbusier and Pierre Jeanneret; the last 4 cover the work of Le Corbusier alone. Reissued in 1995 as a boxed set under the title Le Corbusier: Complete Works 1910–1969.
I, 1910–1929, 6th edn, ed. W Boesiger and O. Stonorov, 1956
II, 1929–1934, 5th edn, ed. W. Boesiger, 1952
III, 1934–1938, 6th edition, ed. M. Bill, 1958
IV, 1938–1946, ed. W. Boesiger, 1946
V, 1946–1952, 3rd edn, ed. W. Boesiger, 1953
VI, 1952–1957, ed. W. Boesiger, 1957

VII, 1957–1965, ed. W. Boesiger, 1965
VIII, Last Works, ed. W. Boesiger, 1970

Le Corbusier Sketchbooks
Published in 4 vols (ed. A. Wogensky and F. de Franclieu, with introduction by M. Besset), Cambridge, Mass./New York, 1981: I, 1914–48; II, 1950–54; III, 1954–57; IV, 1957–1964.

About Le Corbusier

Le Corbusier: une encyclopédie, ed. J. Lucan, Paris, 1987
Becket, D. 'A Study of Le Corbusier's Poème de l'Angle Droit', MPhil thesis, Cambridge University, 1980
Benton, T. The Villas of Le Corbusier 1920–1930, New Haven/London, 1987
Besset, M. Qui est Le Corbusier?, Geneva, 1968
Bloc, A., P. Lacombe and P. Goulet, eds special commemorative issue of Aujourd'hui, Art et Architecture, no. 51, Nov. 1965
Brooks, H. A., ed. Le Corbusier's Formative Years, London/Chicago, 1997
— , ed. Le Corbusier, Princeton, N.J., 1987
Chiambreto, B. Le Corbusier à Cap Martin, Paris, 1987
Cohen, J.-L. Le Corbusier et la mystique de l'URSS, Liège, 1987
— Le Corbusier and the Mystique of the USSR, Princeton, N.J., 1992
Colquhoun, A. 'Formal and Functional Interactions: A Study of Two Late Works by Le Corbusier', in Essays in Architectural Criticism: Modern Architecture and Historical Change, Cambridge, Mass., 1985
Constant, C. 'From the Virgilian Dream to Chandigarh: Le Corbusier and the Modern Landscape', in Denatured Visions: Landscape and Culture in the Twentieth Century, ed. S. Wrede and W. H. Adams, New York, 1991
Curtis, W. Le Corbusier: Ideas and Forms, New York/London, 1986
Eardley, A., and J. Oubrerie Le Corbusier's Firminy Church, IAUS Catalog 14, New York, 1981
Evenson, N. Chandigarh, Berkeley, Calif., 1966
— The Machine and the Grand Design, New York, 1969
Frampton, K. 'Le Corbusier's Designs for the League of Nations, the Centrosoyuz and the Palais des Soviets,

1926–31', in Le Corbusier, ed. Brooks

Gans, D. The Le Corbusier Guide, New York, 1987

Gresleri, G. Il Viaggio in Toscana, Venice, 1987

— and I. Zannier Le Corbusier Viaggio in Oriente, Gli inediti di Charles Edouard Jeanneret, fotografe e scrittore (Fondation Le Corbusier, Paris), Venice, 1984

Gubler, J. 'In Time with the Swiss Watchmakers', in Le Corbusier, Early Works by Charles-Édouard Jeanneret, London, 1987, pp. 121–27

Harris, E. Le Corbusier, Riscos Brasileiros, São Paulo, 1987

Henze, A. La Tourette, London, 1966

Lapunzina, A. Le Corbusier's Maison Currutchet, New York, 1997

McLeod, M. 'Le Corbusier and Algiers', Oppositions, 19–20, Winter–Spring 1980

— 'Architecture or Revolution: Taylorism, Technocracy and Social Change', Art Journal, summer 1983, pp. 132–47

— 'Urbanism and Utopia, Le Corbusier From Regionalism to Vichy', PhD thesis, Princeton University, 1985

Maier, C. S. 'Between Taylorism and Technocracy: European Ideologies and the Vision of Industrial Productivity in the 1920s', Journal of Contemporary History, 5, 1970, pp. 27–61

Moore, R. 'Alchemical and mythical themes in the poem of the Right Angle, 1945–1965', Oppositions, 19–20, Winter–Spring 1980, pp. 111–39

Moos, S, von Le Corbusier, Elements of a Synthesis, Cambridge, Mass., 1979

— 'Urbanism and Transcultural Exchanges, 1910–1935: A Survey', in Le Corbusier, ed. Brooks

— 'Le Corbusier as Painter', Oppositions, 19–20, Winter–Spring 1980

— , ed. L'Esprit Nouveau. Le Corbusier und die Industrie 1920–1925, Berlin, 1987

Oechslin, W., ed. Le Corbusier & Pierre Jeanneret. Das Wettbewerbsprojekt für den Völkerbundspalast in Genf, Zurich, 1988

Papadaki, S. Le Corbusier. Architect, Painter, Writer, New York, 1948

Passanti, F. 'The Skyscrapers of the Ville Contemporaine', Assemblage, 4, 1987

Pauly, D. Ronchamp: lecture d'une architecture, Paris, 1979

— Le Corbusier: The Chapel at Ronchamp, Basel, 1997

Petit, J. Le Corbusier: Lui-même, Geneva, 1970

— , ed. Le Corbusier, Mise au point, Paris, 1966

— , ed. Le Corbusier Parle, Paris, n.d [c. 1966]

Pierrefeu, F. de Le Corbusier et Pierre Jeanneret, Paris, 1930

Prasad, S. 'Le Corbusier in India', in Le Corbusier Architect of the Century, London, 1987

Rafi, S. 'Le Corbusier et les Femmes d'Alger', Revue d'histoire et de civilisation du Maghreb, 4, Jan. 1968

Reichlin, Bruno 'The Pros and Cons of the Horizontal Window: The Perret–Le Corbusier Controversy', Daidalos, 13, Sept. 1984

Rowe, C. 'The Mathematics of the Ideal Villa', Architectural Review, CI, no. 603, March 1947

— The Mathematics of the Ideal Villa and Other Essays, Cambridge, Mass., 1976

Saddy, P. 'Temple Primitif et Pavillon des Temps Nouveaux', in Le Corbusier le passè à réaction poétique, Paris, 1987

Sbriglio, J. Unité, Marseille, Marseilles, 1992

Sekler, E. F., and W. Curtis Le Corbusier at Work: The Genesis of the Carpenter Center for the Visual Arts, Cambridge, Mass./London 1978

Sekler, M. P. M. The Early Drawings of Charles Édouard Jeanneret, 1902–1908, New York, 1977

Serenyi, P. 'Le Corbusier, Fourier and the Monastery of Ema', Art Bulletin, XLIX, 1967, pp. 277–86; reprinted in P. Serenyi, ed., Le Corbusier in Perspective, Englewood Cliffs, N.J., 1975

Stirling, J. 'From Garches to Jaoul, Le Corbusier as domestric architect in 1927 and in 1953', Architectural Review, CXVIII, Sept. 1955

Sumi, C. Immeuble Clarté, Genf 1932, Zurich, 1989

Les Tapisseries de Le Corbusier, Paris, 1975

Taylor, B. B. Le Corbusier at Pessac, Cambridge, Mass., 1972

— 'Piuttosto visionario…', Rassegna, 3 (I clienti de Le Corbusier), Milan, 1979

— Le Corbusier: The City of Refuge, Paris 1929/1933, Chicago/London, 1980

Treib, M. Space Calculated in Seconds: The Philips Pavilion, Le Corbusier, Edgar Varèse, Princeton, N.J., 1996

Turner, P.V. The Education of Le Corbusier, New York, 1977 (PhD, Harvard, 1971)

Vogt, A. M. Le Corbusier, The Noble Savage, Cambridge, Mass., 1998

Walden, R., ed. The Open Hand, Essays on Le Corbusier, Cambridge, Mass., 1977

West, J. P. III Four Compositions of Le Corbusier, n.p. [the author], 1967

Xenakis, I. 'The Monastery of La Tourette', in Le Corbusier, ed. Brooks

Žaknić, I. The Final Testament of Père Corbu [Mise au point, transl. and interpreted by I. Ž.], New Haven/London, 1997

Zervos, C. 'Expositions: Le Corbusier, Painter', Cahiers d'Art, I, no. 20, 1954

Acknowledgments

In addition to the indispensable scholarly entries that make up the remarkably comprehensive and detailed compendium *Le Corbusier: une encyclopédie* (1987), I would like to acknowledge the architectural historians, architects and critics who over the years have made an invaluable contribution to our understanding of this singular figure. Among these, I feel I owe a special debt to Jaroslav Andel, Roger Aujame, Daphne Becket, H. Allen Brooks, Bruno Chiambretto, Alan Colquhoun, Caroline Constant, William Curtis, Anthony Eardley, Norma Evenson, Deborah Gans, Jacques Gubler, Thilo Hilpert, Guillermo Jullian de la Fuente, Mogens Krustrup, Mary McLeod, Stanislaus von Moos, Werner Oechslin, José Oubrerie, Francisco Passanti, Danièle Pauly, Bruno Reichlin, Colin Rowe, Arthur Ruegg, Pierre Saddy, Jacques Sbriglio, Eduard Sekler, Patricia Sekler, Peter Serenyi, Robert Slutzky, Christian Sumi, Brian Brace Taylor, Anthony Vidler, Russell Walden, and Ivan Žaknić. I would like to express my particular gratitude to Jean-Louis Cohen, who, aside from his profound knowledge of Le Corbusier's relations with the Soviet Union, first commissioned the writing of this book. Acknowledgments are due to Ji-Hwan Park and Till Houtermans, who drew a number of illustrations specially for this volume, and to Aliki Hasiotis and Amanda Johnson who worked on various versions of the manuscript. I am particularly indebted to my editor at Thames & Hudson. Finally, I owe an exceptional debt to my family for bearing with me during the trials of bringing this text to fruition.

KF

For illustrations, the author and publishers are indebted to the following: AKG London/Walter Limot 1; W. Boesiger 190; Maurice Culot 138; William J. R. Curtis 9, 12; Lucien Hervé 70, 92, 118, 139, 171; Pierre Joly and Vera Cardot 59, 164; Baltazar Korab 182; Emily Lane 79, 84; J. Lotz 168; Jeet Malhotra 167; Mobilier National, Paris; photo P. C. Buer, Saint-Ouen 55; Bernhard Moosbrugger 147, 152, 157; Musée des Arts Décoratifs, © Éditions A. Lévy, Paris 33; ©Roger-Viollet 41, 160; after Colin Rowe and Robert Slutzky (cf. *Perspecta 8 The Yale Architectural Journal*, 1963) 72; A. Scarnati 133; L. Stynen,

Brussels 165; John Pettit West III (from his *Four Compositions of Le Corbusier*, 1967) 69, 172; and Éditions Hazan (who published *Le Corbusier* by Kenneth Frampton in 1997). Illustrations have also been drawn from *Oppositions* (© The Institute for Architecture and Urban Studies and The MIT Press) 5, 65.

© FLC/ADAGP, Paris and DACS, London 2001:

1; 2–7; 8 (*Carnet du voyage d'orient* No. 3, p. 123); 9; 13 [FLC 30075]; 14 [FLC 19209]; 15 [FLC 19131]; 16 [FLC L2(15)128]; 17 [FLC 18957]; 18 [FLC 19221]; 20–22; 24; 25; 26 [FLC 20208]; 27 [FLC L3(20)9]; 28 [FLC L2(12)120]; 29 [FLC L2(12)50]; 30; 32; 33; 34 [FLC 19083, 19082]; 35 [FLC L2(13)2]; 36 [FLC L2(13)5]; 37 [FLC B2(15)20]; 38 [FLC 30849]; 39 [FLC 29711]; 40 [FLC 31006]; 41 [FLC L3(20)1]; 43; 44 [FLC L2(14)46]; 45 [FLC 24909]; 46–48; 49 [FLC L2(7)5.27]; 50 [FLC FLC L2(7)5.5]; 51; 52 [FLC L2(7)5.19]; 53; 54 [FLC L2(5)7.1]; 55 [FLC 12]; 56; 57; 58 [FLC 31525]; 59; 60 [FLC 8301, 8293, 8295,]; 61 [FLC 8309]; 62 [FLC L1(6)17]; 63 [FLC L1(10)25]; 64 [FLC 10454]; 66 (right); 67 [FLC 19423]; 68 [FLC L1(7)101]; 70 [FLC L3(18)90]; 71 [FLC 23230]; 73 [FLC 23177]; 74; 75; 76; 77 [FLC L4(4)180]; 78 [FLC L3(19)15]; 80; 81; 82 [FLC 2725 1]; 83 [FLC 27249]; 84; 85 [FLC L2(8)22]; 86 [FLC 15328, 15322]; 87 [FLC 13351]; 88; 89; 90 [FLC L5(2)20]; 91 [FLC 32091]; 92 [FLC L1(1)63]; 93 [FLC 14345]; 94; 95 [FLC 30296]; 96–99; 100 [FLC L2(14)32]; 101 [FLC 24146]; 102 [FLC B3(3)268]; 103 [FLC B3(3)200]; 104 [FLC B3(3)283]; 105 [FLC B3(3)243]; 106 [FLC 28619]; 107 [FLC L3(20)60]; 108 [FLC 18238]; 109 [FLC 18252]; 110 [FLC 8982]; 111 [FLC 8980]; 112 [FLC L2(19)16]; 113 [FLC L1(1)104]; 114 [FLC 9249]; 115 [FLC L1(6)146]; 116 [FLC L2(13)75]; 117 [section FLC 633]; 118 [L2(13)102]; 119; 120 [FLC 29995]; 121 [FLC 19368]; 122 [FLC 11(15)443]; 123; 125; 127 [FLC B2(6)257]; 128; 129; 130 [FLC 13973]; 131 [FLC L1(1)6]; 133 [FLC L4(5)5]; 134; 135 [FLC L1(12)53]; 136; 137; 138 [FLC L1(11)13]; 139 [FLC L1(15)89]; 140–143; 145 [FLC 7125]; 146 [FLC L3(2)88]; 148 [FLC 7191]; 149–151; 152 [FLC L1(7)40]; 153 [FLC 1049]; 154 [FLC 1044]; 155; 156 [FLC L1(7)57]; 157; 158; 159; 160; 161 [FLC 16620]; 162; 163; 164; 166; 168; 169 [FLC 6989, 6994]; 171 [FLC L3(8)3]; 173 [FLC 23174]; 174–180; 181; 182; 183; 184; 185; 186; 187; 188; 189; 190 [FLC L3(5)7]; 191.

Index

Page numbers in *italic* refer to illustrations and their captions.

ABC Gruppe 85
Acevido, Tobito 214
Action Française 49
aérateurs 177
'Aérodomes' 48, 150
aeroplanes: C. and 51, 52, 64, 77, 90, 107, 110–11, *111*, 138, *140*, 172, 173, 203–4, *204*
Ahmedabad 193–99; houses 194, (Sarabhai) 193–94, *194*, (Shodhan) 194, *195*; Millowners' Association Building 193, 195–98, *196*, *197*, 215–16
Ahrenberg, Theodor 219
air-conditioning 101–2
Aix-en-Provence 167
Albigensians 202–3
alchemy 200–204, 208–13
Alfortville brickworks 21, 25
Algeria: C. and 109–10, *111*, 166, 208, *208*; *and see* Algiers; Nemours; Oued Ouchaia
Algiers *108*, 109–10, *115*, 121, 208, *208*, 221
The American Architect 112–13
Amsterdam South 48
Andernos 25
Andreini, Roger 214
Antwerp 56, 57, *57*, 72
Apollinaire, Guillaume 27
Après le cubisme 25, 27, 29
Arab architecture 73
Art Deco movement 33
L'Art Décoratif d'aujourd'hui 32, 59, *58*, 60, *61*, 61–62, 87, 90
Art Nouveau influence 9–10
Artsacré (magazine) 174
Arts and Crafts movement 10, 70, 71, 72, 206
Arts Décoratifs, Exposition (1925) 41, 59
ASCORAL 126–29
Association Art et Liberté 25
Association des Constructeurs pour la Rénovation Architecturale: see ASCORAL
ATBAT 161–62
ATBAT Afrique 162
Atelier 5 *166*, *166*
Atelier 35S 43, 59, 62, 63, 68, 84, 100–101, 103, 127–29, 142, 144, 203, 214–29
Atelier des Bâtisseurs: *see* ATBAT
Ateliers d'Art Réunis 12, *12*
Athens 13, *14*, 77; Charter 138, 141, 185–86
Aubert, Georges 17
Aujame, Roger 127, 129, *156*, 214

Badjara: *see* Oued Ouchaia
Badovici, Jean 207

Baizeau, Villa: see Carthage
Baker, Josephine 107, *107*
Banham, Reyner 51
Barcelona 57, 181
Barshch, Mikhail 97
Bata: work for 106, *106*, 137
Baumgart, Emilio 113
Beaudoin et Lods 127
Beck, Arnold 46
Becket, Daphne 212–13
Behrens, Peter 13, 17, 91, 200–201
Benoît-Lévy, Georges 116
Berlage, Hendrik Petrus 46, 48, 84
Berlin 12, 46, 200–201, 224; Unité 163, 164
Bern: Siedlung Halen 166, *166*
béton brut: see concrete
Bézard, Norbert 127, 129
Blanc, Charles 10
Blanchon, Georges 123
bloc à cellules 48, *48*, *50*, 51, 150–51
bloc à redents: see redents
Blum, Léon 121
Bodiansky, Vladimir 162
Bogotá 225
Boll, André 127
Bordeaux: Maison du Tonkin 22
Borie, Henry Jules 48, 150
Boulard, Paul (pseud. of C.) 29
Boulogne-sur-Seine: Maison Cook 45, 71–72, 73–77, *74*, *75*, 197; Lipchitz-Miestschaninoff double house 72
Brasilia: French Embassy 115, *220*, 220, 224
Brazil: C. visits 107, *107*, 113–15, *114*
Breton, André 204
Briand, Aristide 84
Bridgewater: CIAM Congress 129
Briey-en-Forêt: Unité 163, 164
brise-lumière 170
brise-soleil (sun-breakers) 113, *114*, 115, *115*, 153, 160, 162, 189, 191, 194, 198, 211, 220, 228
Broggi, C. 84
Brown-Boveri dynamo 62
Brussels: Maison Canneel 72; exhibition (1935) 68; Palais Stoclet 17, *17*, 36; Philips Pavilion 181–82, *181*, 224
Buenos Aires *112*; C. lectures 68, 71, 88
Burnet, John 84
Burnet Tait & Lorne 91
Burov, Andrei 89, *89*, 91
Cahiers d'Art 39
Cambridge, Mass.: Carpenter Center for the Visual Arts 195, 215–17, *216*, *217*, 224
Canneel, Maison 72
canons à lumière 179, *179*
Cap Martin 207, 207–8, 214, 224–27, 229, *225*, *226*
Caron, Julian (pseud. of Ozenfant) 29
Carré, Louis 142
Cartesian skyscraper 56, *57*, 100
Carthage: Villa Baizeau 71, 194, 195, 215
Carthusian monasteries 11, *11*, 12, 41, 47, 174, 176–77

Cassan, Urbain 127
Cathars 202–3
central heating 19
Centrosoyuz building: see Moscow
Cercle des Amis de *Plans* 121
Chandigarh 43, 184–94, *185*, 198–99; art school 224; Assembly 183, 187, *188*, 189–91, *190*, 193; Capitol 123, 184, 187–94, 206; Governor's Palace 187, 192, 193; High Court 187, 188, *188*, *189*, 193; Martyrs' Monument *188*, 193; the Open Hand 193, *193*, 206; 'peon's house' 186–87; Secretariat 187, 188, *188*, 191, *191*; Tour des Ombres 193; transport 186
Chapallaz, René 10, 18
Chareau, Pierre 103–6
Cherchell 143, *143*
Chiambreto, Bruno 227
Chicago 55–56
Chile: Maison Errazuris 131–33, *132*
churches 167–74, 179, 182–83
Church: library pavilion 62, 72
CIAM 84, 96, 129, 138, *140*, 141, 185–86
Cingria-Vaneyre, Alexandre 15, 16, 17
'Cité Mondiale' 85, *86*, 87, 113, 188
Citrohan, Maison 34–36, 35–36, 37, 41, 43, 72
Claudius-Petit, Eugène 162, 182
Concerning Town Planning: see *Manière de penser l'urbanisme*
concrete 24, 83, 98, 131, 164, 165, 169, 171, 177, 179, 182, 189–90, 193, 196, 198, 224, 225; reinforced 9, 11, 18–19, 21–22, 19, 35–36, 39, 45, 103, 137, 155, 157, 172–73, 177, 196, 217, 221, 224; shuttered (*béton brut*) 129, 146, 156, 162, 164, 169, 171, 192, 198; vaults 24, 35, 131, 137, 142, 186
Considérant, Victor 150
Constant, Caroline 193
La Construction des villes 13, 46
Constructivism 87, 88–89, 90, 95, 98
Cook, Maison 45, 71–72, 73–77, *74*, *75*, 197
Cordemoy, Abbé de 81
Costa, Lucio 113, *114*, 115
Couturier, Alain 174
Cresswell, Denise 123
Cristaller, Walter 149
Cubism 25, 28, 37, 79
Curutchet House 195, 215
curtain wall construction 56, 89, 100, 101–2, 106, 152, 177, 228
Curtis, William J. R. 198
Cuttoli, Marie 67, *67*, 207
Czechoslovakia: C. and 88–89, 106

Dadaism 31, 62, 89
Dautry, Raoul 116, 117, 155, 163
'Défense de l'architecture' 87
Delacroix, Eugène 207, 208
Dermée, Paul 25
Desalle, Hughes 229
Des Canons, des munitions? Merci! Des Logis... S.V.P. 120, *120*

Deutsche Werkbund 12, 13, 31, 46, 60, 200
Devětsil movement 88–89
Dom-ino system 18, *20*, 21–22, 35, 46
dom kommuna 151, 152, 161
Drew, Jane 185
Du Bois, Max 18, 21
Dubreuil, Hyacinthe 116–17, 127, 129
Duchamp, Marcel 62, 213

écoles volantes 144, 144–46
Eiffel, Gustave 31–32
Eisenstein, Sergei 91
Ema: Charterhouse 11, *11*, 12, 150, 174, 185–86
Engels, Friedrich 95
Engineer's Aesthetic 31, 32
L'Éplattenier, Charles 9–10, 11, 12, 13, 17, 46, 206
Errazuris, Maison 131–33, *132*
espace indicible 188
L'Esprit Nouveau (journal) 25–27, *26*, 32, 61, 88, 90, 119, 229
Esprit Nouveau, Pavillon de l' 37, 40–41, 41–42, 47, 52, 59, 62–63, 72, 73, 151–52
Étude sur le Mouvement d'art décoratif en Allemagne 12
eurhythmics 39, 46
Evreinov, Nikolai 97
Exposition d'Art dit 'Primitif' 142

façade libre (free façade) 72, 77, 79
Fallet, Villa 10, *10*
Fatehpur Sikri 195
Favre-Jacot, Villa 17
Fayet (pseud. of C.) 29
fenêtre en longueur 72, *74*, 75, 77
'Ferme Radieuse': see 'Radiant Farm'
Feuille d'Avis (paper) 13
Fibonacci series 213
Firminy-Vert: St-Pierre 182–83, *183*, 217, 224; Unité 163, 164
Fischer, Theodor 46
Fischer, Thomas 12
'Five Points of a New Architecture' 72–76, *74*, 93, 211, *211*
Flégenheimer and Nénot 84
'Four Compositions' 70, 70–79
Fourier, Charles 47, 150, 161
The Four Routes 146–47
'La France d'Outre-mer' exhibition 142
Freud, Sigmund 88
Freyssinet, Eugène 98, 131, 181
Frugès, Henri 22, *22*, 100, 101
Fry, E. Maxwell 185, 187
Fuchs, Josef 89
furniture, furnishings 59–69, 63–66, 68

Gahura, František 106
Gallis, Yvonne (wife of C.) 107, 208, 214
Gandhi, Mahatma 185, 186
Garches: Villa Stein de Monzie 33, 71, 72, 76–77, 75–79, 220
garden cities 22, 46, 49, 96, 117, 135, 184, 185

Garnier, Tony 8, 51, *51*, 55, 81, 150, 183
Gato, C. 84
Gaudí, Antoni 181, 224
Geneva: 'Cité Mondiale' and
  'Mundaneum' 85, *87*, 188; Immeuble
  Clarté 63, 101, *102*, 103, 106, 135;
  École des Beaux Arts 42; League of
  Nations building *80–83*, 81–85, 87,
  91, 93, *200*, 201–2; urbanism 57
Germany: C. visits 12–13, 46; garden city
  movement 46
Gesamtkunstwerk 59, 180, 182
Gilbert, Cass 55
Ginzburg, Moisei 90, 97, 106, 151, 161
Giordani, Jean-Pierre 115
glazing: double 19, *82*, 83, 103;
  ferro-vitreous 101; lenses *102*, 106;
  Centrosoyuz building 93, 103; Maison
  Citrohan 26, 35, 43; Immeuble Clarté
  103, 106; La Tourette 177; rue
  Nungesser-et-Coli (Porte Molitor)
  apartments 106
Golden Section 19, 45, 76, 79, 162, 180,
  213
Gorny, Sergei 96
graphics: C. and 27, 32–33
Grasset, Eugène 10, 11
Gray, Eileen 207, 224
Greece 13, 15, *15*
'Green Factory' 129, 147, 149
Grenoble 123
Gropius, Walter 31
Guadet, Julien 81
'La Guerre? Mieux vaut construire' 119

The Hague: Berlage plan 46, 48
hand motif *122*, 123, 193, *193*, 204–6
hanging gardens 41, *52*
Harding, Gérald 127, 129
Haussmann, Baron 47, 52, 55, 150
HBM (*habitations à bon marché*) 117
Hegemann, Werner 46
heliothermic considerations 56; *see also*
  brise-soleil
Hellerau garden city 46
Hénard, Eugène 46–47, 52
Hennebique, François 11
Henze, Anton 177
Hilberseimer, Ludwig 51
HLM (*habitations à loyer modéré*) 117
Hoesli, Bernard 77, 202
Hoffmann, Josef 11, 17, *17*, 18, 36, 84
Hoffmann, Ludwig 46
Horta, Victor 84
hospital project: *see* Venice
Hoste, Huib 57
housing: *bloc à cellules* 48, *48*, 51,
  150–51; *bloc à redents* 48, 51, 52, 55,
  56, 101, 109; collective dwellings
  47–48, 150–66, *151–66 passim*; high-
  rise projects 47–57; industrialized
  production 117–18; intermediate and
  hybrid technologies 131–49; low-cost
  21, 22, 35, 100, 117, 135; low-rise *51*,
  143; mass-production 31, 37, 100, 135,
  151; middle-class 70–87, 100, 215;

prefabricated 100, 131, *144*, 144–46;
  reform of production 117; roadtowns
  107–10; 'Roq' and 'Rob' 143, *165*, 166,
  186; slum clearance 141, *141*; social
  development and 118
L'Humanité (paper) 49

'Immeuble pour Artistes' 152
'Immeubles-Villas' 41, *42*, 150, 152
India: C. and 184–99
L'Intransigeant (paper) 51
Iofan, Boris 97, 98
Italy: C. visits 10–11

Jacob Delafon 68, 69
Jacquemet, Villa 10, *10*
Jaques-Dalcroze, Émile 39, 46
Jaoul family, houses for: 'log cabin' 143;
  double house *145*, 146
Jeanneret, Pierre 2–3, 27, 187; training
  42–43; partnership with C. 42–43,
  214; relationship with C. 202, 229;
  break with C. over Vichy 123; and
  collectivization of agriculture 141; and
  figurative imagery 202; and furniture
  59, 62, 69; site architect at
  Chandigarh 43
Jeanneret-Gris, Albert (brother) 8, 39;
  house for 38, 39, 42
Jeanneret-Gris, Charles Édouard:
  assumption of pseudonym 'Le
  Corbusier' 8, 27, 201
Jeanneret-Gris, Georges Édouard
  (father) 8
Jeanneret-Gris, Marie-Charlotte-Amélie
  Perret (mother) 8
Jones, Owen 10
Jugendstil influence 9–10, 11
Jullian de la Fuente, Guillermo 215, 222,
  224
Jung, Carl Gustav 201, 203
'Jura culture' 10, 15, 206

Kahn, Louis 224
Kameneva, Olga 91
Klipstein, August 13
Kolli, Nikolai 89, 95–96, 103
Krasin, German 97
Krejcar, Jaromír 88

Labrouste, Henri 83
La Celle-St-Cloud: Maison de Week-end
  135–37, *136*, 142, 143, 193
La Chaux-de-Fonds 8–19 *passim*, 46;
  designs for 10, *10*, 12, *12*, *16*, 16–19,
  18–19
Lagardelle, Hubert 118, 119, 120, 121
La Locle: Villa Favre-Jacot 17
Lamour, Philippe 118, 119, 120
Lannemezan company, housing 143, 146
La Plata 215
La Roche, Raoul 37, 39
La Roche, Maison 37–39, *37–39*, 42, 45,
  59, 62, *70*, 71, 72, 73
La Rochelle-Pallice: Unités 163
La Sainte-Baume 143, 167

La Sarraz Declaration 84–85
Latin America: C. visits 56, 88, 106–7,
  113
La Tourette monastery 174–80, *175*,
  176, *178*, *179*, 222
League of Nations building *80–83*,
  81–85, 87, 91, 93; sculpture 83, *200*,
  201–2
Leao, Carlos 113
Le Corbusier-Saugnier (pseud.) 27,
  28–29, 202
Ledeur, Lucien 167, 174
Leeuw, Kees van der 106
Lefèvre, C. 84
Lège: experimental houses 22
Léger, Fernand 41, 205, 206
Lemaresquier, Charles 84
Le Play, Frédéric 85
Le Pradet: Mandrot house *134*, 135
Le Raincy: Notre-Dame 77
Le Thoronet: Cistercian monastery 174
Le Tremblay: church 183
Liège: exhibition pavilion 172, *172*, 217
linear cities 106, 137, *148*, 149
liners (ocean) 32, *32*, 176–77
Lipchitz-Miestschaninoff double house
  72
L'Isle Jourdain: hydro-electric plant 21
Lissitzky, El 90
Liubimov, Isidor 95
Lods, Marcel 127
London: Crystal Palace 48; Hampstead
  Garden Suburb 46
Loos, Adolf 31, 36, 42, 60–61, 70
Loucheur, Louis 117
Loucheur, Maison *130*, 131, 135, 144, 152
Lunacharsky, Anatoly 91, 95
Lutyens, Sir Edwin 187

McLeod, Mary 109, 116
Magical Realism 89
'Maison d'artiste' 37
La Maison des hommes 123–26, *125–27*,
  208
Une Maison, un palais 81
Maisonnier, André 214
maisons montées à sec: *see* MAS
'Maisons murondins' 143
Malevich, Kasimir 90, 110
'Ma Maison' (1929) 131
Mandrot-Revillod, Hélène de 84, 85;
  house near Toulon (1931) *134*, 135
'Manual of Dwelling' 70
Marinetti, F. T. 27
Marseilles: Unité 155–62, *154–61*,
  164–66, 227
Marseilles-Sud: Unités 163, 220
Marx, Roberto Burle 220
MAS 131, 144–46, *144*
Masson, André 123
mass-production 31, 32, 37, 100, 135
Mathes, Maison aux 135, 142
Matisse, Henri 174
Matté-Trucco, Giacomo 107
Mayer, Albert 184, 199
Meaux: Unités 163

Mebes, Paul 46
Melnikov, Konstantin 90
Mercier, Ernest 116,117
Mercury 203, *210*, 210–11
Mermoz, Jean 107
Messiaen, Olivier 168,180
Meyer, Villa 72–73, *73*
Meyerhold, Vsevolod 91, 97
Mies van der Rohe, Ludwig 13, 202
Milinis, Ignati 106,151
Miliutin, N. A. 106, *148*,149
Mise au point 227–29
Modulor Man 162, *162*, 203, *203*, 210,
  210, 211, 223, *223*
Modulor system 162, *162*, 164,180,192,
  199, 211, 213
monasteries 174–80
Monol, Maison 24, *24*, 35, 60, 131,137
Montevideo 107
Moos, Stanislaus von 17,113
Moreira, Jorge 113,115
Moscow: C. and 88, *89*, 89–99,151;
  Centrosoyuz building 88, 91–96,
  92–94,101,103; garden city proposal
  96; Green City proposal 97;
  Narkomfin apartment block 151;
  Palace of the Soviets 2–3, 81, 87, *96*,
  97–100, *98, 99*; urbanism 53
Moser, Karl 84
Mount Athos 174
Moussinac, Léon 123
mud-brick construction 143
Muggia, A. 84
Mughal architecture 188,192,193,195,
  198
'Mundaneum' 85, 87
Munich 12
murals 207–8, *207*
Musaion (magazine) 87
'Musée à croissance illimitée' 144
'Musée Mondial' 85, *85, 86*, 87
music 168,180,182,222
mythology 201–2, 208

Nagy, László Moholy 32–33
Nehru, Jawaharlal 184–85, 186
Nemours (Algeria) 121, *134*,137
Nénot and Flégenheimer 84
neoclassicism 15, 19, 201
neo-Palladianism 18, 77, 77–79,195
Neue Sachlichkeit 89
New York: C. and 49, 55–56, 100, *112*,
  112–13, 228
Nezval, Vitěslav 88, 89
Niemeyer, Oscar 113, *114*,115, 222, 228
Nietsche, Friedrich 201
nigredo 201, 208, 211
Nivola, Constantino 206

Obus, Plan *108*,109–10,121,221
Oeuvre complète 133–35,144,156–57
office towers 49, 55,191
Olivetti Electronic Centre (Rho-Milan)
  217, 219–22, *221*
open hand motif: see hand motif
OSA *89*, 90, 95,151

Otlet, Paul 57, 85,188
Oubrerie, José 183, 215, 222, 224
Oued Ouchaia 57,152–53, *152, 153*
Ozenfant, Amédée 24–25, *25*, 27,
  28–29, 32, 37, 79, 201, 202; Maison
  Ozenfant 43, *44–45*, 45

Pagès (engineer) 11
painting: C. and 8–9, 16, 25, 28, 29, 37,
  37, *40–41*, 41, 77, 79, 109, 204–13,
  207, 209–12; and see tapestries
Palace of the Soviets 2–3, 81, 87, *96*,
  97–100, *98, 99*
Palladio, Andrea: see neo-Palladianism
pans de verre ondulatoires 176,177,180
Paris 21; Arc de Triomphe 32, *32*;
  Bibliothèque Nationale 83; Cité de
  Refuge 101,103, *105*,106; CNIT
  exhibition hall 228; École des Beaux
  Arts 9, 33; Eiffel Tower 85; Exposition
  des Arts Décoratifs (1925) 41, 59;
  Exposition Universelle (1867) 85,
  (1937) *68*, 69,135; Maisons Jaoul *145*,
  146; Maison La Roche 37–39, *37–39*,
  42, 45, 59, 62, *70*, 71, 72, 73; Maison
  Ozenfant 43, *44–45*, 45; Maison
  Plainex 72; Pavillon de l'Esprit
  Nouveau 37, *40–41*, 41–42, 47, 52, 59,
  62–63, 72, 73,151–52; Pavillon des
  Temps Nouveaux 120, 121,135,137,
  137–42, *138–41*,172, *172*–73,182,
  207; Pavillon Suisse 93, 101, 103, *104*,
  106,135,156, 208; Plan Voisin 52, *53*,
  90, 96; Porte Maillot projects 57,172,
  217; rue Nungesser-et-Coli (Porte
  Molitor) apartments 101, 103–6, *105*,
  135; Synthèse des Arts Majeurs
  pavilion 172, 217; Villa Meyer 72–73,
  73; urbanism 52, *53*,141, *141*
Passanti, Francesco 55
Paucheux, Pierre 215
Pauly, Danièle 171,173
Pavia: Charterhouse 174
Pavillon: see Esprit Nouveau; Synthèse
  des Arts Majeurs; Temps Nouveaux
Paxton, Joseph 48
peasant culture, influence of 15, 35, 72
Peking: plan 53–55
Perrault, Claude 28
Perret, Auguste 18, 25, 43, 77, 81,82
Perret Frères (Auguste and Gustave)
  10–11, 43,101
Perriand, Charlotte 59, 62–69, *63–66*,
  68
Perrin, Léon 10, 17,19
Pessac: Cité-Jardin Frugès 22–23,
  22–23, 49,100
Pétain, Marshal Philippe 123
Petit, Jean 24, 228
Peugeot 64
Peyrissac, Maison 143, *143*
phalanstère 150
Philadelphia: PFSF Building 112
Philippeville: 'Musée à croissance
  illimitée' 144
Philips Pavilion 181–82, *181*, 224

photographs: C. and 13, 32–33,133, 207
Pidoux, Justin 56
Pierrefeu, François de 118,119,121,
  123–26,127,155
pilotis 39, 46, 51, 72, 74, 77, 79, 91, 95,
  97,131,155, *155*,157,163
Pisa 98
pisé construction 143
Plainex, Maison 72
plan libre 22, 45, 70, 72
Plans (magazine) 118–19,120–21
Plan Voisin 52, *53*, 90, 96
Podensac: water tower 21
Le Poème de l'Angle Droit 209–13,
  209–12,214
poème électronique 182
Poésie sur Alger 208, *208*
Poiret, Paul 35
Poissy: Villa Savoye 71, 72, *78*, 78–79,
  177,195
polychromy 23, 42,162,179, 223
Popular Front 121–23,138,142
Prague 88, 89
Prasad, Sunand 194,196
Précisions 194
prefabrication 100,131,144–46, *144*,156
Préludes (magazine) 121
promenade architecturale 43, 79, 83,106,
  194–95
Prouvé, Jean 123,144, *144*, 219, 228
Provensal, Henri 15
pseudonyms: C. and 8, 27, 28–29, 201,
  202
Purism 25, 27–28, 29, 31, 33,149;
  furniture and furnishings 42, 62, 66,
  68–69; house designs 37, 43, 71, 77,
  100,131,195, 207; large public
  buildings 81, 83, 217; poetry 88; in
  Russia; *and* see painting 91
Le Purisme 27

Quand les cathédrales étaient blanches
  113, 206
Les Quatre Routes: see The Four Routes

Raaf, Lotti 39
'Radiant Farm' ('Ferme Radieuse') 127,
  128,129,141, 146–47
rammed earth (*pisé*) construction 143
ramps *38*, 39, *39*, 73, *78*, 79, 85, 93–95,
  94, 97–99, *98, 99*,112, *132*,133
Raymond, Antonin 133–35
Rebutato, Robert 215
Rebutato, Thomas 225
redents: bloc à 48, *50*, 51, 52, 55, 56,101,
  109, *141*; *rue à* 47, 47
Redressement Français 116–17
regulating lines (*tracés régulateurs*) 19,
  19, 76, 79
Reidy, Alfonso 113,115
Renan, Ernest 13
Réponse à Moscou 96
respiration exacte 101–2
Rezé-lès-Nantes: Unité 163–64
RIBA Town Planning conference (1910)
  52

Riemerschmid, Richard 46
Rio de Janeiro 107, *107*, 109, 113–15, *114*
Ritter, William 12, 15
roadtown plans 107–10
Roberto, Marcello and Milton 115
Rockefeller, Nelson 113
Rodin, Auguste 206
Rolland, Romain 88
Romantic Classicism 83
Rome: S. Maria in Cosmedin 179
Romier, Lucien 116, 117
Ronchamp 167–74, *168*, *169*, *170*, *171*,
    173, 180, 182, 217, 222
roof garden (*toit-jardin*) 52, 72, 74, 77
'Roq' and 'Rob' housing 143, *165*, 166
Roquebrune-Cap Martin 229; *cabanon*
    214, 224–27, *225*, *226*; Eileen Gray
    house (E1027) *207*, 207–8, 225
Rowe, Colin 79, *80*, 83, 176
Ruskin, John 10, 15, 206
Russia: *see* Moscow; St Petersburg;
    Soviet Union

SABA (Société d'Application du Béton
    Armé) 21, 25
St-Cloud: *see* La Celle-St-Cloud
St-Dié: Unités 163
Saintes: workers' housing 21
Saint-Exupéry, Antoine de 107
Saint-Gobain glass 129
St Petersburg: German Embassy 200
Salon d'Automne (1922) 36, 48–49,
    (1929) 62–64, *63*–*66*
Salon de la Société des Artistes
    Décorateurs 59
San Francisco: exhibition pavilion 172,
    172, 217
Sant'Elia, Antonio 51
São Paulo 107
Sarabhai, Awand 194
Sarabhai House 193–94, *194*
Sauvage, Henri 117, 153
Savina, Joseph 168
Savoye, Villa 71, 72, 77, 78–79, 79, 177,
    195
Schinkel, K. F. 200–201
Schumacher, Fritz 46
Schwob, Anatole 18
Schwob, Villa 18–19, *18*, *19*, 70
sculpture 168, 200–206
SEIE (Société d'Entreprises Industrielles
    et d'Études) 21
Sellier, Henri 116, 117
Senger, Alexander von 118
Serenyi, Peter 150, 161
Sert, José Luis 215
Shchusev, A. V. 96
Sinco oil company 129
Sitte, Camillo 13, 46
skyscrapers 47, 55–56, *57*, 111–12
slum clearance 141, *141*
Slutzky, Robert 79, *80*–*81*, 83
Socialist Realism 95, 98
Société d'Application du Béton
    (SABA) 21, 25
Société d'Entreprises Industri

d'Études (SEIE) 21
Société des Artistes Décorateurs 59
Sorel, Georges 120
Soviet Union 90–99, 106, 151
Sovrememaia Arkhitektura (magazine) 90
'Sportsman's Gymnasium and Study' 68
stadiums 121, *122*, 141
Stavba (magazine) 87
Stein de Monzie, Villa *33*, 71, 72, 76–77,
    77–79, 220
Stil i Epokha (magazine) 90
Stirling, James 146
Stockholm: art gallery 219; urbanism 57
Stotzer, Villa: *see* La Chaux-de-Fonds
Strasbourg: Congress Hall 217, 222;
    Unité 163, 220
Stroikom group 151, 161
Structural Rationalism 77, 82
Stuttgart: Weissenhofsiedlung 37, 90
Süe, Louis 117
Sullivan, Louis 55
syndicalism 117–19, *117*, 121, 124, *125*
Synthèse des Arts Majeurs pavillon 172,
    217

Tafuri, Manfredo 110
Tait, Thomas 91
tapestries 207, *207*
Taut, Bruno 49
Taut, Max 91
Tavés, Alain 215
Taylor, Brian Brace 100
Taylor, Frederick Winslow 116
Teige, Karel 87, 88
Temple in the Wilderness 137, *172*,
    172
Temps Nouveaux, Pavillon des 120, 121,
    135, 137, 137–42, *138*, *139*, *140*, 172,
    172–73, 182, 207
Tengbom, Ivar 84
Thapar, P. N. 184, 187
Thomas, Albert 116, 117
Thonet bentwood chairs 37, 42, 59
The Three Human Establishments: *see* Les
    Trois Établissements humains
Tivoli: Hadrian's Villa 170
toit-jardin (roof garden) 52, 72, 77
Tonkin, Maison du 22
total art 59, 180, 182
Toulouse: arsenal 21
towers 47, 49, *49*, *50*, *53*, 55–56
town planning 13, 46–57, 147, 161–66,
    184–99
tracés régulateurs 19, *19*, 76, 79
trades unions: *see* syndicalism
transportation 51, 52, 55, 186
Les Trois Établissements humains 129,
    146–47, *147*, 185, 228
Trouin, Édouard 143, 167
Turin: Fiat factory 107

Firminy-Vert 163, 164; Marseilles
    155–62, *155*, *156*, *158*, *159*, *160*, *161*,
    164–66, 227; Marseilles-Sud 163, 220;
    Rezé-lès-Nantes 163–64
Unité (lithographs) 208
United States: C. and 111–13, 124
Unwin, Raymond 46
Urbanisme 13, 28, 49, 90
'Usine Verte': *see* 'Green Factory'

Vago, G. 84
Vaillant-Couturier, Paul *122*, 123, 144,
    206
Valois, Georges 49, 120
Varèse, Edgar 180, 182
Varma, P. L. 184, 187
Vasconcelos, Hernani 113
Vauban, Sébastien Le Prestre de 47
Vauvrecy (pseud. of C.) 29
Velikovsky, B. M. 91
Venice: hospital 222–24, *222*, *223*, 229;
    Loos villa 70
Vers une architecture 8, *14*, 28–32, *30*, *32*,
    41, 59, 62, 70, 77, 88, 89, 90, 100, 106,
    107, 118, 119, 137, 172, *172*, 202, 229
Vesnin, Alexander 89, *89*, 90
'viaduct city' 109, 110
Vichy France 123–27, *125*
Vienna 11, 36, 60
'Villa au bord de la mer' *34*, 35
Ville d'Avray: Church library 62, 72
'Ville Contemporaine' 48–55, *48*, 49,
    51, 52, 150, *see also* city of towers
'Ville Radieuse' 51, 53–57, *54*, 93, 96,
    109, *141*, *151*, 152–53, *152*
La Ville Radieuse 55, 57, 68, 106, *107*,
    108, *111*, *112*, 119, 121, 124, *128*,
    203–4, *205*
ville-tours 47, 55
Vincennes: stadium 121, *122*
Voisin: *see* Plan Voisin
VOKS 91
Voyage d'Orient (1911) 13, *14*, 15, 60, 111

Walter, Jeanne 118
Wanner, Edmond 63, 103
Weber, Heidi, pavilion at Zurich 172,
    219–20, *219*
Week-end, Maison de (La Celle-St-
    Cloud) 135–37, *137*, 142, 143, 193
West, John Pettit III 79, 197
Winter, Pierre 118, 119, 120
Wogensky, André 161
Woods, Shadrach 224
Wright, Frank Lloyd 17

Xenakis, Iannis 180–81, 214

Zaknić, Ivan 227–28
Zehrfuss, Bernard 228
...rvos, Christian 213
...oltovsky, Ivan 97
...n 106, *106*, 137
...la, Émile 150
...rich: Heidi Weber pavilion (La Maison
    de l'Homme) 172, 219–20

141256